FIRST FOUNDERS

New England in the World

GENERAL SERIES EDITOR

Brigitte Bailey, University of New Hampshire

New England in the World promotes new directions in research on
New England topics in a variety of disciplines, including literary studies,
history, biography, geography, anthropology, environmental studies, visual
and material culture, African American studies, Native studies, ethnic studies,
gender studies, film studies, and cultural studies. In addition to its pursuit of
New England topics in general, the series features a special emphasis on projects
that situate New England in transnational, transatlantic, hemispheric, and
global contexts. The series welcomes interdisciplinary perspectives, and
it publishes books meant for academic readers as well as books
that speak to a broader public.

For the complete list of books available in this series,
please see www.upne.com

Francis J. Bremer, *First Founders:*
American Puritans and Puritanism in an Atlantic World

FIRST FOUNDERS

*American Puritans and Puritanism
in an Atlantic World*

FRANCIS J. BREMER

University of New Hampshire Press

Durham, New Hampshire

University of New Hampshire Press
An imprint of University Press of New England
www.upne.com
© 2012 University of New Hampshire
All rights reserved
Manufactured in the United States of America
Designed by April Leidig
Typeset in Caslon by Copperline Book Services, Inc.

University Press of New England is a member of the Green
Press Initiative. The paper used in this book meets their
minimum requirement for recycled paper.

Library of Congress Cataloging-in-Publication Data
Bremer, Francis J.
First founders : American Puritans and Puritanism
in an Atlantic world / Francis J. Bremer.
p. cm.—(New England in the world)
Includes index.
ISBN 978-1-58465-959-4 (cloth : alk. paper)
ISBN 978-1-61168-258-8 (ebook)
1. Puritans—New England. 2. Puritans—
New England—Clergy—History—17th century.
3. New England—History—Colonial period,
ca. 1600–1775. I. Title.
F7.B758   2012
285'.9092—dc23   2011047231

5 4 3 2 1

to my colleagues,
students,
and the administrators
of Millersville University
1977–2011

Contents

Preface

THE MORE I HAVE studied the subject of puritanism in the seventeenth-century Atlantic world, the more I have been impressed with the varieties of belief and practice that lie beneath the standard picture that scholars have painted of early New England. This book is an attempt to explore some of that variety. It is intended for a general audience, and as a result I have dispensed with footnotes. Scholars, who I hope will find the volume of some interest, will know where the quotes come from. I have provided general guidance to sources and further readings at the end of the book. To make the quotes more accessible to the intended readers I have modernized the spelling when I quote from documents.

My studies of puritanism have been shaped by the support of many friends in the scholarly community. I continue to learn from and get support from longtime friends such as Alden Vaughan, John Morrill, Patrick Collinson, Diarmaid MacCulloch, Michael McGiffert, Carol Berkin, Mary Beth Norton, Michael Winship, Walt Woodward, and Tom Webster. In writing this book I have been helped by comments from E. Brooks Holifield, Joel Halcomb, Hunter Powell, John Coffey, Crawford Gribben, Dan Richter, Natalie Zacek, Kristen Block, C. S. Manegold, Jason Peacey, Alden Vaughan, Hal Worthley, Winfried Herget, Christopher Thompson, Susan Lowes, and Agnes Meeker. Much of my understanding of puritanism in the Stour Valley was shaped on trips through the region with Martin Wood. A number of years ago John and Judy Cammack kindly guided me through the geography of puritanism in Lincolnshire. Anne Bentley of the Massachusetts Historical Society was helpful in identifying portraits in the society's collection. Mr. and Mrs. Leverett Byrd were kind enough to allow me to use a portrait of their ancestor, Governor John Leverett.

The dedication recognized my debt to all of those at Millersville University who supported my work in many ways during my thirty-four-year teaching career there. At a time when numerous public figures are appealing for a return to our nation's heritage, it is important that institutions such as Millersville provide environments for scholarly investigation and discussion of that heritage. It is in centers of higher education that value the liberal arts that future generations learn to make sense of the past. Millersville has embraced that mission, and it has provided me opportunities to engage with students in the classroom and the support needed to reach beyond the walls of academe to share my understanding with the broader community through works such as this.

FIRST FOUNDERS

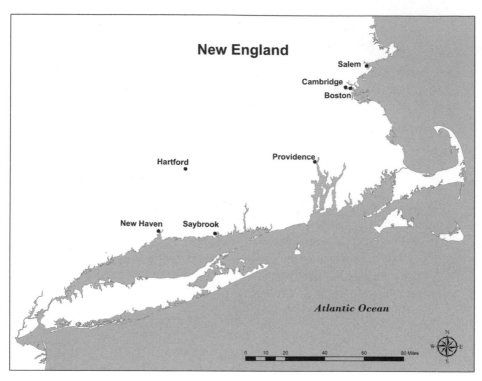

Map of New England
Map by Dana Edsall, Millersville University Geography Department

※

INTRODUCTION

P URITANISM WAS a dynamic force in the shaping of early New England, and its legacy has continued to have an impact on our culture. John Winthrop's call for the colonists to be "as a City upon a Hill" has been cited as the point of origin for America's sense of mission. The town meetings of New England have been called the "seedbed of American democracy." Massachusetts has been applauded as the site of America's first public school and first college. Yet most Americans have little understanding of who the puritans of the seventeenth century were and why they behaved as they did. Some harbor an impression that the puritans were sexually repressed bigots in dreary clothes who executed witches, persecuted Anne Hutchinson, and banned Christmas. Stereotyped over the years by both those who admired them and those who were critical of their legacy, the puritans are largely misunderstood.

This collection of puritan biographies is first of all intended to recover the stories of interesting men and women who lived in a formative period of American history. The individuals include some whose names may be familiar—John Winthrop, Anne Hutchinson—as well as others who are less well known. But the lives I have chosen to investigate have also been selected because their stories illustrate various points about puritanism and the puritan experience in colonial New England. The book is designed to focus on individuals, and I believe that each of the chapters can stand alone as an interesting story. Because of the need to provide some broader context, occasionally I will elaborate on events that precede or follow the biography. Thus, in the chapter on Anne Bradstreet I have briefly traced the career of Simon Bradstreet in the decades that followed his wife's death. I have also tried to provide a specific focus to each chapter rather than cover the entire subject of the featured individual's life. The chapter on John Winthrop, for example, deals in detail with his interior spiritual life, but less with his public career. I would have liked to have included more women in this collection, but the surviving sources are limited, and those that do exist are not as complete as I would wish. I hope that the stories of Anne Hutchinson, Mary Dyer, Lady Deborah Moody, Anne Eaton, Sarah Keayne, and Anne Bradstreet at least suggest the important roles that women played in puritan society.

The thread that pulls together the stories that I have chosen to tell is the narrative of how puritans sought to shape a godly kingdom in America. In the pages that follow, readers will learn how this goal was affected by the surprising diversity of puritanism, the product both of the different experiences and different temperaments of the individuals examined. The stories will illustrate the debates between members of the puritan community over how rigidly to define and enforce orthodoxy and to define the proper relationship between religion and politics. They will illustrate the conflict between the sectarian element of puritanism and its aspiration to become a church. The transatlantic nature of seventeenth-century puritanism will be made evident by following the lives of New England men and women who spent large portions of their lives outside of as well as in the colonies. The various meanings that a godly kingdom had for women and for Native Americans will also be examined.

Some of the stories focus more on the private lives and beliefs of individuals, while others trace the public careers and stands of those that are the focus of the chapter. This is partially intentional, to trace how some men and women shaped their personal lives, while looking at how other dedicated puritans sought to create godly communities. But the different focus also reflects the nature of the surviving evidence. We have abundant sources that enable us to explore the inner lives of figures such as John Winthrop and Anne Bradstreet. There are no surviving diaries or extensive personal letters that illuminate the lives of a John Leverett or a John Sassamon.

One of my intentions in writing this collection was to illustrate the diversity of puritanism. Too often the story of New England is told as if the region were simply Massachusetts (or even Boston) writ large. The fact is that there are important stories to be told about the men and women who lived in all the region's colonies. While most of these essays focus on men and women who are indeed primarily identified with Massachusetts, there are some chapters that focus on individuals that played key roles in the colonies of New Haven (John Davenport and Anne Eaton) and Rhode Island (Anne Hutchinson and Mary Dyer), and others that look at colonists who pursued godly kingdoms outside of New England (Samuel and Stephen Winthrop, Hugh Peter, Sarah Keayne, and Lady Deborah Moody). But the collection fails to be as encompassing as I had wished. There are interesting stories yet to be told of Plymouth's William Brewster and John Cotton Jr., of Connecticut's Thomas Hooker and Roger Ludlow, and of the Bay colony's Daniel Gookin and Thomas Danforth, to mention but a few. Perhaps there are enough to justify yet another book.

WHAT EXACTLY was puritanism, and what brought many of them men and women to America in the seventeenth century? These are questions that provoked different answers in the seventeenth century and that have continued to challenge historians. Part of the difficulty comes from the fact that for most of the movement's history there was no institutional identity that defined puritanism. Whereas other religious movements of the sixteenth and seventeenth centuries—Lutheranism, Catholicism, Calvinism, and others—were or became institutionalized, producing official statements of faith and formal membership in churches, puritanism never achieved that type of clear identity. It was a movement defined in part by the self-identification of men and women who referred to themselves as "godly" or "professors," and partly by their enemies, who scorned them as "precisians," "puritans," and "hypocrites." Some scholars have come to look at puritanism as a temperament and to talk of the "puritan character."

Puritans were members of the Protestant Church of England, created by Henry VIII and Edward VI and restored by Queen Elizabeth following the Marian persecutions of the mid-1550s. Those identified as puritans were reformers committed to raising that church to a higher level of holiness. At the simplest level, puritans were men and women who sought to reform themselves and their society by rejecting the remnants of Roman Catholic teachings and practice to be found in post-Reformation

England. Over the years, their position emerged as an intense version of Reformed Protestantism, drawing inspiration from Calvinist sources. Puritans were particularly concerned that individual believers had access to the scriptures, the word of God, in a proper vernacular translation. This required a commitment to teaching all to read. They agitated for the placement of university-trained preachers in every parish. They believed that England as a political nation must be committed to oppose the forces of Rome throughout Christendom. While Englishmen who were not labeled puritans might support some or all of these objectives, those who did bear the label were seen as most committed and most fervent in advancing them.

Puritans were dedicated to raising the kingdom of God, but the nature of what that kingdom would be was never completely spelled out. It was always an ideal just beyond their reach as they journeyed on a pilgrimage toward an unattainable perfection. They were attempting to build a better society, the best that human effort could achieve. The starting point for making the Earth truly God's kingdom began with the individual's struggle to subject him- or herself to the divine will, a struggle that could not succeed without the blessings of God's grace. Having transformed oneself into a "shining light," the puritan sought to bring others into the kingdom by persuasion and the example of a godly life. Communities of saints, often united by formal or informal covenants, would gather to reinforce each other's faith while also seeking through dialogue to enhance their understanding of God's way. They hoped that their example would bring others to the truth. In many ways some puritans operated in the classic style of a religious sect, jealously guarding their faith. In keeping with this, many puritans sought to huddle together in godly communities while minimizing contact with the ungodly members of their society. Others, however, saw engagement with the ungodly as the only way of bringing their neighbors to the truth. The chapter that presents the story of John Winthrop demonstrates the struggle of one saint to subject himself to God's rule and the personal and familial character of the puritan faith. It also speaks to puritan views on marriage and the family.

Because puritans for a long time had no power other than that of their influence, the struggle to achieve the kingdom of God in late sixteenth-

and early seventeenth-century England was one of witness, puritan men and women such as John and Margaret Winthrop seeking to transform society by their influence. In some areas of the country, godly clergy and magistrates were able to reform individual parishes. But where they had such success, puritans were often dissatisfied with the results. A common complaint of the clergy was that too many of those to whom they preached were "mere professors," men and women who went through the motions of proper worship and who nominally accepted Protestant teachings, but whose hearts weren't engaged. The issue of how to reconcile a sectarian ideal with a church goal was undecided when the New England experiment began.

The puritans who came to the colonies in the 1630s and beyond did so because they found themselves thwarted in their effort to advance the kingdom of God in England. Indeed, it seemed that King Charles I was dismantling what advances their fathers and grandfathers had made. In a new world they hoped to create a new order. But in that new world puritans also possessed political authority. They could if they wished use coercion as well as persuasion to advance the godly order. John Endecott's story explores how one puritan assumed the responsibilities of being a godly magistrate in New England with a mixture of zeal and compassion. The chapter on John Wilson examined how puritan clergy in America used their new freedom to join with fellow believers in creating purified congregational churches in which they could nourish the faith of believers.

One of the challenges faced by the first colonists was how to determine the precise nature of a godly order and how to discern between free discussion that promoted their goal and ideas that threatened it— in short, how and where to position the perimeter fence dividing what was acceptable from what was not. Much of the history of the seventeenth century Bible Commonwealths (as the New England colonies are often referred to) was shaped by debates over where to draw the line between beliefs and behaviors that would enhance the pursuit of the kingdom and those that threatened to erode the foundations of their city on a hill. The task was made more complex by the fact that New England brought together men and women of different temperaments from different parts of England who disagreed in their precise understanding of what the kingdom of God would look like. While they may all be called puritans, there were many different voices engaged in this debate. Each man and woman made sense of the puritan tradition in his or her own way. In contrast to the more moderate Winthrop and Wilson, Thomas Dudley and Thomas Shepard were focused on ideas and people that might undermine the kingdom they were seeking to erect, and emerged as hammers of those they suspected of heresy.

Men were not the only puritans who had ideas about how the society was to be shaped. Chapter 4 discusses four strong women who tested the limits of the emerging orthodoxy. Anne Hutchinson, who became the public face of a challenge to the teachings of the clerical majority in the 1630s, was banished from Massachusetts and excommunicated from the Boston church for her opinions. One of her disciples, Mary Dyer, later became a Quaker. Dyer's challenge to the Massachusetts orthodoxy in the 1650s led to her being hanged on Boston Common. These are familiar stories to anyone who knows the period. Lady Deborah Moody was a resident of early Salem who disagreed with the New England practice of baptizing infants. Rather than confronting the authorities, she withdrew from the colony and resettled among the Dutch in New Netherland. But Moody lent a Baptist tract to Anne Eaton, the wife of the governor of the New Haven Colony. Anne not only challenged the practice of infant baptism, but also crossed what was considered to be the boundaries of proper domestic behavior. She was tried before the New Haven church and excommunicated, but was never banished from the colony and lived uneasily there till she returned to England after the death of her husband.

Different insights into the varieties of puritan life in New England are to be found in the chapter dealing with the Keayne family. Robert Keayne was a prosperous English merchant who migrated to Massachusetts and settled in Boston. A pious puritan, on more than one occasion he clashed with his fellow colonists on how to balance his faith with his desire to prosper. The struggle to reconcile these competing demands troubled him his entire life. His daughter-in-law, Sarah Dudley Keayne, followed her husband, Benjamin, to England in the early 1640s.

There she became a notorious female street preacher and, perhaps as a consequence of radical religious views, engaged in promiscuous sexual behavior.

England's Civil Wars of the 1640s brought puritans to power in that country and provided them the opportunity to create their own godly kingdom. New Englanders lent their assistance to that cause by prayer, advice, and through the return of colonists who fought in the parliamentary armies and accepted ministerial posts. The interaction between puritans on both sides of the Atlantic stimulated new discussion of issues such as the nature of a true church, the limits of toleration, and the extent to which government should advance godly ends. One of the most prominent clergymen to contribute to that cause was Hugh Peter. Serving at various times as an army chaplain, an advisor to Oliver Cromwell, and a popular preacher, Peter was eventually executed as a regicide. Stephen Winthrop, one of the sons of John Winthrop, returned to England and served in the army and in Parliament. His story not only demonstrates the contributions colonists made to the puritan cause in England, but the ways in which that experience could reshape their understanding of their own faith.

John Davenport was the founder of New Haven. He has been neglected because most accounts of New England are focused on Massachusetts. Davenport's story illustrates the beliefs of some who saw New England as a site from which they could advance the millennium. This chapter focuses on his efforts to promote international reform and support those who were transforming England, but it also sheds light on the debate between those clergy and laymen who were committed to the participatory character of congregationalism and those who sought to establish more hierarchical elements in the governance of the churches.

Samuel Winthrop was another son of Massachusetts governor John Winthrop. Seeking to take advantage of New England's expanding trade in the mid-seventeenth century, he eventually settled in the Leeward Islands, first as a merchant and then as the owner of a sugar plantation, a slave owner, and governor of Antigua. His story not only reinforces the fact that the story of New England puritanism was a truly Atlantic phenomenon, but demonstrates how the search for personal godliness could lead to unexpected destinations. Samuel became a prominent Quaker while retaining close ties with his New England kin and friends.

The chapter on John Sassamon, a Native American, explores the efforts of some puritans to incorporate Native Americans into the godly kingdom being erected in New England. Sassamon was an Indian who accepted Christianity and had an important role in trying to bring other natives to the faith. A puritan with one foot in New England culture and the other in native society, he ended up being trusted by neither the English nor his fellow Indians. His death prompted the outbreak of King Philip's War, the most devastating conflict in colonial history. His story illustrates the scope and limitations of puritan evangelical efforts.

The Restoration of the Stuart monarchy in 1660 put an immediate end to puritan attempts to create the kingdom of God in England. The Restoration also carried implications for the colonies. It threatened the virtual autonomy that New Englanders had relied upon in their effort to create a godly kingdom in America. Over the following decades the ability of colonial magistrates to impose their vision of the kingdom eroded until it was totally lost with the revocation of the Massachusetts charter in 1684 and the establishment of the royal Dominion of New England. Step-by-step puritan authority was reduced until the colonists were left in the situation that their ancestors had faced — spreading the kingdom by example, starting with the individual and expanding outward to family, friends, and communities.

The last chapters in this book explore what remained constant and what changed in New England efforts to create a godly kingdom in the decades following the Restoration. John Leverett was governor at the time when King Philip's War broke out. Like Stephen Winthrop, he had served in the puritan parliamentary army. Leverett returned to Massachusetts after the Restoration. His career as governor of the colony in the 1670s is described in a chapter that focuses on conflicts among the colonists as to how to respond to the changing political and social climate of the time and debates over the role of the state in enforcing religious values. The story of Anne Bradstreet, the daughter of Thomas Dudley and a colonist who witnessed the many changes that challenged New England from its earliest days until her death in 1672, illustrates the constancy of the personal and family piety that remained a constant through all of the political changes in puritan political life. A final chapter on Samuel Sewall addresses the final challenges to puritan political control in New England and the return to efforts to base God's earthly kingdom on individuals and their abilities to informally influence those around them. Sewall played a key role in the Salem Witchcraft episode of 1692, and emerged in the early eighteenth century as a critic of the growing African slave trade.

In many ways Sewall and his fellow puritans found themselves in the situation that John Winthrop had experienced in the Stour Valley in the 1630s — trying to live a godly life in an ungodly world and inspire others to follow the path of righteousness. That commitment survived the fall of the puritan political order, fostering continued commitment to education, to participatory government, and to moral reform of society. This became the puritan legacy that continued to shape American history through the following centuries and that remains the reason to get beyond stereotypes and understand these men and women as they truly were.

John Winthrop and the
Struggle to Lead a Godly Life

Before there could be a godly society, there needed to be godly men and women. The seeds of puritan success were planted in the hearts of individuals. As related by John Bunyan in *The Pilgrim's Progress* (1678), the struggle toward godliness was an uneven one, filled with temptations. Having been transformed by God's grace, the saint then sought to bring his family and friends into a godly community by word and example. The effort to accept God's rule in his own life, and to extend the sway of the gospel to include family, friends, and the general society can be traced no more effectively than by an examination of the spiritual life of John Winthrop. Winthrop is best known as the preeminent figure in the founding of New England. But before he was a governor he was a man struggling to understand his relationship with God. His story helps us to understand what made someone a puritan, the social dimensions of that faith, and what made New England puritan.

JOHN WINTHROP was born in the Stour Valley of eastern England, in the village of Edwardstone, in the Armada year of 1588. Edwardstone was one of three closely related communities that included Groton and Boxford. The family had a record of commitment to the further reform of the Church of England. John's grandfather Adam had risen from being an apprentice to become master of the Clothworkers, one of the twelve major London craft guilds. He had purchased the former monastic property of Groton Manor and moved there in 1553 when Mary Tudor came to the English throne. While Adam withdrew to the countryside lest his Protestant affiliation lead to arrest and imprisonment, his son William, John's uncle, stayed in London and became

The statue of John Winthrop in
front of the First Church in Boston
Photo by Barbara A. Bremer

one of the leaders of the Protestant underground church there. William
was in touch with some of the men who were executed for their faith,
preserved their papers, and passed them on to John Foxe, the author of
the immensely popular *Book of Martyrs* (1563). After Elizabeth succeeded
to the throne and the Protestant Church of England was restored, William devoted time and funds to promote the more advanced reforms that
became identified as puritanism.

John's father, named Adam after his own father, had studied at Cambridge University, where he formed friendships with some of the clergy
who would become leaders of the effort to reform religion in the Stour
Valley. Leaving the university without a degree, Adam studied law at the
Inns of Court and was admitted as a barrister of the Inner Temple. But
he came back to Suffolk, managing modest landholdings of his own in
the towns of Boxford, Edwardstone, and Groton, and acting as steward

of Groton Manor for his older brother John, who had inherited the estate. Like his brother William, Adam became identified as a strong promoter of reform, and the Winthrop household frequently hosted puritan clergy who discussed over dinner the state of the church with their host and his family.

John's mother, Anne, was an active participant in these discussions and played a key role in the upbringing of her children. The daughter of a clergyman, she possessed and used a religious library that included a French Bible and a work in Latin by the German reformer Philip Melanchton. When Adam was away from Groton on legal business, or auditing the books of Trinity College, she taught John and his three sisters their lessons and led the family exercises of prayer and scripture reading.

John Winthrop's character was shaped in this godly household. There he, along with his sisters, learned to read and write perhaps when they were as young as four years old. And the children were taught their catechism. A notebook of Adam Winthrop's survives in which he copied out parts of a catechism with which he could instruct his children. Even before he could read, John listened to the stories of the Marian martyrs, and he would have perused the vivid woodcuts illustrating Foxe's classic. These tales and others like them were also woven into his everyday life. From the fields around his home he could see the tower of the church in Stoke, where, according to Foxe, during Mary's reign, the inhabitants, "especially the women that dwelt there, came not to their church to receive [communion] after the popish manner. . . . If there had been few of them, they could have by no means have escaped imprisonment. But because they were so many, the papists thought it not best to lay hands on them." Accompanying his father on trips to Hadley, where Adam had kin as well as business interests, they would have passed the field where the Protestant clergyman Rowland Taylor was burned. Riding south to visit other family members, they traveled through Colchester, where in April 1556 a clergyman and six laymen had been burned in a single fire — Foxe had written that "most cheerfully they ended their lives, to the glory of God's holy name, and the great encouragement of others." And there were many other such stories of men and women who had refused to "bow their knees to Baal" passed on to the youngster and his contemporaries in an effort to make them aware of the sacrifices that had been made on behalf of the reformed faith.

There was more to John's religious upbringing. His parents regularly led the members of the household in daily prayers. Scripture readings, the singing of psalms, and a review of the previous Sabbath's sermon were all part of such domestic exercises. The Winthrops attended services in Groton or Boxford, and occasionally traveled farther to hear the word of God preached in neighboring communities such as Kersey. Afterward they gathered, sometimes with neighbors, to review the sermon they had heard and discuss its meaning. Such practices encouraged each individual to personally explore matters of faith, but also to test his or her understanding against the judgment of trusted fellow pilgrims. For the Winthrops, religion was often the topic at the dinner table, with clerical friends of Adam such as Henry Sandes and John Knewstub joining the family.

John grew up admiring such clergymen. Since his father had little land for him to inherit, a clerical career offered the best opportunity for the young man to make a mark for himself. He matriculated at Trinity College, Cambridge, in 1602 with the intention of preparing for the ministry. But two things happened to derail these plans. On the one hand, his uncle John, the lord of Groton Manor, a ne'er do well who had deserted his wife and quarreled with the neighbors, left England for Ireland, presenting a chance for John and his father to purchase the manor, which would open up the possibilities of a different career. And, accompanying a college friend, William Forth, to visit the latter's kin in Great Stambridge, Essex, he met and fell in love with Mary Forth. The two were married in 1605 and settled originally in Great Stambridge.

When his father was able to raise the funds to purchase Groton Manor on his behalf, John returned to the Stour Valley. His wife Mary died in 1615, leaving John with four young children. John shortly thereafter married Thomasine Clopton, who also lived in Groton and whom he had known since they were children. Thomasine died in childbirth a year later, and in 1618 John married Margaret Tyndal of Little Maplestead, a town on the Essex side of the Stour. Over the course of a marriage that lasted almost thirty years, the couple would have eight children, only four of whom survived to adulthood.

THROUGH THESE YEARS of youth and early adulthood, Winthrop was deeply concerned with the state of his soul. Like most English Protestants, puritans believed in predestination, a doctrine that asserted that only God could save man from the consequences of his sinfulness. In the late sixteenth and early seventeenth centuries, puritan clergy worked to help men and women such as Winthrop understand Christian doctrine while also trying to provide pastoral counsel that would help them make sense of their individual spiritual situation. The ministers struggled to balance their belief in God's inalterable decrees with the need to guide believers to experience God's healing and converting graces, and to instruct them on how to lead responsible, godly lives. Most clergy sought to focus on suggesting to the faithful how they could *know* they were saved, rather than on how they *could save themselves*. Only God could save, but in doing so he transformed the elect in ways that could be discerned. Pastors and authors increasingly set forth elaborate guidance on identifying behavior that could be seen as evidence of a saving transformation.

There were a number of dangers to this approach that were debated in the broader puritan community. One concern was that in practice some individuals were likely to misapprehend their godly acts as the cause rather than the result of salvation and drift toward Arminianism, a viewpoint that diminished the role of God by asserting that people had an active role in determining their fate. Another consequence was that as the path of godliness was spelled out in greater and greater detail, many of the very people this was meant to reassure began to experience doubts about whether their lives measured up to the high standards being set forth. This could lead to doubt and sometimes despair instead of assurance. A growing minority of believers, some of them labeled Antinomians by their opponents, tried to cut free from this situation by rejecting any connection between works and the state of the soul and arguing that only the experience of God's caress could truly identify and bring comfort to the elect.

John Winthrop's spiritual diary allows us to trace these concerns in the life of a single puritan believer. John had first experienced the stirrings of grace at about the age of ten. He later recalled, "In some great frightening or danger, I . . . prayed unto God, and . . . found manifest answer." A few years later, he "began to have some more savor of Religion, and I thought I had more understanding in Divinity than many of my years; for in reading of some good books I conceived that I did know divers of those points before." But he was troubled by the fact that he "was still very wild, and dissolute, and as years came on my lusts grew stronger, but yet under some restraint of my natural reason."

At the age of fourteen, in his first year at Cambridge, John became ill and turned to God for help, believing God "to be very good and merciful, and would welcome any that would come to him, especially such a young soul, and so well qualified as I took my self to be." He expressed sorrow for his sins and "was willing to love God, and therefore I thought he loved me." But, recovering, he found himself drawn again "to former lusts, and grew worse than before." It is likely that his sinful urges had to do with his emerging sexuality, and this might have contributed to his rush to marriage.

Living in Great Stambridge, John profited from the teachings and counsel of the clergyman Ezekiel Culverwell, but he also found that the puritan community of southeast Essex was different from that which he had previously known. Perhaps because they were in the ascendancy, puritans in the Stour Valley were more tolerant of different views and practices in their communities. In Great Stambridge, puritans were an embattled minority and more determined to maintain strict standards. Some of his neighbors criticized John for hunting game birds along the area creeks, and called his piety into question. Striving to live up to these greater expectations of godliness, he soon "came . . . to some peace and comfort in God and in his ways." Speaking of Culverwell, he wrote that he "honored a faithful minister in my heart and could have kissed his feet." He later wrote of how he "grew full of zeal (which outran my knowledge and carried me sometimes beyond my calling) and very liberal to any good work. I had an insatiable thirst after the word of God and could not miss a good sermon, though many miles off, especially of such as did search deep into the conscience. I had also a great striving in my heart to draw others to God." He took any opportunity that presented itself "to draw men to God."

As members of a movement without official support, puritans joined in informal social networks to bolster one another's faith. John recollected that he "grew to be of some note for religion (which did not a little puff me up) and divers would come to me for advice in cases of conscience; and if I heard of any that were in trouble of mind I usually went to comfort them; so that upon the bent of my spirit this way and the success I found of my endeavors, I gave up myself to the study of Divinity, and intended to enter into the ministry, if my friends had not diverted me."

At this stage of his spiritual self examination, Winthrop was seeking assurance, as many others did from their works, assuming that good behavior was evidence that God had saved him. But was he really taking credit himself for what had to be the work of God? For a time pride kept him "from making any great question of my good estate." He "knew by the word of God," of "better assurance by the seal of the spirit . . . but could not, nor durst say that ever I had it; and finding by reading of [the puritan clergyman] Mr. [William] Perkins and other books that a reprobate might (in appearance) attain to as much as I had done: finding withal much hollowness and vain glory in my heart, I began to grow very sad." He now doubted that he was one of God's chosen, but he "knew not what to do" because he "was ashamed to open my case to any minister that knew me; I feared it would shame myself and religion also, that such an eminent professor as I was accounted, should discover such corruptions as I found in myself, and had in all this time attained no better evidence of salvation." When he gathered with others in discussions of faith, these encounters now spurred anxiety. He felt himself a hypocrite and "grew very sad, and melancholy" when others praised his sanctity.

Winthrop struggled for a time, acting like a godly Christian, but without the assurance that he was saved and fearing that he was a hypocrite, deluding himself and others. Yet occasionally in prayer he felt what he thought might be the presence of God. And then he suffered "a sore affliction"—Thomasine's death—whereby he felt that God "laid me lower in mine own eyes than at any time before, and showed me the emptiness of all my gifts and parts." He stopped struggling, accepted that he was powerless to save himself or others, and in doing so finally received comfort. The "good spirit of the Lord breathed upon my soul," he later wrote, "and said I should live. Then . . . could my soul close with Christ, and rest there with sweet content, so ravished with his love, as I desired nothing nor feared anything, but was filled with joy unspeakable, and glorious and with a spirit of Adoption." In later years this sense of joy would occasionally fade. He would look again to his works for comfort, but then worry that he was placing too much reliance on his actions, as if they were the causes rather than the fruits of his election. Troubled, he would again feel God's caress, an overwhelming love that he would often compare to the intensity of sexual love between husband and wife. His own difficult progress toward assurance made him sympathetic to the spiritual struggles of others. It is possible that in drawing assurance from both his experience of God's caress and the behavioral evidence of a spiritual transformation, Winthrop was typical of many puritan men and women, whose lives denied the notion that assurance could only come from one source.

At the same time, unlike some puritans who believed that the receipt of God's grace made them superior to others, Winthrop never lost his awareness of the fact that he was by nature a sinner and that anything he had was an unmerited gift from God. Many years after the event he recalled how, as a youngster, he had "spied 2 small books lie cast aside, so I stole them, & brought them away with me." On another occasion he recorded a list of his sins in his spiritual diary, which one of his descendants expunged from the copy of the diary he made available.

WHEN WINTHROP sought assurance that he had bent his will to God, he measured his actions against a common puritan understanding of what constituted a godly life. The clergyman Richard Baxter wrote that "overdoing is the ordinary way of undoing," and this is perhaps the best guide to understanding puritan morality. Puritans believed that all of creation was a gift of God and intrinsically good. Sin came not from using what God had made available, but from abusing it. And no matter how excellent something was, it could be overdone. Thus, for example, drinking alcoholic beverages was appropriate, but drunkenness was a sin. As governor of Massachusetts, John would serve wine and beer to his guests, but would reject the custom of offering numerous toasts because of his concern that this would lead to excess. As a magistrate he would license alehouses, but also pass sentence against those who were arrested for drunkenness.

The idea that puritans condemned alcohol is but one of many misconceptions about these men and women that developed in the nineteenth century and have proven difficult to undo. Another fallacy concerns the question of how puritans dressed. In keeping with their belief that there were appropriate and inappropriate ways of doing things, puritans condemned fashions that were designed to make a person appear better than he or she was, as well as styles that were designed to be sexually provocative. These qualifications being made, puritans dressed as other Englishmen of their class. The wardrobes of men and women included silk and satin garments in a variety of colors, including scarlet and canary. As a leader of his society, John Winthrop's portrait shows him dressed in a fine black suit (black being the most expensive color to manufacture), with an elaborate starched ruff around his neck and fine gossamer silk gloves in his hand. Of course, in this as in other matters, deciding where to draw the line between what was appropriate and what was not was difficult, and often became a matter of dispute between puritans of different dispositions. Winthrop favored allowing each individual to reach his or her own conclusions, but during a period when his political influence had been reduced, his fellow Massachusetts magistrates adopted sumptuary laws, which condemned certain popular fashions in clothing.

PURITANS BELIEVED that the earthly kingdom of God began with the surrender of the individual soul to God's will and the ensuing struggle to live a godly life. The saints were to draw others to God's way by their

exemplary behavior and by their words. The first place they would hope
to have success was the family. The London clergyman William Gouge
published a treatise on *Domestical Duties* in 1622 that set forth the puritan ideal. The family was as a little commonwealth, and "if the head
and several members of a family would . . . perform their own particular
duties, what a sweet society and harmony would there be." Within this
small society, each member had a role, and wives were to be obedient to
their husbands just as children and servants were to obey both parents.

At the heart of the family was the married couple, and Gouge explained that it was mutual duty of husband and wife to love and desire
one another, and to share in family obligations. While he bowed to the
traditional belief in the female's natural subordination, Gouge urged
the husband to make his wife "a joint governor of the family with himself, and refer the ordering of many things to her direction, and with
all honorable and kind respect to carry himself towards her." Whereas
traditional Christian teachings had emphasized the purpose of marriage
as procreation, puritan writers such as Gouge asserted the importance of
companionship and mutual support. Sex became an expression of love
rather than simply a means to produce children.

John Winthrop had been raised in a household that in many respects was a reflection of these new attitudes, but he found it difficult to
apply that pattern to his own first marriage. Both he and Mary Forth
were young, and it is likely that sexual attraction had been the force
that brought them to wed. Tensions were soon evident in the marriage,
and also between John's wife and his mother. Mary had not been well
educated and, more importantly, did not share John's intense faith. She
would not have been able to teach their children as John's mother had
taught him. His attempts to draw her to God by discussion of religious
matters led to quarrels, though he later persuaded himself that she had
eventually shown a greater interest in matters of faith.

Thomasine Clopton, John's second wife, was a perfect soul mate. He
had known her from the time when they were both children in Groton.
She was literate and a zealous Christian, whose piety impressed all who
knew her. This was an ideal puritan marriage, and John was devastated
when she passed away following childbirth (the baby also died) a mere

year after they had wed. His account of her last days is a moving testament to their love, as well as to her faith and concern for others.

It was John's third marriage, to Margaret Tyndal, that would become one of the great love stories of early American history. Margaret was the daughter of one of the judges in England's national courts and the niece of the clergyman Stephen Egerton. She had been taught to read and write and was noted for her piety. John rested his suit for her hand on their spiritual compatibility, but the letters he sent to her during their courtship reveal a deep emotional connection as well. Addressing her as his "sweet love," he talked of their love as, in the "springtime of our acquaintance" putting forth "no more but the leaves and blossoms" of what was to come, while "the fruit lies wrapped up in the tender bud of hope." "Love bred our fellowship," he wrote, "let love continue it. And love shall increase it until death dissolve it."

Margaret embraced her role as mother of John's children from his first marriage as well as to their own children. Because John would often be away from Groton as a member of the Suffolk bench, on legal business in London, and in preparations for the Great Migration to New England, the two often had to rely on correspondence to sustain their union. Those letters attest to the ways in which their love continued to increase over the course of their lives. They attest to a physical longing for one another, which was in keeping with puritan ideals. While puritans condemned fornication, adultery, homosexuality, bestiality, and other sexual indulgences outside of marriage, intercourse between husband and wife was viewed as a means of strengthening the love that was the cement of a proper marriage. Winthrop as well as other puritans drew comparisons between the joy experienced in union with Christ and the joy of sexual love between husband and wife. Clearly, this was a comparison that would not have been made if puritans viewed sexuality as such as sinful. Margaret was also a counselor and support to her husband, and bore much of the responsibility for raising their children. Their household became, as John had hoped, a godly kingdom.

Expanding God's realm to the broader society proved an increasingly daunting task for Winthrop and other puritans in the 1610s and 1620s. Winthrop had never relaxed his efforts to live an exemplary life, and when he was named to the Suffolk Commission of the Peace in 1615 following his return to Groton, he aspired to follow the path set by the godly magistrates he had known as a youth in applying puritan moral concerns to the task of government. But he found that the character of the bench had changed and that many of his fellow justices were more focused on their own interests than those of the people. While he found some congenial colleagues who shared his commitments, he saw other justices who had succumbed to the temptations of glory and wealth and who ridiculed those who chose a godly path, calling them "puritans, nice fools, hypocrites, hare-brained fellows, . . . and all that naught is."

Faced by such challenges, Winthrop drew support from his community of puritan friends, just as he had when he was living in Essex. As early as 1613 he had joined with Henry Sandes, John Knewstub and other clergy, as well as lay men and women, in a spiritual association, pledging to meet at least once a year to confer, and "in the meantime every of us each Friday in the week to be mindful one of another in desiring God to grant the petitions that were made to him that day, etc." Such friendships were critical to puritans. As Winthrop once explained it, "having occasion of conference with a Christian friend or 2, God so blessed it unto us, as we were all much quickened and refreshed by it; the matter of our conference was not doubtful questions to exercise our wits, etc: but a familiar examination of our own experiences."

Some Englishmen, especially some in authority, viewed such private meetings of the godly as inherently subversive, leading ordinary men and women to reach their own conclusions on matters of faith. England's lay and clerical leaders had been divided since early in the Reformation as to how far to trust lay judgment and how far to involve the lower clergy and the laity in the shaping of policies. But in the Stour Valley clergy and sympathetic magistrates encouraged this inherently democratic system of godly conferencing in which believers learned to value and trust one another as a means of striving toward a better and mutual understanding of God's will. Conferencing was a means whereby the clergy and the laity would achieve a shared understanding of broad principles of faith and practice and achieve the unity (not necessarily uniformity) that created a puritan hegemony over the region. It became a hallmark of the godly kingdom of the Stour Valley and would be an important element in the evolution of New England institutions.

THE THREAT to godliness that Winthrop detected in the changing nature of the Suffolk bench of justices continued to grow in the 1620s. Puritans had hoped that King James would be sympathetic to reform when he came to the English throne in 1603, but those hopes were soon dashed. The king's insistence on conformity led to a crackdown on some puritan practices. In the latter years of James's reign his failure to come to the support of the Protestant forces in the Thirty Years War (1618–1648) on the Continent led many puritans to criticize his foreign policy. At about that time King James also began to create bishops who were less committed than their predecessors to Calvinist orthodoxy. These churchmen, especially men such as Lancelot Andrewes, Richard Neile, and William Laud, began to promote "the beauty of holiness," a program that included high ceremonies, the return of altars to the chancel, communion rails, fine music in worship, and other elements that evoked memories of discarded Catholic practices.

Puritan concerns grew with the accession of Charles I to the throne in 1625. The new king continued to resist pressure to intervene in the Continental struggle, and his marriage to a French Catholic Queen and tolerance of her Catholic retinue further called into question his commitment to Protestantism. Charles showed himself to be a strong supporter of William Laud and other bishops who puritans feared were seeking to bring England back to Rome. The new king and his bishops discouraged anti-Catholic rhetoric, and traditional ties with Reformed churches on the Continent were allowed to decay. Most important, the king was not content with mere formal assent to his will. The bishops he appointed and promoted were less tolerant of nonconformity and more energetic in enforcing the use of disputed ceremonies than their predecessors. Controversial innovations in worship were introduced. Altars were required to be railed in and communicants instructed to kneel to receive the sacrament. Churchgoers were expected to stand during the Creed, the Epistle, and the Gospel. Wearing hats in church, a common practice, was forbidden. Sports and other recreations that the puritans had sought to ban on the Sabbath were explicitly allowed by royal authority. Lectureships, which gave puritan clergy a pulpit to preach their views without requiring them to participate in disputed ceremonies, were subject to new controls.

The new initiatives supported by Charles I affected puritans throughout the land, both in areas where godly minorities gathered in holy huddles, and in regions such as the Stour Valley where for a time they had come close to establishing a godly hegemony. Puritans in parish ministries found that conformity was no longer negotiable with local bishops. Some ministers were suspended, others were deprived of their livings, and still others saw the handwriting on the wall and began to consider emigration. Ireland, where the Protestant church was considered closer to the puritan ideal, became a destination for some, but new policies implemented by Charles I for that kingdom closed off that option. Other clergy and lay puritans immigrated to the Netherlands, long a refuge for English Protestant reformers. But others began to consider a third option—the New World.

AS THE SKY DARKENED over the godly kingdom of the Stour Valley, John Winthrop was one of those who began to think of a new England in America where he and his fellow puritans could rebuild the type of spiritual communities they had known and still cherished. He joined with like-minded puritans in the Massachusetts Bay Company, and was one of the leaders who agreed to personally migrate to New England if allowed to take the corporate charter with them. His fellow investors chose him to be the governor of the company, and thus of the colony as well. There were other, more promising puritan colonial ventures, headed by more distinguished leaders. But it was Massachusetts that would become what many viewed as a City on a Hill, exemplifying the godly kingdom that puritans aspired to.

Poised to depart for America in 1630, Winthrop preached a lay sermon to his fellow emigrants in which he set forth the ideals that he believed should shape the creation of such a society. "Christian Charity," as the sermon became known, was a restatement of the main points of the social gospel that puritan clergy had long been preaching to their flocks, together with an application of what specifically it meant for those preparing to journey to New England. Reflecting his puritan faith, Winthrop rejected the "me first" spirit of individualism that was emerging at the time, and asserted that a person's true meaning was to be found as a member of a community and that people should be concerned with the common good rather than their own selfish desires.

Recognizing that the men and women gathered before him represented different parts of the puritan tradition, Winthrop sought to meld them into a single body, and his "Christian Charity" repeatedly used words such as "consortship," "cohabitation," and "company," as well as "community" and "communion" to rhetorically drive home the lesson. They were a "company professing ourselves fellow members of Christ." They were undertaking their task by a "mutual consent." In agreeing to join this venture they had made an implicit covenant with one another and, more important, had entered into a covenant with God—indeed a "near bond of marriage" with the Lord—and God would "expect a strict performance of the articles."

What were those articles? What had the colonists pledged themselves to? As expressed by Winthrop, their goal was "to improve our lives, to do more service to the Lord," and "to increase the body of Christ whereof we are members, [so] that ourselves and our posterity may be the better preserved from the common corruptions of the world." They were to "serve the Lord and work out our salvation under the power and purity of his holy ordinances." In essence, they were to continue to expand the scope of God's rule, from themselves, to their families, and now to the general society that they proposed to found. They were called "to do justly, to love mercy, to walk humbly with our God," to "delight in each other, make others' conditions our own; rejoice together, mourn together, labor and suffer together—always having before our eyes our commission and community in the work, our community as members of the same body."

Winthrop was not prepared to offer a detailed blueprint for the society. The closest he comes to giving such direction is his statement that "whatsoever we did or ought to have done when we lived in England, the same must we do and more also where we go. That which most in their churches maintain as a truth in profession only, we must bring into familiar and constant practice, as in this duty of love." A generally over-looked phrase in the "Christian Charity" is arguably among the most significant. In talking about how God would reward the colonists if they adhered to the covenant, Winthrop said, "He will command a blessing upon us in all our ways, so that we shall see much more of his wisdom, power, goodness and truth than formerly we have been acquainted with." For puritans such as the new governor, the journey toward the kingdom of God would not end but continue when the colonists reached New England. Much of the history of the region would be a struggle between those who were satisfied to impose the truth as they then understood it, and those, such as Winthrop, who sought to continually seek for a better understanding.

ONCE IN MASSACHUSETTS, Winthrop played a key role in shaping the colony's character. Contemporaries cited the importance of his example in making this a godly society. Putting his puritan values into practice, he shared his own supplies with others in need during the difficult first months of the colony. He worked in the fields with his fellow colonists. As a magistrate he showed an awareness of the new circumstances that the men and women of Massachusetts found themselves in and applied the law with discretion and understanding.

Winthrop also guided his fellow colonists in defining their forms of government. He sought to incorporate into the charter framework the familiar patterns of English government, with the Massachusetts mag-istrates acting as an English county commission in administering affairs, levying rates, and serving as the colony's ultimate judicial authority. The members of the Court of Assistants (the equivalent of a corporate board of directors) were empowered as justices of the peace and met four times a year in Quarter Sessions. Winthrop also pushed his fellow leaders to expand freemanship to all adult male residents who applied and were of good character. A few years later it was determined that only church members would be eligible.

In establishing the Massachusetts Bay Colony the New England pu-ritans faced important questions that they had not had to confront while still in England. From the beginnings of the movement, puritans had sought to advance God's design by their individual personal reformation, to achieve a better understanding of that design by discussion with fellow saints, and then to influence others to join them by their words and example. They were interested in gathering true saints rather than mere professors. In New England, for the first time, they had the authority to impose what they saw as God's will on all members of their society. They had to decide how to best use that authority. Everyone agreed on the need for the government to encourage the formation of godly congregations and to shield the faithful from gross heresies. But how precisely should the government dictate how churches were to be formed and operate? If the government erected a perimeter fence marking the boundary between acceptable and unacceptable belief and behavior, would this stifle godly discussion that would shed further light on the faith? But if there was no such fence would this allow truly subversive views that would undermine the effort to advance the kingdom? In dealing with these issues Winthrop's instincts led him to favor broad (but not unlimited) discussion of religious matters, and to discourage efforts to precisely define a New England orthodoxy.

Not all of New England's leaders shared his humility and openness. From 1630 until his death in 1649, John Winthrop was the preeminent leader of Massachusetts, but his judgment was often questioned, and for some of those years others were voted to be governor. Magistrates such as Thomas Dudley and ministers such as Thomas Shepard sought to define faith and practice more precisely. Such men effected the banishment of Roger Williams despite Winthrop's doubts. They spearheaded the attack on the religious views commonly associated with Anne Hutchinson. They imposed sumptuary laws that proscribed various aspects of dress and behavior. This is not to suggest that Winthrop himself believed in a broad religious freedom. As governor he pronounced the sentences of banishment for John Wheelwright and Anne Hutchinson. But he also expressed his temperamental uneasiness with closing off the discussion of religious matters. When, on his deathbed, he was presented with a warrant to banish someone as a heretic, he refused, stating that he "had done too much of that work already."

In 1645 some of Winthrop's foes secured his trial before the General Court on charges of having exceeded his authority. He was easily acquitted, but as he defended his actions, he took the opportunity to expresses his understanding of the human condition. Magistrates were, he said, "men subject to passions as you are. Therefore, when you see infirmities in us you should reflect upon your own." For this puritan, his conviction that God had numbered him one of the saints remained coupled with his awareness of his fallibility as a man.

※

John Endecott

Godly Magistrate

When we think of the lay leaders of early New England the name that first springs to mind is that of John Winthrop. But before Winthrop there was John Endecott, who was sent to the New World by the leaders of the New England Company in 1628 to lay the foundations for the puritan experiment in America. After 1630, Endecott became a loyal lieutenant to his friend and colleague Winthrop, and after the latter's death in 1649 it was Endecott to whom the colonists turned to lead them through the trials of the 1650s and early 1660s. As a local magistrate and then again as a colony leader, he sought to work with New England's clergy and his fellow lay leaders to shape the godly kingdom that he had committed himself to. A soldier of the Lord, he was always zealous in his pursuit of what he was persuaded to be God's will.

THE PURITAN view of the godly magistrate was set forth in England in numerous sermons and speeches, nowhere better than in 1618, when the clergyman Samuel Ward addressed the Suffolk magistrates at the annual Assizes. John Winthrop, who had been added to the Suffolk County Commission in 1615, was among those present to hear the sermon. Ward stressed the importance of a magistrate serving the common good rather than his own self-interest. Magistrates, according to Ward, needed to be men of ability, God fearing and truthful. He was critical of the "politician of our times, learned in the wisdom of the newer state, and acquainted with the mysteries of the market, that knows how to improve things to the best for his own time and turn, and to let the common body shift for itself." He reminded the magistrates that "offices are not livings and salaries, but charges and duties" and

John Endecott
Courtesy of the Massachusetts Historical Society

criticized those who "come into them and execute them not with a mind of doing good, but of domineering; not of providing for others' welfare, but for their own."

Ward was calling for a kingdom of God built through the efforts of magistrates who had internalized puritan values and who sought to co-operate with godly clergy. He was *not* calling for a theocracy run by cler-ics. Civil affairs were to be run at the county level by godly magistrates functioning in their formal capacities as justices of the peace. In local communities pious town officials were to institute a culture of discipline that would bend people toward godly behavior. This included regulating the number of alehouses, supervising markets, tending for the poor and infirm, and punishing breaches of the peace. The role of the clergy was to meet formally and informally with civil leaders to provide advice as to how godly values should be applied to the broader society. Such cooperation was the pattern that Endecott and his fellow colonial leaders sought to put into practice in the New World.

WHILE THE PILGRIM separatists had founded the Plymouth Colony in 1620, the first true effort to build a puritan society in America was taken in June of 1628 when the New England Company sent John Endecott to take control of colonial settlements that had first been established as fishing outposts, and whose settlers had been consolidated at Naumkeag, which the colonists renamed Salem. Endecott was himself one of the six original patentees of the New England Company, and one of those who had been willing "to engage their persons in the Voyages as opposed to simply directing the affairs from England. Charged with governing the colony, he departed from England on the *Abigail*, accompanied by fifty or more fellow planters and their servants. He was described by those who sent him as "a man well known to divers persons of good part," and a contemporary who came to know him in New England referred to him as "a fit instrument to begin this wilderness work, [a man] of courage, bold, undaunted, yet sociable, and of a cheerful spirit, applying himself . . . as occasion served."

Though he would become one of the most significant figures in seventeenth-century New England, Endecott's life prior to emigrating is shrouded in mystery. It is believed he was born in England in the Armada year of 1588. It is likely that he was from the southwest, probably Devon, and that he moved to London in his early twenties. In London, Endecott may have studied law at one of the Inns of Court or Chancery. That would have been where he encountered the great jurist Sir Edward Coke, and the young Roger Williams, who was a protégé of Coke. From his later correspondence we know that Endecott fathered an illegitimate child around this time and made arrangements for it to be raised in London. The boy bore his name, John Endecott, and the father placed him with the family of Roger Dandy, a collier living in the parish of St. Andrew, Holborn, providing funds to enable Dandy to send the boy to school, and then to apprentice him in some good trade. The incident may have led Endecott to leave his place at the law schools and to enlist as one of the English volunteers fighting in the Netherlands under Sir Edward Harwood or Sir Horace Vere.

Volunteers for the Netherlands were billeted in Lincolnshire in 1623 and 1624, and it was there that in all probability Endecott encountered Samuel Skelton, the chaplain of the Earl of Lincoln. When Skelton himself came to New England he was described as someone "well known" to Endecott, and someone from whom Endecott had "formerly received much good from his ministry." Within a few years Endecott had rehabilitated his reputation and married Anne Gower, the cousin of Matthew Craddock, a prominent London merchant. He also had acquired the contacts and financial status to become one of the patentees of the New England Company.

IN AGREEING to take control of the settlements in New England Endecott was taking on a formidable task. The initial efforts to establish settlements in New England faced significant obstacles. First of these was the voyage itself. Depending on the time of year and the direction of the prevailing winds, emigrants might expect to spend anywhere from weeks to months crossing the Atlantic. Five weeks was the fastest one might expect, and the typical voyage was eight to twelve weeks. For all but the most fortunate passengers most of this time was spent below decks, in crowded quarters with hammocks and sleeping mats shoved into every nook and cranny and little or no privacy. There was little ventilation or light, and the air was foul with the odor of the unwashed passengers and with traces of vomit and feces that missed the buckets provided, and could never be adequately scoured from the decks. Food was plain and on longer voyages threatened to run out. Storms were terrifying. Those who had never before set out on the sea experienced for the first time how "the wind blew mightily, the rain fell vehemently, the sea roared, and the waves tossed us horribly." Many sickened, some died, all were weakened by the voyage.

Arrival in the New World brought no relief. Until prosperous farms and settlements were established to provide the needs of new arrivals, the emigrants were thrown on their own resources in their struggle with the wilderness. As one of the early colonists expressed it, they must "have victuals with them for a twelve-month" for they "must have meal, oat-meal, and suchlike sustenance of food until they can get increase of corn by their own labor." Hopefully, they had prepared well, for "when you are once parted with England you shall meet neither with taverns, nor alehouses, nor butchers, nor grocers, nor apothecaries' shops to help what things you need, . . . [nor] markets nor fairs to buy what you want." They needed to bring with them "meal for bread, malt for drink, woolen and linen cloth, and leather for shoes, and all manner of carpenter's tools, and a good deal of iron and steel to make nails and locks for houses, . . . furniture, . . . plows and carts, and glass for windows, and many other things." Those hoping to supplement their diet with milk and meat needed to bring livestock with them, for the New World did not have cattle, chicken, swine, or sheep. Domestic livestock were crammed into the ships, adding to the smells and noise of the voyage, and the animals consumed some of the passengers' precious food supplies. It was not un-usual for over half the cows, mares, and goats to die en route. Livestock that survived faced unaccustomed predators in America that included wolves and bear, as well as poaching by natives and the challenge of a new environment.

The environment was a shock to the colonists as well as to their ani-mals. The New England winter was much harsher than what the settlers would have been accustomed to. The frost came earlier and the thaw later, and in between the colonists experienced colder temperatures and much heavier snows. One of the early colonists wrote of how "in the winter season for two months space the earth is commonly covered with snow, which is accompanied with sharp, biting frosts, something more sharp than is in old England." Summers were "somewhat more fervent in heat than in England," a way of saying that the colonists had never experienced the hot sun of the New England summer. Cattle did best when able to graze in the salt marshes along the coast and in the tidal reaches of the region's rivers. Much of the land was wooded, which required clearing but also provided wood for building and warmth. But the woods also made it more difficult to hunt the native wild fowl, one colonist commenting that "it is harder to get a shot than it is in old England."

The combination of these factors led to a struggle for survival in the first years of colonization. The *Abigail*'s journey to America was a long and difficult one that took over two months. Arriving in early September, Endecott was faced with a grim prospect. Roger Conant, who had been in charge of the fishing settlements, had gathered the remaining settlers together and relocated them along the coast, where a small river flowed into a fine harbor, called Naumkeag by the natives. But the survivors had inadequate food and shelter, and the new arrivals had little time to get established before the onset of the New England winter. Endecott quickly directed everyone to build shelters. Some simply dug caves into the local hillsides. Endecott had to reassure the Conant party that there would be a place for them in the new order.

Endecott's instructions called for him to explore the region and make preparations for additional settlements. On one such foray he encountered the site of a small English settlement which the Plymouth Pilgrims had recently attacked. In 1624 Thomas Wollaston had established a trading post near the future site of Quincy, to the south of Massachusetts Bay. When Wollaston moved off to Virginia, Thomas Morton, together with other members of the original outpost, remained behind and continued to trade with the natives. To achieve success, Morton was willing to sell alcohol, guns, and powder to the natives, which was troubling to the Pilgrims and other Englishmen in the region. Christening the site Ma-Re Mount, he erected an eighty-foot maypole and invited natives to join in revelry that reportedly involved acts of sodomy and fornication.

The Plymouth authorities, having warned Morton not to sell weapons to the Indians, dispatched a small military expedition under Miles Standish that seized Morton and shipped him to England. Endecott must have heard of all this prior to seeking out the site of Ma-Re Mount (which he referred to as "Mount Dagon," Dagon being one of the gods of the Philistines in the Old Testament) on one of his exploratory expeditions. Finding the maypole itself still standing, he cut it down, and warned Morton's remaining followers to avoid committing further offenses.

The bitter climate, joined with the debilitating effects of the long voyage, and the lack of time to provide comfortable shelters, led to serious sickness among the Salem settlers. Endecott sent a message to the Plymouth colonists asking for aid, and the Pilgrims—perhaps impressed with the reports of Endecott's visit to Ma-Re Mount—dispatched Samuel Fuller, a physician who had come over on the *Mayflower* in 1620 and seen disease take a similar toll during the Pilgrims' first winter. Despite Fuller's help, many died in Salem, including Endecott's wife Anne.

WHILE ENDECOTT was trying to bring order to the affairs of the colony in America, the backers of the venture had reached out to additional investors in order to place their operations on a more secure footing. Because a puritan refuge would require clergy, the company, now with a new charter as the Massachusetts Bay Company, selected, with the approval of the Reverends John White and John Davenport, Francis Bright, Samuel Skelton, and Francis Higginson to serve the religious needs of the colony. The three clergymen journeyed to America in the spring of 1629. Bright was dispatched to an outpost that had been established on Boston Bay at the future site of Charlestown. Skelton and Higginson remained in Naumkeag, recently renamed Salem (the ancient form of the word Jerusalem, related to the Hebrew name for peace), where they quickly set about organizing a church. Because one of the functions of a godly magistrate was to nurture the church, Endecott appointed July 20 as a day of fast and humiliation for the colonists to shun worldly cares and focus on God's work. The first part of the day was devoted to prayer and preaching, after which Skelton and Higginson were questioned by their fellow settlers about their spiritual callings. Those gathered decided that the two men were blameless in their lives and qualified by education and the gifts of the Spirit to preach and guide the godly. A written vote was conducted in which the men present indicated their choice of Samuel Skelton to be the pastor of the congregation and Francis Higginson to be the teacher, the role of the former being in theory primarily to offer pastoral guidance in his sermons, while the teacher was to explain doctrine in his preaching. Some of the "gravest" laymen present, including Endecott, then placed their hands on the two clergy and prayed that they might indeed be ministers of God.

In the following days Higginson drew up "a confession of faith and church covenant according to scripture" and shared it with those who had taken part in the activities of July 20. An invitation was also sent out to the members of the Plymouth congregation to join in the formal organization of the Salem church. On August 6, after Skelton and Higginson preached, thirty members of the community swore to the covenant, thus officially constituting the church. Lay elders and deacons were formally chosen, and the two clergymen were ordained by the laying on of hands. Governor Bradford and the Plymouth delegation were delayed in their arrival by contrary winds, but did get there in time to extend the right hand of fellowship to the new church.

Once the covenant was sworn to, the church was formed. But one of the questions that still needed to be answered was how additional members were to be added, and this was tied up with questions about Baptism. Higginson had consulted with Plymouth's elder William Brewster and the two men found themselves in agreement. They believed that children should be baptized and when they became adults they would be admitted into the church upon demonstrating their knowledge of the faith and their swearing of the covenant on their own behalf. This recognized the validity of infant baptism in the Church of England, but at the same time denied those who were so baptized the rights of members until they were accepted into a gathered congregation in New England. Higginson's own son, who would also become a noted clergyman, came over to New England with his parents at the age of fifteen. He was examined on his knowledge by Samuel Skelton and then publicly owned the covenant before being admitted to the Lord's Supper. Some newly arrived immigrants whom the clergymen had known in England were denied the Lord's Supper until the new church had judged them worthy.

It is possible that while spending time in Salem tending the settlement's sick during the winter of 1628–1629, Plymouth's Samuel Fuller had engaged the new arrivals in discussions of his own colony's situation and the Pilgrims' religious practices. Plymouth was a colony of separatists who renounced all ties to the Church of England. Massachusetts puritans maintained that they were still in communion with the national church, the church in which their faith had been nurtured. Three thousand miles from the nearest bishop, however, the differences in the two groups' practices paled in comparison to their commitment to lead godly lives. This was evident when, following Fuller's visit, Endecott wrote to Governor Bradford. He thanked the Plymouth governor for the aid that had been tendered and urged that the two colonies "may, as Christian brethren, be united by a heavenly and unfeigned love; bending all our hearts and forces in furthering a work beyond our strength, with reverence and fear, fastening our eyes always on him that only is able to direct and prosper all our ways." As far as Endecott was concerned, the members of the two colonies were "servants to one master, and of the same household." "God's people," he wrote, "are all marked with one and the same mark, and sealed with one and the same seal, and have for the main, one and the same heart, guided by one and the same spirit of truth; and where this is, there can be no discord, nay, here must needs be sweet harmony." Throughout his career Endecott would be a stern judge of those who were outside his understanding of what comprised God's people, but he would always hold a broad understanding of who bore God's mark and seal.

The formation of the Salem church under Endecott's oversight was a pivotal event that set the course for the religious development of the Massachusetts Bay Colony. But it would also be a controversial event. In his account of the colony, Higginson rejoiced, writing, "Thanks be to God, we have here plenty of preaching and diligent catechizing, with strict and careful exercise and good and commendable orders to bring our people into a Christian conversation. . . . And thus we doubt not but God will be with us; and if God be with us, who can be against us?" They would soon find out. In Salem itself two of the colony's councilors, John and Samuel Browne, were sharply critical of the way worship was conducted. The Brownes had invested in the company and journeyed to New England in the spring of 1629. John Browne was described as "a man experienced in the laws of our kingdom," and both he and Samuel had been appointed to Endecott's governing council. Though they must have been involved in the formation of the church, they soon were concerned about the forms of worship. It would appear that Skelton and Higginson largely, if not entirely, dispensed with the liturgy prescribed in the Book of Common Prayer, which offended some of the more traditionalist members of the community. Those individuals began to absent themselves from the church and to assemble at the Brownes' to conduct meetings with readings from the Prayer Book. They accused the Salem church of separatism.

The goal of the Massachusetts Bay Company was to establish proper worship, not freedom for anyone to worship as he would. While differences might be tolerated within the community of the church, separation from it was not acceptable. It was the responsibility of the godly magistrate to defend the churches. Endecott summoned the Brownes before the council, where the two men argued that they were the ones who properly held to the orders of the Church of England, while Skelton and Higginson were separatists who would be shown to be Anabaptists (who rejected infant baptism) as well. The two ministers denied these charges but acknowledged that "they came away from the Common Prayer and ceremonies, and had suffered much for nonconformity in their native land, and therefore, being in a place where they might have their liberty, they neither could nor would use them, because they judged the imposition of these things to be sinful corruptions in the worship of God." Evidently, the "generality" of the colonists supported this position. Unable to persuade the Brownes, Endecott and the council determined to ship them back to England, charging them for the cost and reimbursing them for their investment in the colony at a low valuation. The English leaders of the company later settled with the Brownes to quiet them.

The Massachusetts Bay Company appointed ministers to serve the needs of its members, and those ministers determined how, in the absence of established English parishes, they could best do so. In the end, as the historian Stephen Foster has argued, "quite simply, the earliest New England ecclesiastical foundations were the only way according to both theology and practice (at about 1630) that professing Christians [in New England] could have been organized in a church way." Endecott followed the lead of the community's ministers and was zealous in implementing their plan and opposing those who challenged the Salem consensus.

WITH THE ARRIVAL of John Winthrop and the first wave of the Great Migration to Massachusetts in the summer of 1630, Endecott assumed a secondary role as a member of the colony's Court of Assistants and as a local magistrate in Salem. But on occasion he would emerge on the center stage of the colony's history, more than once due to his enthusiasm for the ideas of his friend Roger Williams. Following his arrival in Massachusetts in 1631, Williams decided to settle in Salem after he determined that the Boston puritans had not sufficiently cut themselves off from the Church of England. After a brief stay there, Williams moved on to Plymouth. There, according to Governor Bradford, Williams "began to fall into some strange opinions, and from opinion to practice, which caused some controversy between the church and him." Some of those opinions were "that it is not lawful for an unregenerate man to pray, nor to take an oath, and in special not the oath of fidelity to the civil government; nor was it lawful for a godly man to have communion, either in family prayer, or in an oath, with such as they judged unregenerate; also, that it was not lawful so much as to hear the godly ministers of England, when they occasionally went thither." Here we find the genesis of Williams's insistence on the need for total separation of church and state to prevent any impingement on God's sovereignty, but we also find the seeds of his unwillingness to even join in prayer with family members who may not have been saved. These positions were more than the Pilgrims were ready to accept.

Disappointed with Plymouth, Williams returned to Salem, where he preached unofficially and continued to express radical ideas. Recognizing the young clergyman's zeal for purity, Endecott became his ally as well as his friend. Williams asserted that women should wear veils when they went abroad, but especially in church services, as a sign that they had inherited Eve's corruption. He questioned the appropriateness of the red cross of St. George as a symbol on the English flag. He took the position that it was inappropriate for the king to have granted a charter to Massachusetts since the monarch had no true claim to the land he was dispensing. Williams had developed this last argument in a manuscript treatise that he had shared with Plymouth's governor Bradford, and he continued to elaborate on the argument after returning to Salem. He was not concerned so much with the natives' rights to the lands as he was convinced that European powers that claimed the right to grant lands on the basis that they were "Christian nations" or parts of "Christendom" were wrong because the claims were blasphemous, there being no such thing as a "Christian" nation.

Williams was a figure of extraordinary charisma, respected and admired by many colonists, including John Winthrop and John Endecott. At this time it was customary for matters of faith and practice to be openly debated in the churches of Massachusetts as the colonists sought further light on what they should believe and how they should behave. In early March 1634, Williams's position on women's veils was raised in the Boston church by John Endecott, who would have been in Boston for the meeting of the General Court and Court of Assistants. John Cotton took the position that "where (by the custom of the place) they were not a sign of women's subjection, they were not commanded by the apostle." Endecott objected, and in this instance the debate became heated, prompting Governor Winthrop to intervene to bring an end to the discussion.

A growing number of the Bay's leaders feared the consequences of Williams's views. His challenge to the king's authority in granting the charter might, if it reached English ears, pose a potential threat to the security of the colony and was not a matter to be openly debated. The issue was of particular concern at the time since early criticisms of New England had led the king's Privy Council to appoint a special Commission for Regulating Plantations that was to be headed by, of all people, Archbishop of Canterbury William Laud. John Winthrop, who admired Williams's fervor, took steps to dampen the potential danger. He reviewed the treatise and managed to persuade both Williams and John Endecott that the argument was at best impolitic. In December 1633 the General Court took up the matter and sought the advice of "some of the most judicious ministers," who found Williams's argument erroneous and chastised him for citing uncomplimentary verses from the Book of Revelation that he "did personally apply to our present king, Charles." The Salem minister appeared before the court and, prepared by Winthrop, promised not to repeat his complaints about the charter. When the Court of Assistants again reviewed the controversy in January 1634 they called in Boston's two ministers, Cotton and Wilson, who advised them to not take any further action, since the treatise was "very obscure" and subject to various interpretations.

Then, in November 1634, John Endecott cut the red cross from the royal ensign being used by the Salem trainband (militia), which had begun to drill more often due to the threat of English action against the colony. His explanation was that "the red cross was given to the king of England by the pope, as an ensign of victory and as a superstitious thing, and a relic of Antichrist." Williams, of course, had made the same point earlier and both Winthrop and John Cotton agreed in theory that the "cross in the banner" was "the image of an idol, and the greatest idol in the Church of Rome." But Endecott had put the theory into practice in a dramatic and highly public manner. It was not proper, he believed, for Christian magistrates to temporize or to compromise with evil.

Endecott's action plunged the colony into discord, as once again debate raged as to what was acceptable and what was not. Thomas Hooker, Thomas Dudley, and some of the other leaders believed that the Reformation had weaned the people from idolatrous uses of such symbols, and that the cross in the flag might therefore be used. Everyone could agree, however, that defacing the king's flag could be the final event that would bring action against the colony. The Court censured Endecott and deprived him of his eligibility to hold office for a year. Since many in the colony supported his stand, the reason given for his punishment was that he had acted rashly without first bringing his concern to the colony authorities. Meanwhile, the debate over further use of the king's flag with the cross continued until a compromise was worked out whereby that flag would continue to fly over Castle William, in Boston harbor, but new colors without a cross were devised for the town trainbands.

Roger Williams continued to challenge the colony's leadership. With

John Winthrop no longer governor and Endecott removed from the magistracy for defacing the royal ensign, in October 1635 the General Court ordered the clergyman to be expelled from the colony. Informed by John Winthrop of a plan to seize him for this purpose, Williams left the Bay in mid-winter and journeyed to the Narragansett Bay, where he founded the town of Providence.

Endecott was restored to office in 1636. Over the following decade he supported John Winthrop on matters that concerned the colony as a whole, but was mostly content to make his mark as a local magistrate. The General Court had recognized the burden that the growing population was placing on the legal system and had divided the colony into separate counties, each with its separate court to handle its own administrative and judicial matters. Salem was in the new Essex County, and Endecott presided as a godly magistrate over the quarterly meetings of that court, which generally met in Salem. Here his focus was transforming the puritan moral code into a culture of discipline through the application of the laws of the colony.

The Essex court heard cases that dealt with a wide range of issues and offenses. Drunkenness was a common charge; a Mr. Burrell was fined and ordered to sit in the stocks on the next training day for drunkenness. James Smith was to be whipped for stealing and disobedience to his parents. Mary Boutwell of Lynn was sentenced to be whipped but was given clemency and only admonished; her crimes were living idly and stealing, "taking away others' victuals pretending community of all things." Robert Adams was set by the heels in the stocks for being uncharitable to a poor man in distress. Reuben Guppi ran away from his pregnant wife but was caught and whipped for that crime as well as for theft and lying to the officials. Hugh Browne's wife was severely whipped for breaking her husband's head, threatening that she would kill him, throwing stones at him, which caused his face to bleed, calling him beast, and wishing him hanged. Servants who ran away were often caught and brought before the court. Elizabeth Johnson, a servant, was whipped and fined for "unseemly practices between her and another maid." Robert Cocker was whipped and fined for contracting himself to one woman when he was already betrothed to another. In the 1640s, the court began to see cases that involved public disturbances resulting from the spread of views opposing the practice of infant baptism. Endecott earned a reputation as a strict judge in his dealings with those who offended against the established orthodoxy of the colony, one litigant complaining, "It was better to go to hell gate for mercy than to Mr. Endecott for justice."

The court also exercised administrative functions. Endecott and his colleagues on the bench took seriously the need for education. They assigned responsibility for engaging a schoolmaster for Salem and made sure that parents paid for their children's education, though "if any poor body hath children or a child to be put to school and not able to pay for their schooling that the town will pay for it." The concern extended to servants as well. On one occasion Joseph Armitage was required to post bond to insure that his servant, "Tage Omoholme, son to Direman oMajonie, shall be taught to read the English tongue."

FOLLOWING THE DEATH of John Winthrop in 1649, the colonists elected Endecott as governor. He was returned to that office in all but two of the annual elections from that date until his death in 1665. Retaining his home in Salem, he found relaxation from public cares by paying attention to his farm, called Orchard Hills, and in particular to his pear trees. But to better exercise his responsibilities as governor, Endecott established a Boston residence, acquiring a home in what is now Scollay Square, though he did not transfer his church membership until 1664.

Under his leadership, in 1652 Massachusetts sent an expedition to explore and establish its northern border. The commissioners identified the source of the Merrimac River, the stipulated boundary, at what is now known as the Weirs, on New Hampshire's Lake Winnipasaukee. Endecott Rock still marks the spot. Also in 1652 the colony established a mint and began to issue its own currency. In the latter 1650s Massachusetts extended its authority over what is now southern Maine, then designated as the Bay's York County. Endecott was a strong supporter of England's Puritan Revolution and the rule of the saints there under

Oliver Cromwell. Indicative of these feelings, he welcomed the regicides Edward Whalley and William Goffe when they fled to the colonies after the Restoration of the Stuart monarchy in 1660.

During the 1650s New England was challenged by the arrival of Quaker missionaries. Endecott engaged some of these individuals in dialogue, but had no problem with imposing punishments on them when they proved resistant to what he believed to be the truth. In 1658 Massachusetts enacted the death penalty on Quaker missionaries who returned from banishment. Endecott imposed this sentence on three Quakers, but bowed to the king's prohibition of future executions in 1661. While he accepted that royal directive, Endecott resisted other attempts by the crown to curtail the autonomy that Massachusetts claimed by virtue of its charter. Recognizing this, in 1664 Charles II demanded that the colonists replace Endecott at the next elections. But the governor died in March 1665, before this demand would have been tested. His contemporary John Hull remembered him as "a man of pious and zealous spirit. . . . He died poor, as most of our rulers do, having more attended the public than their own private interests."

⁂

John Wilson

Puritan Pastor

One of the hallmarks of the puritan program to reform the Church of England and to build a godly kingdom in America was an insistence that every community have a well-educated clergyman whose preaching would inform the faithful of the nuances of faith and guide them toward godly living. John Wilson was one such individual, and his life illustrates the many aspects of the task—preparing and delivering sermons on Sunday and designated lecture days, visiting and catechizing members of his flock, and counseling troubled souls. In the congregational system of church governance that New Englanders as well as many other puritans embraced, the clergyman also met with lay elders to manage the affairs of the particular congregation, engaged with the general membership to decide issues before them and to determine possible censure of erring brethren, and joined with other clergymen to shape a common path for their churches. In an ideal world, the minister would also cooperate with the godly magistrate in working toward the creation and maintenance of a social order that reflected godly values. Where such cooperation was lacking, the clergyman might become a prophet, calling errant leaders and citizens to the path of righteousness. While the way in which each individual responded to these demands varied considerably, there is a pattern that identifies men such as John Wilson as puritan pastors.

B EFORE HE became a pastor, John Wilson became a puritan. But this was something that many would not have anticipated, since he grew up within the Protestant establishment of the Church of England. His father, the Reverend William Wilson, had been a chaplain to Archbishop of Canterbury Edmund Grindal and had married Grindal's niece, Isabel Woodhall of Walden, Essex. Grindal, one of the Marian exiles, had supported some reforms in the church and had been suspended by Queen Elizabeth for his refusal to suppress prophesyings, clerical gatherings where respected clergymen discussed the meaning of scripture with less educated colleagues and, occasionally, a lay audience. The suspension of his patron did not bring an end to William Wilson's advancement, since he was willing to conform to what his superiors expected of him. William went on to hold a number of prestigious church positions, including the posts of canon of St. George's Chapel at Windsor and chancellor of St. Paul's Cathedral. His son John was born at Windsor in 1591 and was educated at Eton before matriculating at King's College, Cambridge, at the age of fourteen. His family expected these to be the first steps toward a distinguished career in the church establishment.

There was a long tradition of evangelical, or puritan, ideas at Cambridge. The young Wilson was influenced by one of the puritan leaders, William Ames, on whose advice he took to hosting a gathering of fellow religious seekers in his college rooms, where they engaged in fasting, prayer, and discussion. Informal gatherings of individuals to further their spiritual growth was one of the activities that separated puritans from other Englishmen. Richard Rogers had identified this as an important way of bringing oneself and one's neighbors into godliness in his popular *Seven Treatises* (1603). Browsing in a Cambridge bookseller's shop, Wilson purchased a copy of Rogers's book and was so impressed by the volume that he traveled to the Stour Valley to hear Rogers preach in his Wethersfield parish. He heard that clergyman urge upon his listeners the importance of living gospel lives and putting into practice the biblical demand to serve God through helping the least of one's brethren. Impressed by this social gospel message, Wilson took to visiting local prisons to minister to the inmates.

His growing association with puritans led the young Wilson to distrust some of the ceremonies of the established church that he had previously observed, practices that he now saw as remnants of Catholicism. With little sympathy for such views at his college, there was talk of his expulsion. Relations with his father became strained, since the elder Wilson could not understand how his son could throw away the glittering prizes that his education and connections offered him in the church. For all of these reasons, John left Cambridge about 1608 and began a study of the law at London's Inner Temple.

By 1613, however, Wilson had returned to Cambridge and received his degree. He was drawn back to the Stour Valley, where Richard Rogers had made such an impression upon him, and by the end of the decade he was preaching in rotation in the parishes of Steeple Bumstead, Stoke-by-Clare, Clare, and Cavendish. Around 1617 some parishioners of All Saints parish in Sudbury heard Wilson preach and arranged an invitation for him to become lecturer at their church. He initially demurred, requesting that the parishioners as a whole confirm the call. Following a day of fasting and prayer with neighboring ministers present, the call was repeated, and Wilson was installed in the post. This was an extraordinary example of the ways in which laymen were invited to participate in such decisions in some parishes in the Stour Valley, and indicates the trust that Wilson was willing to place in the judgment of godly laymen at this time. Though the Elizabethan reformer Dudley Fenner had asserted that "ministers should be appointed to their office by the covenant of the people," it was still rare in England at this time.

As he stood in the pulpit of All Saints, Wilson faced a mixed body of English men and women. Some were individuals who had experienced what they believed was God's caress. For such men and women the preacher's task was to provide them spiritual food to nourish their faith. Such men and women brought their Bibles with them to check the scriptural references, took notes of the key points in the sermon, and expected to carry away points to ponder. At the other extreme, mixed in the congregation, were those who were ignorant of all but the most basic concepts of Christianity. They might have memorized the Commandments and the Lord's Prayer, but had little comprehension of what it all meant. It was the task of the preacher to get such parishioners to

understand and internalize the principles of faith. Most challenging for
the clergyman were those who were often referred to as "mere professors"
— those who understood the faith and acknowledged the need to serve
God, but who didn't think that God demanded as much of them as the
puritans maintained. These were men and women who were likely to
disrupt the service by chatting with those around them, or, on occasion,
to miss the service to bowl, fish, or devote their Sabbath to other recreations. Often the preacher would seek to indict the behavior of such
lukewarm Christians, verbally lashing their shortcomings. Designed to
break through their self-satisfaction, such attacks could also breed re-
sentment among those so targeted and thus lead to friction in the parish.

Wilson recognized that it was his task to minister to all who sat in the
pews before him. While he might have distinguished between those of
his listeners who were saints and those who were sinners, he would have
understood that God might act through his sermons to convey saving
grace to some of those who appeared "ungodly." During his years at
Sudbury he earned a reputation as a powerful and affecting preacher. Just
as he had traveled from Cambridge to hear Richard Rogers, so now students such as Thomas Goodwin, Jeremiah Burroughes, William Bridge,
and Henry Jessey traveled from the university to hear him.

There are a variety of stories that were told about Wilson that, true or
not, indicate the type of reputation that was likely to grow around a clergyman noted for being one of God's chosen. A tradesman of the town,
"much addicted to vicious practices, among them pilfering," who regularly absented himself from services, saw a throng of people flocking to
hear Wilson preach on one occasion and decided to find out what drew
so many to hear the clergyman. Attending the service, he heard a sermon
that seemed aimed directly at him on the text "Let him that stole, steal
no more," after which he repented and became noted as a pious Christian.
On another occasion, Dr. John Duke of Colchester encountered Wilson
shortly after the physician left the sickbed of a man who had informed
against Wilson and other puritan clergy to the bishop. Duke offered
his judgment that the informer would recover, but Wilson responded,
"you are mistaken, Mr. Doctor, he is a dead man," and shortly thereafter
Duke received the news that his patient had, unexpectedly, perished.

On yet another occasion, Wilson's young son John, about four years old, fell from a fourth-story loft where he had been playing. The state of his broken and bloody body led spectators to believe that he would soon die, but his father's prayers were answered by his full recovery.

The puritan clergyman was expected to play a role in the civic affairs of his community. Sudbury was an incorporated market town of three parishes that had its own elected mayor and local officials, and had the right to send two representatives to the national Parliament. It faced many of the social and economic problems common to such communities. Civic leaders took care to regulate the moral climate of the town, and consulted with the town's clergy on such matters. In 1622 they paid for a new ducking stool for the punishment of scolds. In 1624 they drew up regulations for a new house of corrections "for the safe-keeping, punishing, and settling to work of rogues, vagabonds, sturdy beggars, idle persons, and such as are not able to find for themselves habitations, nor to sustain themselves and their children." Wilson would have been involved when they used a bequest to distribute shirts and smocks to poor men and women of the town parishes.

As part of the effort to create a godly kingdom, clergy and their lay allies used their influence to place other godly men in positions of authority not only on the local and county level, but also on the national level. In 1624 Sir Robert Crane, a local justice and member of Parliament himself, sought (unsuccessfully) to use his influence to have the citizens of Sudbury elect John Winthrop of nearby Groton, along with Crane himself, to be their representatives in the coming Parliament. Wilson likely supported Winthrop, and this was not the only instance of his electioneering. Another example came a few years later, when he corresponded with Sir Francis Barrington, one of the leaders of the godly on the Essex side of the Stour Valley, about another parliamentary election, indicating that the godly were committed to the support of Sir William Spring and Sir Nathaniel Barrington for one of the county seats.

WILSON WAS AMONG those who accompanied Winthrop to New England in 1630 and was the clergyman the governor had chosen to minister to the congregation he would himself belong to. Having settled in Charlestown, to the north of Boston harbor, the particular band of settlers that included Winthrop set out to organize itself for religious worship. On July 30, 1630, they observed a day of fasting to ask God's support, with the services held under a shady oak tree. Such fast days were critical events in the struggle to advance the kingdom of God, focusing the colonists on their inadequacy and their reliance on the help of the sovereign God—just as days of thanksgiving recognized that what blessings they had were gifts from God. Following the service in Charlestown, those present discussed their "godly desire" to worship God properly. John Wilson, along with the laymen Isaac Johnson, John Winthrop, and Thomas Dudley, entered into a covenant whereby they did "solemnly and religiously . . . promise and bind ourselves to walk in all our ways according to the rule of the Gospel and in all sincere conformity to His holy ordinances, and in mutual love and respect each to other, so near God shall give us grace." Over the following days others were admitted into the covenant, and on August 2 the congregation elected John Wilson as their minister. Similar congregations were formed in the other communities being established in the colony. In the fall of 1630, with fresh water being scarce at Charlestown, the majority of the community, including Winthrop and Wilson, moved across the bay to relocate at Boston.

ALL OF THESE CHURCHES reflected congregational principles that rooted the formation and control of the individual church in the actions of lay believers. While many identified such churches as separatist, there were other precedents that the New England colonists were able to draw on. During the Marian era, English Protestant exiles had viewed themselves as remnants of the true Church of England and banded together to form congregations in various cities of northern Europe. More significant was the example of the over two dozen English congregations that were functioning in the Netherlands in the early seventeenth century. Early in Queen Elizabeth's reign, Bishop Edmund Grindal had extended permission to the clergy of the merchant chapels abroad to adapt to their local religious environment, including the right to use the Prayer Book selectively, to place greater emphasis on the sermon, and to dispense with the surplice. Various congregations, such as the English church established at Amsterdam in 1607, largely followed this pattern. As different from the organization and forms of worship of the English church as some of these churches were, they were still considered part of the English national church. There were also congregations that gathered around the English regiments stationed in the Netherlands. Not under the close supervision of any English bishop, these churches, like those of the merchants, became self-governing and adopted many of the reforms being advocated by the godly at home. Yet, they were not regarded as separatist congregations either, but as part of the national church.

In England itself, the idea that a true church was formed by the agreement of its members rather than the authorization of the hierarchy, and that the individual congregation should determine its own affairs was being debated within the puritan community. Certain parishes, like St. Stephen's in London's Coleman Street, had the right to choose their own rector. John Wilson had refused to accept the call to All Saints in Sudbury, Suffolk, unless the members of the congregation signified that it was their desire that he do so. We know that John Cotton entered into a separate covenant with godly members of his Boston, Lincolnshire, parish (and possibly nonparishioners such as the Hutchinsons), thus forming in essence a gathered church within the parish. More striking was the London church gathered by covenant under the leadership of Henry Jacob. Separate in that it was not a parish church nor in any other way recognized by the church authorities, it firmly declared its place in the communion of the Church of England. Such experiments influenced the formation of the Salem church, and were elaborated on by Wilson and the founders of the other churches of early Massachusetts.

PURITAN CONGREGATIONS in New England ideally had two clerical leaders, a pastor and a teacher. In theory, the teacher preached mostly on doctrinal matters while the pastor addressed issues involving the application of Christian principles to the individual's life. In practice there was little distinction. In October 1633 the newly arrived John Cotton was installed as the teacher of the Boston church. Wilson was the pastor. As had been the case in Sudbury, Wilson devoted himself energetically to the needs of his flock. But his role was larger. In Sudbury he had been a lecturer, preaching but not administering the sacraments. In the Boston church more was expected of him.

Wilson rapidly established himself as a beloved pastor. John Winthrop called him a "very sincere, holy man." Another contemporary praised him as being "eminent for love and zeal" and cited his key role in sustaining the faith of the congregation during the first months of the settlement, months during which many sickened and died. Edward Johnson, a contemporary who knew and revered Wilson, spoke of him as having a weak constitution, but as being tireless in nurturing the sick and keeping up the spirits of the survivors. Tradition tells of a sermon he preached on one occasion in which he took as his text Genesis 35:19, the death of Rachel when she and Jacob were journeying to Canaan in accord with God's will. Even the chosen people, en route to the Promised Land, could expect to suffer.

Wilson was convinced that the New Englanders were chosen by God for great things. Commenting on "a great combat" between a mouse and a snake witnessed by settlers in Watertown, in which, "after a long fight, the mouse prevailed and killed the snake," Wilson offered the interpretation that "the snake was the devil, the mouse was a poor contemptible people which God hath brought hither [to New England], which should overcome Satan here and dispossess him of his kingdom." On the same occasion, Wilson revealed that he had had a dream in which "he saw a Church arise out of the earth, which grew up & became a marvelous goodly church."

Along with Cotton, Wilson presided over the weekly Sunday services. The churches of New England discarded the liturgy set forth in the Book of Common Prayer and developed forms of worship comparable to the practices of the English congregations in the Netherlands. The morning service in the Boston meetinghouse began at nine o'clock with Wilson offering prayers of intercession and thanksgiving lasting about a quarter of an hour, including special intentions put forward by members of the congregation. Either Wilson or Cotton would then read and expound on a passage from scripture, which would be followed by the congregation singing one of the psalms. One of the ministers would then preach a sermon of an hour or longer; that also was followed by a psalm. A lengthy extemporaneous blessing and prayer would conclude the normal service. At two o'clock in the afternoon the congregation reassembled. The pattern of worship was the same as in the morning, with the clergyman who had not preached then giving the afternoon sermon. The sermons were the centerpieces of the services, designed to sustain the faith of the saints and to help those awaiting God's call to prepare for it.

Once a month Wilson administered the Lord's Supper after the morning service. He baptized the children of church members after the afternoon service when there was an infant to be joined to the church. He visited the members of his congregation as their pastor, and catechized the youth of the church. He also met with those who aspired to join the church to discuss their spiritual condition and help them to come before the congregation.

In England puritans had complained of the failure of church authorities to exercise proper discipline in correcting sins and excluding sinners from the sacraments. In New England the colonists employed various measures to bring those who erred in doctrine or behavior back to a proper relationship with God and their fellow saints. Wilson, as pastor, had the task of bringing errant members before the congregation and passing official judgment on them as the members of the church determined appropriate. The records of the church are filled with examples of this. The first formal step, after informal efforts to persuade the offender, was usually a formal admonishment. If this failed to produce the desired result, a sentence of excommunication was passed, but this was a last and serious tool used in the hope of producing reformation and reacceptance into the parish. Judith Smith, admonished for various unnamed errors, for "obstinate persistence therein," and "for sundry lies" was "cast out of the church with joint consent." Anne Walker, having been on more than one occasion privately admonished for "drunkenish, intemperate, and unclean or wantonish behavior, and likewise of cruelty towards her children" was "with joint consent of the congregation cast out of the church." James Mattock was "by our pastor [John Wilson] (in the name of and with the consent of the church, taken by their silence) cast out of the church" for scandalous behavior in Old and New England, including having "denied conjugal fellowship unto his wife for the space of two years," for having physically abused her, for having had sexual relations with a married woman, and for drunkenness. In most of the recorded cases excommunication had the desired result; the sinner did repent and was readmitted into the church.

In some cases the sin committed was also a crime, and the magistrates handed down the civil punishment. On more than one occasion Wilson found himself accompanying a convicted felon to the gallows to encourage the individual to publicly repent. In December 1638 Dorothy Talby was hanged for having murdered her three-year-old daughter. Wilson and Hugh Peter, the pastor of Salem, were unsuccessful in getting her to acknowledge her sin. William Hatchet was sentenced to death in December 1641 for the crime of buggery with a cow on the Lord's Day. On the day of execution the cow was slaughtered, Wilson offered a lengthy prayer, and Hatchet was hanged.

While his primary responsibility was to the Boston church that had called him as its pastor, Wilson reached out beyond that community. On various occasions he travelled to preach to settlers in new towns that had not yet organized a church. His outreach extended beyond his fellow Englishmen. During the early days of the colony a small community of Indians lived in the Charlestown area. When the natives suffered from disease, Wilson visited them and tried as best he could to communicate the basics of Christianity while tending to their physical needs. In the process he struck up a friendship with the tribal leader, Sagamore John, who was described as "of gentle and good disposition." In 1632, the Sagamore himself contracted smallpox. Wilson visited him and brought him what physical and spiritual comfort he could. Edward Johnson recorded that on his death bed Sagamore John expressed regret that he had not embraced Christianity, and entrusted his only child to Wilson, asking him to raise the boy in English and Christian ways, which the clergyman did.

WILSON RECOGNIZED that in a system that rested on the right of each individual congregation to reach its own decisions on matters of faith and practice, it was critical for the clergy to work formally and informally to promote unity. He supported the practice of regular clerical conferences, similar to those that had united puritan clergy in the Stour Valley. He also promoted less formal gatherings. By the mid-1630s most of the colony's clergy traveled to Boston each week to hear John Cotton's Thursday lecture day sermon and then retired to John Wilson's house for refreshments and discussion. Wilson in turn regularly led members of his church to nearby towns to hear the Bay's other clergy, the Boston group singing psalms on their journeys.

Through such means, the clergy strove for symmetry and cultivated toleration for divergent opinions in cases where unity was not possible. The spirit of clerical communion that Wilson became noted for was best expressed in the words of one of his fellow ministers, John Eliot, who advised one of his clerical colleagues, "Brother, learn the meaning of these three little words — bear, forbear, forgive." From the earliest days of the colony Wilson saw it as one of his tasks to work to bring about consensus among the colonists, and to heal divisions when possible. When a dispute arose between John Winthrop and Thomas Dudley in the summer of 1632, the latter critical of Winthrop's leniency in dealing with the colonists, Wilson was one of the key figures seeking to reconcile the two leaders. When the two magistrates quarreled again in 1636, Wilson again mediated successfully. He accompanied Winthrop on a visit to Plymouth in October 1632, where they discussed religious and civil policies with the Pilgrim leadership. He continued to serve the colony this way throughout his career. In 1641 he labored to heal the division between the Rev. Stephen Bachellor and his congregation in Hampton, New Hampshire. In 1647 he was one of the messengers delegated by the Boston church to extend "brotherly care" to the divided church at Hingham. In 1652 he was one of the messengers sent by the Boston church to Malden in response to that congregation's concerns about the irregular ordination of its pastor. In 1659 he was a member of a similar delegation dispatched to help settle divisions in the church at Hartford.

When John Cotton joined Wilson in the ministry of the Boston church, the two men quickly settled into a comfortable relationship. Together they encouraged the members of the congregation to join them in seeking further light on their faith and practice. The two men complemented each other in their understanding of the process of salvation. They differed on the extent to which the elect could draw assurance of their salvation from the first stirrings of grace as opposed to from sanctified behavior. This was an area where puritans in general had been unable to reach agreement, but the dialogue between those who trusted in the witness of the Spirit and those who looked for behavioral fruits of spiritual rebirth helped individuals better understand their own condition. In Boston, John Wilson sought to help listeners find grounds for assurance in their lives, recognizing the witness of the Spirit as a gift given only to some. He represented what might be called the "eclectic middle of puritan practical divinity." Cotton preferred to preach on the experience of God's caress. But each respected the views of the other, and they could agree on whether or not given individuals were qualified to enter the Boston church as full members.

In 1634, when Wilson returned to England for a time on family business, Cotton was left as the sole preacher in the Boston church and the element of dialogue was no longer evident in the pulpit. Cotton's emphasis on the Spirit was not tempered by reminders of the law. At the same time, the Boston church had grown, its membership augmented by new immigrants who had been radicalized by the recent attacks on puritanism in England. The influx of new members and new ideas resulted in vigorous exchanges that led some to call the Boston congregation at this time "the most glorious church in the world."

Though some of the new arrivals, such as William Hutchinson and his wife Anne, and Sir Henry Vane, were more sympathetic to Cotton's spiritist emphasis, godly men and women of different beliefs were still able to see the root of the matter in each other and join in holy communion, and this continued for a time after Wilson's return. One observer, Giles Firmin, described an occasion when a discussion broke out in the Boston church. Wilson, preaching on Mark 2:5, indicated that he believed that "the palsy-man had Faith, because Christ tells him *his sins were forgiven*" and there is no forgiveness without Faith. "Up rose" a member of the congregation, who indicated that "he was not satisfied" with this reading, "then another after him" also expressed doubts. John Cotton then intervened and agreed with Wilson, following which others, "one after another," disputed the position. According to Firmin, "Sir Henry Vane was the man that did embolden" those who asked such questions, because "when ministers had done preaching, he would find questions to put to them." This was also the case when visitors preached to the church.

The harmony of the Boston church was shattered in 1636. The clergyman Thomas Shepard, who had arrived in the colony the previous year and settled in Newtown, questioned John Cotton's views on certain disputed doctrines, and began to preach a sermon series in which he raised questions about the beliefs being discussed in the Boston church. The resulting Free Grace controversy, which will be explored in more detail in the following chapter, divided not only the Boston congregation, but the entire colony. Shepard, together with others who favored restricted freedom to explore new religious insights, attacked members of the Boston church who claimed to be disciples of John Cotton, accusing John Wheelwright, Anne Hutchinson, and Henry Vane (who had been elected governor), among others, of antinomianism and other heresies. These individuals responded by accusing Shepard and his supporters of preaching a covenant of works that implied man could save himself.

As the Free Grace controversy was dividing them, the colonists were faced with another serious threat in the form of the Pequot War. Tensions had arisen in southern New England as a result of the conflicting land claims of various European groups— settlers from Massachusetts, the Plymouth colony, and the Dutch, as well as the representatives of a new colonizing venture headed by Lord Saye and Sele and Lord Brooke—which were matched by the claims of a variety of native peoples. The murder of a number of English traders had led to the dispatch of a military expedition under John Endecott, which was designed to bring the guilty to justice. Instead, Endecott had precipitated a rising of the Pequot tribe against the English settlements. Each of the New England colonies raised forces for the conflict.

John Wilson accompanied the Boston area troops as chaplain, having been chosen by lot. This had to be an extraordinary experience for Wilson, who had never seen a battlefield of any kind before, and who found himself tramping through the wilderness and coming under attack from skirmishing natives. When the troops of the various colonies gathered at Hartford, Wilson addressed them. He assured them that they were fighting in a just war to defend their "affectionate bosommates" and "harmless prattling and smiling babes" and to impose justice on the Pequots and their sachem Sassacus. Some of the English soldiers, he indicated, would die, "not because they should fall short of the honors accompanying such noble designs, but rather because earth's honors are too scant for them, and therefore the everlasting crown must be set upon their heads forthwith." Thus, they should "march on with a cheerful Christian courage in the strength of the Lord and the power of his might," for God would "forthwith enclose your enemies in your hands, make their multitudes fall under your warlike weapons, and your feet shall soon be set upon their proud necks."

The Pequot War was short and bloody. A force consisting of troops from the Bay, Saybrook, and the Connecticut River towns attacked the fortified Pequot village at Mystic in May, 1637. An initial attack revealed the difficulties of storming the native palisade. Had they breached the walls, the colonial forces would have had to advance into the densely packed village and engage in wigwam-to-wigwam combat against superior numbers. As a result, the English commanders, John Mason and John Underhill, withdrew their troops to the perimeter and set fire to the village. Over six hundred natives—women, children, and the elderly as well as warriors—were burned in the village or killed trying to escape the flames. In the following months small tribes that had allied themselves with the Pequots sued for peace. Another English military expedition pursued the remnants of the tribe and dealt them another serious blow in the "Great Swamp Fight," killing many and capturing over two hundred. Sassacus and some of his fellow chiefs escaped the English cordon and sought refuge with the Mohawks. Their hoped-for protectors killed them and sent the scalp of Sassacus to the English.

With the war over, Wilson returned to Boston to find the religious divisions worse than when he had departed. As the colony had polarized, individuals who sought to hold a moderate middle position were criticized by the Free Grace party as being no better than Shepard and his allies. Wilson, Winthrop, and their supporters were shunned in the town. Some members of the Boston trainband had refused to serve in the Pequot War because Wilson was the chaplain. The relationship between Wilson and Cotton became frayed. When Wilson rose to preach or pray, "many of the opinionists, rising up and contemptuously turning their backs" upon him, left the meetinghouse.

Eventually, the moderates emerged victorious. A synod consisting of representatives of the churches of New England, with Wilson in attendance, identified a list of errors that no one should uphold. A turning point was the election of 1637. The place of election had been moved to Newtown (later renamed Cambridge) in the hope of diminishing the turnout from Boston radicals. On May 17, 1637, men from all over the colony gathered on the Newtown common. The gathering threatened to degenerate into a riot as freemen from the opposing sides exchanged sharp words and blows and the election was endangered. Recognizing this, John Wilson climbed into the lower branches of a large oak growing in the field and harangued the assembly. He reminded them of the great enterprise they had embarked on by coming to New England, and how their divisions threatened everything that they had tried to do. The much embattled clergyman, a man who truly believed in moderate dialogue, won the day. The majority indicated their support for proceeding to the election. When the votes were counted, John Winthrop was restored to the governorship, with Thomas Dudley deputy governor, and Henry Vane not even chosen to be one of the Assistants.

Henry Vane returned to England. The most radical members of the Free Grace party, including John Wheelwright and Anne Hutchinson, were banished. As Cotton came to recognize that many of his proclaimed supporters had indeed been driven to adopt ideas that he could not tolerate, he and Wilson were able to begin to repair their relationship. Wilson presided over the church trial in which Hutchinson was excommunicated. Cotton joined in the judgment.

The controversy was probably the low point in Wilson's career. The pastor who had shared the sufferings of the early months of settlement with his flock, who had visited them in their homes and baptized their children, had been vilified by members of his own congregation. At the height of the controversy, according to John Winthrop, "all (save five or six) [members of the church were] so affected to Mr. Wheelwright and

Mrs. Hutchinson and those new opinions, as they slighted the present governor [Winthrop] and the pastor, looking at them as men under a covenant of works, and as their greatest enemies." Yet neither Winthrop nor Wilson joined the heresy hunters in trying to root out everyone who may have been the least tainted by errors. They tried to keep as many as possible within the newly drawn perimeter fence that defined orthodoxy. According to Winthrop, the two men bore their abuse "patiently, and not withdrawing themselves (as they were strongly solicited to have done), but carrying themselves lovingly and helpfully upon all occasions" they won over those who had shunned them, so that "the Lord brought about the hearts of all the people to love and esteem them more than ever before, and all breeches were made up, and the church was saved from ruin beyond all expectation, which could hardly have been . . . if those two had not been guided by the Lord to that moderation."

WILSON CONTINUED to serve the Boston church for another thirty years. In 1649 his longtime friend and ally John Winthrop passed away. In 1653 his colleague in the Boston ministry, John Cotton, died. After three years during which Wilson was the sole clergyman, the Boston church chose John Norton as its new teacher. But when Norton died in 1663, Wilson alone would minister to the church until his own death in 1667. Two religious issues concerned Wilson in his last years in office, the need to modify baptismal practices and the influx of newcomers to New England who did not share the values of the puritan founders.

The failure of many baptized children to be sure that they had experienced saving grace upon reaching their maturity led to a crisis for the churches in midcentury. Many of these young men and women were reluctant to present themselves for full church membership, which meant that they could not have their own children baptized. Dorchester's Richard Mather proposed modifying church procedures by allowing those who had been baptized on the basis of their parent's membership to in turn have their children baptized. This "Half-Way Covenant" was briefly discussed at the Cambridge Assembly of 1648, approved by a majority of delegates at a synod in 1657, and then recommended to all the churches by the Massachusetts General Court following another synod

in 1662. Such recommendations notwithstanding, the decision to imple-
ment the change was one to be made by each church individually, and
the Boston congregation was deeply split. Though Wilson himself favored the proposal, he was careful to avoid pushing it to the point where
the congregation might divide as it had in the 1630s. Instead he worked
to hold the church together while moving toward the more liberal re-
quirements in small steps. His ineffectiveness in swaying the congregation made him question the power of the laity and favor a greater role
for the clergy within churches and councils of clergy over the churches,
a position many ministers came to share as the century advanced.

The 1650s and 1660s also saw Wilson's New England threatened by
the arrival of Quaker missionaries, challenges that the Restoration government posed to the charter, and a perceived moral decline that had
come about with the influx of new, non-puritan immigrants. In his last
sermon to the Boston church he addressed those threats and sought to
call his listeners back to the cause for which he and their forefathers had
come to the American wilderness. The Quakers, he said, were dreamers
who sought to bewitch the colonists. He warned his congregation "not
|to| hearken to those dreamers, but hearken to the voice of the Lord,
by his ministers in their speeches and writings." "I have known New
England about thirty-six years," he reminded them, "and I have never
known such a time as this that we live in." The first settlers had come so
that they, their children, and their grandchildren might be "under the
ordinances of God, that they might be as plants in the Lord's house." Just
as the colonists would not let a thief come into their homes to rob them
of their jewels or money, so they should resist those who would "come to
rob you of the ordinances of God, and of his faithful ministers." They
were, he reminded them, to "trust not in men. Trust not in the Governor. Trust not in the Magistrates. Trust not in your Captains. Trust not
in your Castle or ammunition. Trust not in your own righteousness, but
trust in this—that if the Lord be your God, and if you walk worthy of
the Lord, . . . that he will be with you."

By the time Wilson had preached his warning about the threats to
the puritan experiment, he was noticeably weak and in ill-health. His
voice frequently failed him. But he continued his regular visitations to

the members of his congregation, engaging them in discussions to test
their knowledge of the faith and offering them counsel as they strove
to live godly lives. At some point in the summer of 1667 he preached a
sermon on the last five psalms as a guest in the Roxbury church of his
son-in-law Samuel Danforth. He ended by claiming, "If I were sure this
was to be the last sermon I should preach, and these the last words that
ever I should speak, yet I would still say, Hallelujah! Hallelujah! Praise
ye the Lord." It may well have been the last time he spoke from a pulpit.

He was soon confined to his home, where various ministers and magistrates came to visit him. On August 7 he felt the end was near and he
spoke to those gathered by his bedside. He railed against what he saw
as the sins of the time that were provoking God, and in particular upon
three contentious issues: the Half-Way Covenant, the role of synods,
and the authority of clergy within a congregation. He spoke of "our
neglect of baptizing the children of the church, those that some call
grand-children," and "not subjecting to the authority of synods, without
which churches cannot long subsist." When offered the post of lecturer
at Sudbury early in his career, Wilson had insisted that he would accept
only if the parish members voted that they desired his ministry. Like
most of the clergy of the first generation he had come to New England
believing in the independence of the individual congregation and trust-
ing the authority of the lay members of the church. Experiences, starting
with the Free Grace controversy of the 1630s and ending with the dispute
over the Half-Way Covenant in the 1660s, had led him to question the
judgment of the laity. At the end, he complained of the people rising up
against their ministers, saying it had become "nothing for a brother to
stand up and oppose, without scripture or reason, the word of an elder."
Such a man, he said, "if he do not like the administration (be it baptism
or the like) will turn his back upon God and his ordinances, and go
away." With night approaching, as his friends prepared to depart, he
turned to prayer: "The Lord pardon us and heal us, and make us more
heavenly, and . . . make us burning and shining lights by our heavenly
doctrine and example." He comforted himself by saying that he would
soon be with his old friends such as Dr. Ames, Dr. Preston, Mr. Cotton,
and others, and passed quietly away.

Thomas Dudley and
Thomas Shepard

Hammers of Heretics

When historians seek to highlight the variety of religious viewpoints in early New England, they more often than not examine the differences between those who found themselves outside the bounds of acceptable behavior—Roger Williams, Anne Hutchinson, Baptists, and Quakers and the "orthodox" majority who sought to keep such troublers out of the puritan Zion. But it is equally important to recognize the diversity of outlook within the so-called majority. If John Winthrop and John Cotton represent in some sense those who were willing to believe that they could profit from open discussion of matters of faith and practice, Thomas Dudley and Thomas Shepard can stand for those who more closely fit the stereotype of the narrow-minded, persecutory puritan.

W HEN JOHN Endecott, John Winthrop and John Wilson immigrated to New England the threat to English puritans was looming on the horizon. As the decade of the 1630s progressed, that threat became reality. William Laud was elevated from Bishop of London to Archbishop of Canterbury and used his authority to inquire into the efforts of his bishops to enforce directives aimed at curbing puritan influence. Clergy such as John Cotton, Thomas Hooker, and John Davenport were among those who found their situations in the church no longer tenable. The Laudian initiatives served to drive conforming clergy such as these to leave England, and also served to radicalize other members of the puritan movement. The shifting dynamics of the English religious scene meant that the puritanism of those who came to New England during those years might differ significantly from that of those who had built the religious foundations of the region.

New ideas brought to America stimulated fresh discussions of faith and practice, the type of discussions that earned for the Boston church the reputation of being "the most glorious church in the world." Leaders like John Winthrop, who had anticipated that in the New World "we shall see much more of His wisdom, power, goodness and truth, than formerly we have been acquainted with," welcomed the exchange of new ideas as a way to further enlightenment, and desired only that all who participated acknowledged the possibility that they might be wrong. Other leaders, such as Deputy Governor Thomas Dudley and the clergyman Thomas Shepard, believed that the foundations were fine as they were and viewed the newcomers and their notions with suspicion.

A TYPICAL SUNDAY morning in the fenland town of Boston, England, in 1620 would have seen men and women converging on the church of St. Botolph. Many were inhabitants of the town. Others traveled a distance to hear John Cotton preach. The Dudley family would have likely been there. Thomas Dudley was the steward of the Earl of Lincoln. His family frequently made the fifteen-mile journey from the Earl's Sempringham estate to Boston on a Saturday so that they could attend the Sabbath services in St. Botolph. Dudley and his wife, Dorothy, were usually accompanied by their daughter Anne, then eight years old, and their son Samuel. On at least some such occasions, the Dudleys may have encountered another family that journeyed far to hear Cotton. William Hutchinson and his wife Anne are believed to have often traveled the twenty-four miles from Alford, a journey of six hours, to attend to Cotton's ministry. After the services, it was customary for Cotton to gather the godly members of the congregation for additional prayers. There the Hutchinsons and Dudleys would have joined others, such as Boston alderman Thomas Leverett—men and women who were recognized as saints and sought communion with one another. This wasn't the sort of sermon gadding, the journeying from parish to parish to hear various preachers, that was common in John Winthrop's Stour Valley and other parts of the land. The Dudleys, Hutchinsons, and other puritans who traveled to hear Cotton were not supplementing the preaching of a local godly minister, they were coming in search of what they couldn't find elsewhere. This was the situation throughout most of the Midlands and the Northeast of England, where clusters of the godly struggled in the midst of indifferent or hostile neighbors.

Thomas Dudley, born in 1576, had been orphaned at the age of twelve and taken in by a puritan kinswoman of his mother. His grandfather had evidently been a zealous Catholic who was believed to have plotted against both Henry VIII and Edward VI, left England to become one of the Catholic Knights of Malta, returned in Mary's reign to further the Catholic restoration, and then worked against Elizabeth following that monarch's accession. Needless to say, Thomas, who had a conversion experience around the age of twenty and became a zealous puritan, had little to say about his grandfather. He devoted his own career to seeking to eradicate Catholicism and other forms of religious error.

Mrs. Purefoy, the woman who took Dudley in when his parents died, provided him with an education and placed him in the household of William, Lord Compton (who became Earl of Northampton), when he was fourteen. There Thomas learned the workings of an aristocratic household that would stand him in good stead later in his life. At the age of eighteen he became a clerk to Judge Augustine Nicolls, a member of the bench of the Court of Common Pleas. Motivated perhaps to free himself from the taint of his grandfather's reputation, Dudley joined a force of English volunteers fighting for the French Protestant king Henry of Navarre. A story passed down to the early New England historian Thomas Prince relates that none of the youth of Northampton were willing to enlist until Dudley was named captain, after which eighty signed up to fight under his command, a story that suggests a charisma that doesn't elsewhere emerge from the scant records of his life. Following the capture of the city of Amiens by the force he was with, Dudley returned to England and the service of Judge Nicholls. He encountered the puritan ministers Arthur Hildersham and John Dod, among others. It was Dod who was responsible for his conversion, and who presided over Dudley's marriage in 1603. Through Dod, Thomas also established contacts with Sir Richard Knightley, William Fiennes, and other members of the puritan gentry in Northamptonshire.

Following the death of Judge Nicolls, William Fiennes recommended Dudley to his young cousin Theophilus when the latter inherited the title of Earl of Lincoln along with a debt of perhaps £20,000. The earl hired Dudley as his steward and the Dudleys moved to the earl's principal estate of Sempringham Manor in 1619. Through rigorous management Dudley was able to pay off the estate's debts and right the earl's finances, though in doing so he earned for himself a reputation as a hard man by cutting wages and imposing other economies. He did well enough himself to send two of his sons to Cambridge to study under John Preston, who occasionally preached at Sempringham when he traveled to Boston to visit with his friend John Cotton.

Dudley was a zealous puritan, whose library included works of Richard Rogers and Arthur Hildersham. He was sure of his election and confident that he knew God's will, so much so that he was viewed as a hard man in religious as well as business matters. When he died he recorded in his will, "I hated & do hate every false way in religion, not only the old idolatry and superstition of popery which is wearing away, but much more (as being much worse), the new heresies, blasphemies, & errors of late sprang up."

Toward the close of the 1620s puritan concerns about the direction that England was moving in were growing, and the Earl of Lincoln was one of the gentry who opposed the loan that Charles I demanded of his subjects in 1626. Charged with "evil speaking among his servants against this new form of exacting money," the earl was one of a large number of refusers who were called to court to answer for their actions and speech. He was sentenced to the Tower in March of 1627. Dudley also refused to pay the loan and was suspected of harboring some other opponents of the act. Though he was not a significant enough figure to be jailed, his family must have lived in a state of anxiety for some time. While the immediate crisis passed and the earl was released early in 1628, the future of reform appeared bleak, and, like the Stour Valley reformers, some Lincolnshire puritans began to consider emigration.

In June 1629 the Earl of Lincoln hosted a meeting on his estate where various groups who had been contemplating the creation of a puritan refuge in America gathered to lay the plans for what would become the Massachusetts Bay Company. John Winthrop was at that meeting, as was Thomas Dudley. Winthrop was selected as the governor of the company and its colony in October of that year, with John Humfry as deputy governor. When Humfry chose not to migrate at the last moment, Dudley was chosen in his place.

JOHN WINTHROP and Thomas Dudley represented two sides of puritanism. Whereas Winthrop was humbled by an awareness of being unworthy of God's saving grace, and inclined to reach out to and learn from others in whom he detected the spark of godliness, Dudley's conviction that he was one of the elect made him confident in the rectitude of his beliefs. Whereas Winthrop recognized that men of faith might disagree on issues of faith and practice, Dudley was convinced he knew the truth and was inflexible in defending it. The differences between the two men were reflected in other ways. Whereas Winthrop was noted for leading by example, working in the fields with his fellow colonists during the struggles of the early months, Dudley sought to maintain a distance from the ordinary colonists, believing that this was necessary for him to be respected and obeyed. Adorning his house with expensive wainscoting was one of a number of ways in which he sought to establish his status. While Winthrop gave of his own food supplies to feed the hungry, Dudley was accused of lending corn at interest. Winthrop believed in discretionary justice and that in the difficult circumstances of a new world laws should be applied with leniency. Dudley believed in the full application of the law to all and suspected Winthrop of courting popularity. On more than one occasion Dudley threatened to resign his office because of disputes with the governor. Eventually, clergy and fellow magistrates persuaded the two men to bury their differences for the sake of the colony as a whole. That truce was furthered when one of Winthrop's daughters married a son of Dudley's.

THERE WAS what some have called a political revolution in Massachusetts in May 1634 when the colonists voted for Thomas Dudley as their
governor and Roger Ludlow as deputy governor. This was the first time
that John Winthrop was relegated to the fringes of power—he was an
assistant (one of the magistrates who served as the governor's council),
but it was Dudley and Ludlow who would drive the colony's affairs for
the next year. That faction also produced the governor and deputy governor in the following year's elections. Those who had been elevated
to the top level of colony government represented a more conservative,
harder element of the puritan leadership. During their ascendancy the
colony passed laws that limited judicial discretion such as had been practiced by Winthrop. Rather than trust to the judgment of individuals,
they banned certain practices and mandated new penalties for behavior
they disapproved of. Smoking tobacco was prohibited in public places.
Sumptuary laws prohibited new fashions in clothing and personal appearance. But, most significantly, the magistrates acted against religious
opinion that they considered dangerous.

Roger Williams had arrived in the colony in 1633. He was a charis-
matic leader whom Winthrop recognized as "a godly minister," but his
strong views soon caused controversy. New Englanders had proceeded
to structure their own congregational churches and to reform patterns
of worship in accordance with their puritan emphases, but despite their
fundamental differences with the Church of England they insisted on
asserting a communion with that mother church in which they had been
nurtured. Williams wanted to take the logic of colonial practice one step
further and refused to join the Boston congregation because it would not
publicly separate from the Church of England. He moved on to Salem,
spent some time in the Plymouth colony, and then returned to Salem.
During this time he developed additional views that were highly controversial. He believed that in keeping with scriptural precepts women
should wear veils. He argued that the red cross in the English flag was
a papist symbol—prompting John Endecott to cut the cross from the
flag used by the Salem militia. He argued that regular meetings of the
colony's clergy were undermining congregational autonomy, paving the
way toward Presbyterianism. He rejected the authority of the king to

have granted the charter. And he argued that since an oath was a religious act it was sinful to contaminate the ceremony by administering oaths to unregenerate individuals. It is likely that he also began to raise questions about the legitimacy of infant baptism.

John Winthrop was governor when Williams first became a center of controversy. With the help of some of the other clergy he was able to persuade Williams to temper his views and avoided a major division in the colony. Controversy again flared up in 1634. While it is true that Williams had pushed his beliefs to a more extreme level, the fact that less tolerant leaders controlled the colony government was also important. In April 1635, with Dudley presiding, the authorities called Williams before them to answer for his views. A few months later Williams was again summoned to answer charges. Among the views that he was called to account for were that it was wrong for magistrates to enforce violations of the first table of the Ten Commandments, and that it was wrong for saints to even join in prayer with those who were not of the elect. The Salem church had been prepared to choose Williams as their pastor, but the magistrates applied pressures on that congregation to change their mind. Williams was ordered to desist from promulgating his controversial views. This he refused to do.

It is important to realize that no one, not even Roger Williams at this time, was prepared to tolerate the practice or advocacy of errors. Williams, for example, didn't simply desire that he and others who had objections to oaths be allowed to avoid them. He insisted that the colony authorities were violating God's wishes in doing so. He was as intolerant of the errors of the majority as his chief critics were of him.

In October 1635 the magistrates ordered that Williams be sent out of the colony. The implementation of the verdict was originally deferred till the following spring, but when Williams continued to meet with others and promulgate the views that had been condemned, orders were sent to seize him and immediately ship him to England. John Winthrop warned Williams, giving his friend the chance to flee to the area around Narragansett Bay, where the land he settled on would become known as Providence, in what became the Colony of Rhode Island. There Williams would continue to search for further truth, briefly becoming a

Baptist before abandoning the hopes for a pure church created by men and formulating a position calling for broad religious toleration. Winthrop would continue to correspond with Williams over the following decades. While he came to recognize that the views of the Rhode Islander could not have been tolerated in Massachusetts, he continued to recognize him as a man sincerely seeking for a better understanding of God's truths. Thomas Dudley showed no regrets for having played a key role in cutting the poisonous infection of Williams's thought out from the body of Massachusetts.

EVEN BEFORE Williams was banished, new challenges to the perimeter fence that Dudley was seeking to build around Massachusetts orthodoxy were arising. The man who would alert Dudley to the threat and help him to purge it from the colony was the clergyman Thomas Shepard. As a student at Cambridge University in England and then as a young clergyman, Shepard had found ample reasons for concluding that he, like all men, were born into sin. In his diary and autobiography he recorded various instances that proved the point, including one instance when he woke up hung over in a field outside the university. Precisely because he was so aware of his shortcomings, Shepard struggled to achieve certainty of his election. At one point he questioned the teachings of those puritan divines who taught that sanctification (godly behavior) was evidence of spiritual transformation—good fruit from a sanctified tree—and considered antinomian and radical views such as those of the Family of Love (Familists), a sect whose perfectionist stance supposedly relieved the saints from adhering to traditional formulations of the law, arguing that assurance came from opening oneself to the overpowering work of the Spirit. Having been tempted by such arguments, Shepard committed himself to being, as it were, a hammer of heretics, dedicated to saving others from like temptations.

When Shepard arrived in Massachusetts in 1634, settling in Newtown (soon to be renamed Cambridge), Dudley and his fellow magistrates were in the process of protecting the colony from the contagion of the views of Roger Williams. Meanwhile, the Boston church, with an influx of newcomers, had become the center of spirited religious discussions.

THE
PARABLE
OF THE
Ten Virgins
OPENED, & APPLIED:
Being the Subſtance of divers
SERMONS
on *Matth.* 25. 1,---13.

Wherein, the Difference between the Sincere Chriſtian and
the moſt Refined Hypocrite, the Nature and Characters of Saving
and of Common Grace, the Dangers and Diſeaſes incident to
moſt flouriſhing Churches or Chriſtians, and other Spiritual
T R U T H S of greateſt importance, are clearly
diſcovered, and practically Improved,

BY
THOMAS SHEPARD
late Worthy and Faithfull Paſtor of the Church of Chriſt at
Cambridge in NEW-ENGLAND.

Now Publiſhed from the Authours own Notes, at the deſires of
many, for the common Benefit of the Lords people,

By {
Jonathan Mitchell Miniſter at *Cambridge*,
Tho Shepard, Son to the Reverend Author,
now Miniſter at *Charles-Town*
} in NEW-ENGLAND.

LUKE 21. 36.
Watch ye therefore and pray alwaies, that ye may be accounted worthy to eſcape all theſe things
that ſhall come to paſſe, and to ſtand before the Son of man.

LONDON,
Printed by *J.H.* for *John Rothwell*, at the Fountain in Goldſmiths-Row in Cheap-ſide,
and *Samuel Thomſon* at the Biſhops Head in *Pauls* Church-yard. 1 6 6 0.

Title page of Thomas Shepard's *Parable of the Ten Virgins*

At the heart of these discussions were newcomers such as Henry Vane, the puritan son of a member of the king's government; William and Anne Hutchinson, a London merchant and his wife from Lincolnshire; and the Londoners William and Mary Dyer. Puritans encouraged the laity to ask questions during church services and to meet separately to further explore matters of faith. In the New Haven Colony, such lay groups would regularly gather every Tuesday. One of those who hosted such gatherings in Boston was Anne Hutchinson. John Winthrop later recalled that Mrs. Hutchinson "had more resort to her for counsel about matters of conscience, and clearing up of men's spiritual estates, than any minister . . . in the country." "Her ordinary talk," according to Winthrop, "was about the things of the Kingdom of God," and she conducted herself always "in the way of righteousness and kindness." Similarly, John Cotton indicated that "all the faithful embraced her conference, and blessed God for her fruitful discourses." But her voice was but one among many as the godly sought to better understand their relationship with God. There were different voices in the Boston church with different views, among them Henry Vane. But the congregation was united by what historian Michael Winship has correctly identified as "mutual forbearance [and] common standards of behavioral orthodoxy," the success of the elders in managing a "well-functioning, satisfying church," and the shared sense of many members that they were one in helping to achieve the kingdom of God on Earth. This unity also depended on what Winship has called a "tolerance for linguistic idiosyncrasies among people perceived as godly."

Just as John Wilson led Bostonians to hear other clergy, so lay men and women from other towns in the Bay came to Boston to hear Cotton and Wilson preach. In the process visitors mingled with members of the host congregation and became familiar with members of other churches and with what was being discussed in them. Henry Vane, with his aristocratic demeanor, his good looks, and his zealous piety drew the interest of many, and in the colony elections of 1636 the freemen elected him governor, an extraordinary sign of approbation for someone so young and so new to the Bay—and the third election in a row in which John Winthrop was not chosen to lead the colony.

Perhaps one reason why the Boston church was held in such high regard was the fact that its members had set the perimeter fence around their church wide enough to encourage fruitful discourse—indeed, the very point was that nonconfrontational exchanges of different spiritual insights helped to advance the kingdom of God by allowing everyone to achieve a better understanding of their faith. Godly men and women of different beliefs were able to see the root of the matter in each other and join in holy communion. While in retrospect many would look back on the disruptions that followed as the inevitable consequence of such open airing of views, there is no indication prior to 1636 that anyone in that church—not John Winthrop, not John Wilson—found anything troubling about these exchanges.

All that we know about the controversial ideas that emerged from the discussions in the church and private homes of Boston come from accounts written down after the controversy that disrupted the colony and led to the political banishment and congregational excommunication of many of the key figures. Because those accounts were shaped by the agenda of the authors, and because they also focused on the expressions of religious belief that came at the height of the controversy, after polarization pushed people to more extreme formulations of their ideas, caution must be exercised in speculating on what notions were initially being put up for discussion.

Excited by the freedom to worship and debate as they wished, some of the members of the Boston congregation abandoned the caution with which many customarily pursued the secrets of God's work. Most puritans believed that sanctification was the restoration of the righteousness that Adam had when originally created. William Dyer and Henry Vane denied this, Dyer arguing that Adam had not been made in the image of God, and Vane asserting that Adam had never received the seal of the Spirit. Anne Hutchinson likewise questioned whether God's image in Adam consisted in holiness. Vane may also have been developing views on Christ's active and passive obedience to the will of God that some would label anti-Trinitarian when he later expressed them in England. Anne Hutchinson may have also been drifting toward anti-Trinitarianism by questioning the eternal sonship of Christ. In taking the positions she did, Anne felt that she was directly inspired by the Spirit in her understanding of scripture. She, Vane, and others who claimed a union with the Holy Spirit were worried that the emphasis many clergy and laypeople placed on behavior indicated that such individuals were in danger of drifting into a reliance on the covenant of works, the belief that a person could be saved by good behavior. Some of their critics felt that Vane and Hutchinson were suggesting that the presence of the Spirit made the instructions of scripture superfluous. Hutchinson also considered whether the resurrection of the body was possible. Many of these ideas had been circulating in the English puritan underground for some years, but it would be wrong to simply see these lay men and women as disciples of English radicals and dismiss the possibility that they were adding their own glosses to ideas they had previously encountered.

All of this was anathema to Thomas Shepard, and it was he who first sought to brand some of those views as heterodox. The Newtown clergyman took it upon himself to act the part of heresy hunter in attacking what he was convinced were the false teachings of Cotton and the erroneous beliefs of his disciples. By doing so he initiated a process of polarization where individuals of various opinions gradually abandoned dialogue and began to hurl negative labels at one another with about as much accuracy as one finds in modern political campaigns. Simplify, exaggerate, and demonize your opponents became the strategy adopted by both emerging camps. As each side came to believe the categorization they had shaped to define their opponents, they hardened their own stance in ways that must have surprised anyone who had observed the dialogue and tolerance that once categorized the affairs of the colony.

In the ensuing controversy, which is described in greater detail in the following chapter, Thomas Shepard and Thomas Dudley played the lead roles in trying to condemn errors and narrowly define what would be acceptable in the puritan "City on a Hill." It was Shepard who mobilized the majority of ministers in the region to oppose the doctrines originating in Boston and threatening to infect members of their own congregations. Dudley played a key role in the prosecution of Anne Hutchinson during her civil trial in 1637, and at one point sought to implicate John Cotton in her views in a way that would have made it impossible for that clergyman to remain in Massachusetts. Though he had been a follower of Cotton in England, Dudley started to probe Cotton's beliefs, but Winthrop cut him off before he could proceed down that road. Winthrop clearly was focused on keeping Cotton within the perimeter fence of orthodoxy.

Shepard played a decisive role in the subsequent church trial that led to Anne's excommunication from the Boston congregation. At one point it appears that Cotton and the clergyman John Davenport (newly arrived from England) had weaned Anne from her positions to the degree that she might have been reconciled with the congregation. It was Shepard who provoked her into retreating from compromise. Shepard took the lead in attacking Hutchinson, whom he identified as "a very dangerous woman to sow her corrupt opinions to the infection of many." In his least fine hour, he challenged her, and she rose to the bait, making assertions that put her back in danger. He concluded that she was "of a most dangerous spirit, and likely with her fluent tongue and forwardness in expressions to seduce and draw away many, especially simple women of her own sex," and warned, "If any of this congregation . . . do hold the same opinions, I advise them to take heed of it, for the hand of the Lord will find you out."

Despite their successes, Dudley and Shepard did not achieve all they hoped for. Winthrop and Davenport brought John Cotton and John Wilson to agreement, and created a middle way that was broad enough to save Cotton and others who had originally dabbled in the controversial views. While the perimeter fence defining orthodoxy was not redrawn to encompass as much variety of expression as Winthrop would have liked to include, it was not drawn as rigidly as Dudley and Shepard would have wished. It is likely that they would have preferred it if a synod that was called to confute errors had defined what everyone should believe rather than merely identifying a host of false doctrines. Some of the men and women whom they would have wished expelled were able to remain in the colony. Nevertheless, following the episode the types of lay prophesying that had been common in New England became less so (though perhaps not as uncommon as some scholars have believed). During the midst of the controversy, Harvard College was established to ensure a continuing supply of educated and orthodox clergy, and it was situated in the newly renamed Cambridge, where, as the local minister, Shepard could guard against any dangerous opinions that might arise there.

IN THE YEARS that followed, Shepard and Dudley continued to guard against any views they believed would threaten puritan orthodoxy as they understood it. The Cambridge synod of 1637 had identified religious errors, but had not spelled out true belief and practices. In the 1640s Shepard played a key role in correcting that, advocating for a new assembly that would develop a Confession of Faith and ecclesiastical practice, a goal that was realized in the Cambridge Platform of 1648. During England's Puritan Revolution of the 1640s, Shepard wrote a number of treatises urging the New England system upon his English readers. He was troubled by the explosion of various new opinions that arose in England due to the uncertain situation prompted by that conflict, and feared that God would punish England if the godly did not "seasonably suppress and bear public witness against such delusions which fill the land like locusts." He did, however, recognize the need to "show the utmost forbearance to godly men if for a time deluded," and accepted that the English situation might require for a time that the "state may tolerate all because of necessity they must, the numbers being so many and the hazard more." But he called for "axes and wedges" to "hew and break through this rough, uneven, bold, yet professing age." He died in August 1649.

One of the views that Shepard feared was gaining currency in the 1640s was Anabaptism, the rejection of the practice of infant baptism. Many who took this position were respected puritans who believed that the purity of churches and the Lord's Supper would be advanced only if adults who had experienced God's grace were baptized. They explained their stand by reference to the "further light" that Winthrop himself had hoped would emerge from the puritan experiment. Roger Williams had been attracted to this position for a time in his own search for perfected churches, and had participated in the formation of a Baptist church in Providence. Many English puritans who rejected this position nevertheless tolerated Baptists, even within their congregations. It is hard to know how many colonists privately sympathized with Anabaptism. Henry Dunster, the man who as president raised Harvard to respectability in the Atlantic world, was an Anabaptist, though this didn't become evident until he failed to present his son for baptism in 1653. Presumably he kept those positions to himself through most of the decade of the 1640s as he worshiped in Thomas Shepard's Cambridge congregation. When he came to suspect Dunster's views, Shepard sought to persuade the Harvard president of his error, but came away with "a strange confusion and sickliness upon his spirits" which "interrupted his study for the Sabbath" as he contemplated what he found as "venom and poison" in Dunster's views. Yet no action was taken against Dunster until he made his stand public in 1653.

The threat of Anabaptism was considered serious enough in 1644 for the Massachusetts magistrates to pass an order banishing those who maintained the position after attempts to correct them of their errors. The order was attributable to the fact that the more restrictive element in the colony's leadership had again been placed in office—John Endecott was elected governor in 1644 and Dudley in 1645. John Winthrop's son Stephen, who was then in England, wrote criticizing the measure, and John's nephew George Downing commented, "The law of banishment for conscience . . . makes us stink everywhere." A group of colonists petitioned against the law in 1645. Winthrop, who was one of the colony assistants, appears to have at least favored suspending it, but the Dudley-led Court refused to do so. Meanwhile, leading clergymen marshaled arguments against Anabaptism. George Phillips of Watertown, Thomas Cobbett of Lynn, and John Cotton all wrote treatises defending infant baptism in the 1640s, and Shepard wrote an extensive letter (not published until 1663) to one of the members of his congregation against Anabaptism.

Winthrop was returned to the governorship in 1646 and was reelected each year until his death in 1649. Dudley continued to push Winthrop to take the threat of heresy seriously. When the governor was on his deathbed, Dudley came to have him sign an order for the banishment of an accused heretic, but Winthrop refused, saying "he had done too much of that work already."

Dudley was a man who would be memorialized by his loving daughter Anne Bradstreet as being "to sectaries, a whip and maul." As noted previously, when he died in 1653 he left behind a statement "for the use and example of my posterity . . . that I hated & do hate every false way in religion, not only the old idolatry and superstition of popery which is wearing away, but much more (as being much worse), the new heresies, blasphemies, & errors of late sprang up in our native country of England, and secretly received & fostered here more than I wish they were." A poem found in his pocket warned, "Let men in courts and churches watch over such as do a toleration hatch, lest that ill egg bring forth a cockatrice to poison all with heresy and vice." It ended by stating "my epitaph is 'Died no Libertine.'" He was, as one student of the period has put it, "one of those characters in which virtue does not put on her gracious aspect."

THERE IS NO question that Thomas Shepard, Thomas Dudley and, to a lesser extent, John Endecott represent a spirit of intolerance in New England puritanism that frequently controlled the affairs of Massachusetts. But it would be wrong to overemphasize their differences with John Winthrop and those who argued for more openness to different voices in the community. Like virtually all of their contemporaries in the Western world, all of these men were committed to the belief that there was one true faith and one ideal form of worshipping God. They all agreed that some religious beliefs and practices were beyond the pale. Their differences were over which views were to be allowed as contributing to a search for greater understanding and which were to be condemned as threatening to poison the spiritual commonwealth. Those differences are important to recognize if we wish to understand the complexity of early New England, but with few exceptions all the colonists were playing variations on the same tune.

Four Strong Women

Anne Hutchinson, Mary Dyer, Lady Deborah Moody, and Anne Eaton

Thus far all of the characters we have examined have been men. This is partly attributable to the fact that the public role of women was strongly restricted in the early modern world, and partly to the fact that relatively few women left a record of their experiences and beliefs. But Protestants believed that all men and women should have the opportunity to engage with God's word directly in the scriptures. This meant that they believed it important for all girls as well as boys to learn to read. Wives were expected to lead their families in worship and catechize members of the household when their husband was absent. While women were not allowed to attend grammar schools or to study at the universities, many men taught their daughters Latin and modern languages and encouraged them to discuss matters of faith so that they would be better prepared as wives and mothers. John Winthrop's mother had a French Bible and theological works in German. John's correspondence with his wife Margaret shows her to have been well educated and thoughtful. Anne Bradstreet's broad education is revealed in her poetry. While thinking women, both Margaret Winthrop and Anne Bradstreet accepted the orthodox teachings of early New England and supported their magistrate husbands. Other women interpreted scripture in ways that led them away from orthodoxy and behaved in ways that challenged the New England Way.

ANNE HUTCHINSON was the daughter of the Reverend Francis Marbury, a clergyman in the Church of England who had been sharply critical of the failures of the church to adequately serve its members, on one occasion stating that "the bishops of London and Peterborough and all the bishops in England are guilty of the death of as many souls as have perished by the ignorance of the ministers of their making whom they knew to be unable." Having been suspended from his living for a time, in 1580 Marbury was named to serve the small Lincolnshire parish of Alford. It was there that Anne was born in 1591. Shortly after this, Marbury was again suspended from his ministry. Clearly, Francis was willing to speak truth to power, and this was a characteristic that Anne would also demonstrate. Francis devoted himself to the education of his children, all of whom were girls. Restored to his ministry in 1594, a decade later he moved to a London parish. The teenaged Anne was exposed to the vitality of the nation's largest city and the diversity of its religious life, with her father there to encourage her inquiries about the political and religious disputes of the time.

Francis Marbury died in 1610. Two years later Anne married William Hutchinson of Alford, whom she had known since her childhood. The couple settled in that Lincolnshire town, where the clergyman who had succeeded her father in Alford was a moderate typical of the conservative religious scene in that region of England. While there is no direct contemporary evidence to support the claim, the abundance of reports that attest to it make it likely that the Hutchinsons journeyed occasionally to the Lincolnshire town of Boston, twenty-four miles away, to listen to the preaching of John Cotton. After 1623, they would occasionally make the shorter journey to the nearby town of Bilsby, where John Wheelwright was a powerful puritan preacher. Both Cotton and Wheelwright emphasized the role of the Spirit in directing the faithful, and this may have particularly resonated with Anne, who, unable to regularly travel to hear such clerical counselors, relied on her own interpretations of the scripture to chart her course.

In 1632 John Wheelwright, who had married Anne's sister Mary in 1629 was removed from his ministry for selling his church living back to his patron. Pressured by the authorities, John Cotton resigned his ministerial living in 1633. Anne was thrown on her own resources and those of other puritan laity in the region, joining with them in sessions where they shared their views and reinforced one another's faith. When Cotton immigrated to America, the Hutchinsons decided to follow. They settled in Boston and soon became respected members of the community. William was chosen one of the town's deputies to the General Court in May 1635. He was named a magistrate in 1636, and also served as a Boston selectman (in essence, one of the town council). In November 1636 the church elected him to the office of deacon. Anne earned a reputation as a caring mother and a devoted comforter of the town's sick, and also served as a midwife. It is likely that she participated in the prophesying session during worship. She also reviewed sermons in her home with other women, and her religious insights soon prompted male neighbors as well to engage her in discussions.

Reports of the dynamic religious discussions in Boston soon spread throughout the colony, and some of these excited the suspicions of the newly arrived Thomas Shepard. Shepard, as noted in the previous chapter, was particularly concerned about teachings that emphasized the role of the Spirit in guiding believers as opposed to measuring one's progress to grace by reference to obedience to God's laws. He feared that John Cotton was encouraging, if not himself preaching, dangerous opinions and wrote a letter challenging Cotton to explain what was going on. Cotton felt no need to justify himself, and a meeting of clergymen gathered for the October 1636 session of the Massachusetts General Court initially appeared to clear suspicions about what might be going on in the Boston church. But then Anne Hutchinson was asked to join the gathered ministers. One of those present later recalled that Anne had asserted that "there was a wide and broad difference" between the teachings of Cotton and John Wheelwright (who had recently arrived in the colony) on the one hand, and the rest of the clergy on the other, and that she accused the other ministers of not being "able ministers of the new testament" and of preaching a covenant of works.

This prompted Shepard to continue his public assault on those whom he viewed as dangerous enthusiasts, and other ministers joined him in raising the alarm about Familist and other heretical influences. Church

The statue of Anne Hutchinson
in front of the Massachusetts State House
Photo by Mark Andrew Higgins

meetings—and not just in Boston—became "full of disputes" as men
and women whose views were being questioned began to "grow bold, and
dare to question the sound and wholesome truths delivered in public by
the ministers of Christ." In the Boston church, those who saw themselves as disciples of Cotton had become critical of John Wilson, and
when he rose to preach or pray, "many of the opinionists, rising up and
contemptuously turning their backs" upon him, left the meetinghouse.

In an attempt to heal the growing divisions, at its December 1636
session the General Court appointed a day of fast and prayer to be held
in all of the colony's churches to seek God's aid in reconciling those
who were drifting apart. In what may have been a conciliatory gesture,
John Wheelwright was asked to preach on the occasion. After Cotton
preached in the morning on the need for peace and reconciliation, in

the afternoon Wheelwright delivered what can only be described as an inflammatory sermon. He announced that Christ had recently withheld his presence from Massachusetts because of the actions of an anti-Christian people who advanced a covenant of works. It was time for the true believers to "prepare for spiritual combat," "to show themselves valiant" and "have their swords ready," and to "fight and fight with spiritual weapons." They must "kill" their anti-Christian enemies "with the word of the Lord," but also "be willing to be killed like sheep" if that was the Lord's will. Warning against indulging in behavior that might "give occasion to others to say we are libertines or Antinomians," he branded their enemies as being the ones who were "the greatest enemies of the state that can be."

The extremity of Wheelwright's sermon strengthened the resolve of the orthodoxy party, and the General Court charged him with sedition. In the May 1637 colony elections John Winthrop was chosen governor, replacing Henry Vane, who was identified with the Hutchinson faction in the Boston church. Recognizing the ascendancy of those who viewed his opinions as dangerous Vane soon left the colony. The General Court called upon all of the churches to send representatives to a synod that, meeting in Cambridge in August 1637, identified a list of eighty-two religious errors. John Cotton acknowledged that he "esteemed some of the opinions to be blasphemous, some of them heretical, many of them were erroneous, and almost all of them incommodiously expressed." It is to be noted that the synod sought not to precisely define what had to be believed, but pointed to views that would not be tolerated. In November of that year the General Court banished the unrepentant John Wheelwright and a number of prominent members of the Boston church who had petitioned aggressively on his behalf.

The same session of the General Court called Anne Hutchinson to answer charges. The trial was conducted in accordance with English and Massachusetts precedents, with magistrates examining the accused as well as rendering judgment. This was a civil trial, and Mrs. Hutchinson was accused of undermining the foundations of the society by her attack on the ministers. For two days the magistrates tried to get her to incriminate herself, with little effect until she asserted that her beliefs were based on immediate revelation and that it had been revealed to her that if the colony continued on its existing course the magistrates would "bring a curse upon you and your posterity." She was convicted and sentenced to be banished. While her gender was an aggravating circumstance, it was not the cause of the actions against her, and to suggest that it was is to actually diminish the significance of her ideas.

The final episode of the story took place in the following spring, when Anne Hutchinson went on trial for her religious views before the Boston church. Because she was awaiting execution of her sentence of banishment, following her civil trial Anne had been placed under the supervision of Joseph Welde, brother of the clergyman Thomas Welde, in the town of Roxbury. Lodged two miles away from her home, she had little contact with her family over the months when heavy snows blanketed the path from Boston to Roxbury. Her husband, William, made the trek, but it is unlikely that her children—six of whom were ten and under—accompanied him. She was also largely isolated from the men and women whom she had counseled over the previous years.

Various clergy did visit her in efforts to persuade her to recant, Shepard himself engaging her on three occasions. Meanwhile, John Davenport, a prominent clergyman recently arrived in Boston, joined with Wilson and Cotton in trying to heal the divisions in the Boston church. On March 15 Anne appeared before the congregation to answer for various heretical views that she had been accused of. Robert Keayne took notes of the trial in his sermon notebook. Wilson opened the proceedings by asking everyone to put aside his or her feelings as "father, mother, sister, brother, friend, enemy" and judge according to the "rules of God's word," yet to "proceed in love." Winthrop seemed interested in engaging Anne in discussion. Davenport treated her with more sympathy than many of the clergy had, and for a time it seemed that she might be sent into exile in good standing with the Boston church. After a one-week adjournment, she in fact recanted the errors that she had been charged with. But Shepard provoked her into new expressions of her earlier beliefs. Winthrop and Cotton both tried to remedy the damage, but Cotton himself eventually lost patience with Hutchinson, and that proved decisive. He acknowledged that many had profited from conferences with Hutchinson, but warned that they "not let the good you have received from her make you to receive all for good that comes from her." The church found her guilty of lying and heresy and Pastor John Wilson passed sentence of excommunication upon her. As she exited the church, accompanied by her friend Mary Dyer, she was purportedly heard to say, "Better to be cast out of the church than to deny Christ."

Those who try to interpret this controversy as a struggle pitting the forces of intolerance against toleration, and Anne Hutchinson as consciously promoting religious freedom are guilty of rewriting history to satisfy their own polemical purposes and advance their own values at the expense of truth. The fact is that neither side accepted the legitimacy of the opposing views. In calling the majority of magistrates and ministers anti-Christian, and prophesying that God would pass judgment upon them unless they abandoned their teachings, Anne Hutchinson was asserting that there was no place in a godly kingdom for such men as Wilson and Shepard and the doctrines they taught.

Because the civil sentence of banishment would have stood even if Anne had been exonerated by the church, William Hutchinson, William Coddington, John Clarke, William Dyer, and others who had been identified as her supporters had planned to move on from the Bay colony. They set their sights on Aquidneck Island, in the territory that became Rhode Island, and signed a civil contract with William Coddington as their first governor. Moving to the region, they purchased land they settled from the sachems of the Narragansetts. Much of Anne Hutchinson's life had been spent in traveling to achieve spiritual comfort. It is likely that she made the long trek from Alford to Boston to listen to John Cotton. When the light of the gospel dimmed in England, she immigrated to the new England. Now her convictions were responsible for moving again. Following her trial she and her family, including her younger children, journeyed overland to the Narragansett Bay. Their possessions loaded on horse-drawn carts, the family crossed the largely unsettled regions to the south of Boston, at times trudging through the snow that remained on the ground, struggling through mud where the snow had begun to melt. There were no inns or homes to break their journey. After a week of travel they reached Roger Williams's Providence, and from there sailed to Aquidneck. Whereas the Hutchinsons had arrived in Boston at a time when substantial homes had replaced the primitive shelters of the first years, now they were to find out what carving a new home from the wilderness was all about.

We know little about Anne Hutchinson herself during the early years of this new settlement. The settlers named the town they settled Portsmouth and created a political entity that they declared to be under the kingship of Christ, with William Coddington as "judge," a position akin to the type of chieftain identified by that name in the Old Testament. Within a short time some residents began to chafe under this system and to assert the types of rights and processes that they were familiar with from England and from Massachusetts, causing political friction in the settlement. In the spiritual sphere, there was no organized church. John Clarke, one of the settlers, appears to have preached on occasion, and it is likely that lay men and perhaps women shared their religious beliefs freely when the community was gathered. It was said that Anne preached more than she had in Boston, but this may have been primarily in domestic settings.

The Massachusetts authorities gathered news and rumors from the south. When Anne miscarried toward the end of her sixteenth pregnancy in May 1638, news of the "monstrous birth"—likely a mass of tissue with separate transparent lumps now known as a hydatidiform mole—was viewed by the orthodox as a visible manifestation of the horrendous errors she had birthed, and the providential sign was widely broadcast by Winthrop and others as a vindication of the righteousness of her excommunication. At the same time, however, excommunication was seen as the ultimate effort of the church to chastise erring brothers and sisters in the hope of bringing them to their senses and eventually reuniting them to the church. Therefore, in 1640, the Boston church sent three emissaries to Aquidneck in an attempt to bring their "wandering sheep" back into the fold of orthodoxy. Anne refused to acknowledge the church that had sent them as a true church and rejected their overtures. But it should be noted that her eldest son, Edward, did return to Massachusetts and made his peace with the authorities there. He would serve in a variety of civic functions over the following decades.

Without a common enemy to unite them, the religious zeal that had animated these men and women and divided the Boston church drew members of the group in different directions. Some began to preach under what they claimed to be the direct inspiration of the Holy Spirit. Embracing the experience of being possessed by the Spirit, many would later join the Society of Friends, or Quakers. Others seemed to have moved toward a true antinomianism in which they claimed that their actions were directed by God and not subject to the judgment of men. The divisions in Portsmouth led Coddington to leave the town and settle on the southern part of the island, at a place he called Newport. Drawn perhaps by the greater commercial potential of the new settlement, many of those with mercantile backgrounds followed him there. In Portsmouth the remaining settlers chose William Hutchinson as judge.

New divisions soon arose over land distribution. William Hutchinson died around the turn of the decade, the exact date being unknown. Coddington was able to gain control over Portsmouth as well as Newport, making Aquidneck something of an island republic for a brief period. It proclaimed itself "a democracy or popular government," on the basis of the right of freemen to elect their leaders and approve all laws (though only about half of the male residents and no women were freemen). The "republic" did vote for a form of religious liberty, which was probably the only course for a society with so many fragmented and distinct religious groups. At the same time, Coddington and a small group of fellow elders were regularly chosen to the top positions in the government, making the "republic" more like an oligarchy.

In the meantime, following the death of her husband, Anne Hutchinson decided to move one more time. She had again been visited by representatives of the Boston church, who commiserated with her loss and hoped yet to bring her back to orthodoxy. She rejected these overtures as she had the earlier ones. She was not yet ready to settle for other people's faith, and it is likely that a growing dissatisfaction with the religious and civic affairs of Portsmouth led to her leaving. She sought and received permission from the Dutch authorities to settle in New Netherland, along what is now known as Pelham Bay in the New York City borough of the Bronx. In the summer of 1643 she and the members of her household were killed there by Native Americans. Again, her former enemies interpreted her personal misfortune as a providential judgment.

ANNE HUTCHINSON's friend Mary Dyer and Mary's husband William had left the London parish of St. Martin-in-the-Fields and travelled to New England in 1635. London at the time was a hotbed of new religious ideas, many of which emphasized the role of the Spirit in the lives of the saints. William was a milliner and member of the Fishmongers Company and set up trade in Boston as a merchant. An educated man, William served as clerk for the development of the fortifications on Fort Hill. During the controversy that divided the Boston church in the mid-1630s, John Winthrop had identified both William and Mary as having "a piercing knowledge in many things" and being very active in the faction that questioned the teachings of John Wilson.

Mary Dyer had been particularly close to Anne Hutchinson, took her friend's hand when Hutchinson was sentenced to excommunication, and accompanied her out of the Boston church. The attention this drew to her led to an exhumation of a child of hers that had been stillborn about a year earlier and quietly buried. Upon examination the infant was found to be grossly misshapen, and—as would later be claimed in reference to Anne Hutchinson's 1638 stillbirth—her enemies saw this as a manifestation of the monstrous opinions she had embraced.

Moving to Rhode Island, the Dyers first settled in Portsmouth but then moved on with William Coddington to Newport. When the towns of the region became organized as the Colony of Rhode Island and Providence Plantations in 1644, William served the colony in a variety of capacities. In the 1650s Mary returned for a time to England, perhaps accompanying her husband. There she found an affinity between the spiritist views she had long espoused and the teachings of the Society of Friends, or Quakers, who taught that the inner light of God was within all men and women. She became a Quaker and returned to New England determined to witness to this truth. In 1657 she arrived in Boston with a fellow Quaker, Anne Burden. Dyer was not the only supporter of Hutchinson who was drawn to the teachings of the inner light, a fact that led the Massachusetts magistrates to make a connection between

The statue of Mary Dyer in front of the Massachusetts State House
Photo by Mark Andrew Higgins

the threat of this new movement and that of the old. Legislation had been passed in 1656 stipulating that Quakers were to be banished. When Mary arrived with Anne Burden, the Massachusetts authorities committed the two women to prison. After a few months, Burden was sent back to England. Dyer, who claimed ignorance of the 1656 statute, was released to her husband.

It soon became clear that the effort to keep the sect out of New

England actually stimulated Quaker efforts to pierce the walls of the kingdom. John Hull made a perceptive observation when he wrote, "In those parts of the country where they might with freedom converse (as in Rhode Island . . .), they take no pleasure to be." Instead they came to Massachusetts, where "they seemed to suffer patiently, and take a kind of pleasure in it." Over the following years Quaker men and women threw themselves into the assault, many returning after having been banished.

The Massachusetts authorities responded to this behavior by ratcheting up the penalties to be imposed on Quakers. In October 1657 fines were increased for harboring members of the sect, and offending enthusiasts who returned from banishment were to have an ear cropped. Yet another appearance would lead to the loss of the other ear. Returning yet again from banishment would lead to the offender's tongue being bored. The last two penalties were never imposed as the law continued to change. Previously, when dissenters had been cast out from the godly kingdom they had accepted their exile and stayed away. But this was different. The General Court passed a law imposing the death penalty on Quakers who persisted in returning after banishment.

In the summer of 1659 the Quaker Marmaduke Stevenson, hearing of the Bay's latest legislation, felt the call of God to travel to the Bay. He was joined there by William Robinson, Nicholas Davis, and Mary Dyer. The four were arrested and banished. Within weeks of their departure, Robinson, Stevenson, and Dyer were back and were arraigned before the General Court. They were quickly sentenced to death. On October 27 the three were brought to the Boston Common, Mary Dyer holding the hands of her two friends. Stevenson and Robinson were hanged and buried beneath the gallows. Dyer, whose husband had again interceded on her behalf, was reprieved, being dismissed into the custody of her son, who brought her back to Rhode Island. So great was the crowd that had gathered to witness the executions that the drawbridge over Boston's Mill Creek collapsed under the weight of those returning home, with some killed and others injured in the accident.

The following spring saw Mary Dyer return yet again to Massachusetts. The merchant John Hull saw her "come audaciously through the town at high day." Urged by some to leave, "she answered she had a strong power to go forward, but no strength to go back." Hull commented parenthetically, "He must needs go whom the devil drives." Arraigned before Endecott and the General Court, Mary denied the authority of their law and claimed to have returned to bear witness against it. Once again she was convicted, and once again she was brought to the gallows on the Common. Offered yet another reprieve if she would swear never to return, she declined, saying, "In obedience to the will of the Lord I came, and in his will I abide faithful unto death." Mary Dyer's execution prompted many to rethink the policy that had been adopted toward the Quakers. Yet Dyer wasn't the last Quaker to be executed in Massachusetts. William Leddra was hanged in March 1661. At the foot of the gallows he said "All that will be Christ's disciples must take up the cross."

Like Anne Hutchinson, Mary Dyer had found her own understanding of God and his will and was willing to speak up for that view. Also like Hutchinson, she had no doubt that the light she had acquired was the truth and that she was compelled to spread that message to all.

ANOTHER STRONG WOMAN who challenged the Massachusetts authorities was born Deborah Dunch in London in 1586. Her father was a lawyer and a member of Parliament at the time of her birth. Her mother came from a line of clergymen noted for advocating radical religious reforms. Like many other women of her class she was taught how to read and write. In 1606 she married Henry Moody, who was shortly thereafter knighted by King James I, which made Deborah Lady Moody. Henry served, as her father had, as a member of Parliament. When Henry died in 1629, Lady Deborah moved to London. It is likely to have been there that she came to doubt the validity of infant baptism. Because puritans were focused on limiting access to the Lord's Supper to those who were ascertained to be God's elect, some questioned the validity of infant baptism. These Anabaptists claimed that only adult believers should be baptized.

King Charles had decreed that members of the upper class must spend less time in London and more on their country estates, and Lady Deborah was prosecuted in 1635 for defying this order. Shortly thereafter she immigrated to Massachusetts, where she acquired a farm of 500 acres she called Swampscott as well as a house in Salem. As noted previously, many puritans had doubts about who should be baptized and what forms the sacrament should take. In England during the 1640s many puritan congregations would include supporters of both infant and adult baptism. In New England infant baptism was the practice accepted by the civil and ecclesiastical authorities, though Harvard president Henry Dunster came to reject the practice (and was forced to leave his post as a result), and other clergy such as John Davenport expressed sympathy for Anabaptists. Thomas Goold, one of the early Baptist leaders in Massachusetts, was a friend and tenant of the Winthrops.

Lady Moody had joined the Salem church in May 1640, though she would have disapproved the baptismal practices of the congregation. She may have met with some sympathy there, since when Roger Williams had ministered there he had been moving toward the adoption of Baptist principles. When Lady Moody's views on the sacrament became known in December 1642, the colony authorities charged her with holding Anabaptist beliefs. Like Anne Hutchinson and Mary Dyer, she was convinced of the righteousness of her views. Unlike Hutchinson and Dyer she was not willing to assert that contrary views were necessarily sinful. John Winthrop referred to her as "a wise and anciently religious woman." Differing from Winthrop, John Endecott saw Lady Moody as "a dangerous woman." After various clergy failed to dissuade her from her views, she left Massachusetts in 1643 "to avoid further trouble," and settled on the Dutch portion of Long Island, becoming the founder of the town of Gravesend.

Lady Moody was joined at Gravesend with some supporters from the Salem area, and some Englishmen who had been residing in New Amsterdam. Gravesend was threatened for a time by Indian attacks, but by 1645 it was well established. The Dutch authorities had granted Lady Moody a charter, allowing Gravesend considerable self-government and guaranteeing "free liberty of conscience according to the custom and manner of Holland." That freedom meant that the residents of the town could practice their faith privately without being molested, but it did not allow them to worship publicly. Lady Moody embraced this policy of toleration and would defend it against both Dutch and English authorities who later challenged it. She used the privilege to shield Quakers in the community. Some have suggested that she herself became a Quaker, though there is no specific evidence of that. She died late in 1658 or early in 1659.

WHEN TRAVELLING from Salem to New Netherlands, Lady Moody had stopped to visit friends in the New Haven settlement that John Davenport and Theophilus Eaton had established on the north side of Long Island Sound in 1638. Among those friends was Anne Eaton, the wife of the colony's governor. Like Lady Moody, Anne came from a privileged background. She was the daughter of George Lloyd (Bishop of Chester from 1604 until his death in 1615). Anne was well educated and prosperous in her own right when she married the successful London merchant Thomas Yale. Following the death of Yale she wed Theophilus Eaton, himself a widower, who was a prominent merchant engaged in the Baltic trade. In 1637 Theophilus decided to accompany his pastor and friend John Davenport to New England. Accompanying the couple were their own two children as well as Anne's sons David and Thomas Yale, her daughter Anne Yale Hopkins, Theophilus's two children from his first marriage, and his aged mother.

Counting servants, including two African slaves, up to thirty individuals resided in the governor's home. Managing such a large household would have been difficult under any circumstances. For Anne Eaton the situation would have been made more difficult because of the presence of her mother-in-law, who had been accustomed to running Theophilus's household between the death of his first wife and his marriage to Anne. Anne's relationship with her step-daughter Mary, about thirty at this time and unmarried, was likewise difficult. Theophilus, focused on his public responsibilities, was disinclined to interfere in household affairs, even when Anne asked him to support her actions. Despite the relative elegance of the Eatons' home, the comforts available were far less than what Anne had been raised with and that she had enjoyed in their London residence.

Faced with these difficulties, Anne would have welcomed the support of her married daughter, Ann Yale Hopkins, but she had moved on to Hartford with her husband, Edward Hopkins, soon after the families arrived in the New World. Worse, in the early 1640s Ann Hopkins began to lose her sanity. In April 1645 John Winthrop reported that Edward Hopkins, then governor of Connecticut, had brought his wife to Boston in hope of finding a treatment for her. Ann, referred to by Winthrop as "a godly young woman, and of special parts," had "fallen into a sad infirmity, the loss of her understanding and reason, which had growing upon her for divers years." Concern about her daughter would have only added to the burdens Anne Eaton bore.

At some point, possibly even before she settled in New Haven, Anne Eaton had begun to question the legitimacy of infant baptism, doubts that may have been encouraged by earlier contact in London with Lady Deborah Moody. When Moody visited Anne on her way to Long Island, the two women discussed the issue of baptism. Anne "importuned her [Lady Moody] to lend her a book made by A. R." The book in question was Andrew Ritor's *A Treatise of the Vanity of Childish-Baptism* (1642), which Anne proceeded to "read secretly, and as secretly engaged her spirit in that way." She didn't discuss the ideas with her husband, her pastor, or any of the church elders, though she did share it with some other women who she thought might be sympathetic. Suddenly, on one Sabbath late in 1643 or early in 1644, as the congregation was preparing for the Lord's Supper, Anne got up from her favored position on the front bench of the meetinghouse and walked down the aisle and out of the service. That afternoon, she left after the sermon was concluded and the congregation prepared for an infant's baptism. Over the following weeks she would occasionally absent herself from public worship in general.

At one of the congregation's regular Tuesday discussion meetings, "some of the brethren desired that Mrs. Eaton would declare her reasons." She explained that she rejected the normative puritan view that infant baptism was justified as the Christian equivalent of circumcision. Davenport asked her "whether if that point were cleared she would be satisfied," and she appeared to assent. Davenport borrowed Ritor's book from her and on the following Tuesday "began to speak to the first part of it in the meeting of the church." On the next Sabbath he began to preach a series of sermons in support of baptizing infants. Anne was not convinced. Further private efforts to shift her from her position likewise failed. Davenport "marveled at the hand of God herein, which to me seemed dreadful, fearing that, as before she would not seek light, so now God would not give her a heart to receive light."

While the efforts to win Anne Eaton back to orthodoxy slowly proceeded, new concerns arose about her treatment of members of her household. The records show that Davenport was clearly reluctant to give credence to the rumors that had begun to circulate, presumably because he would not have welcomed having to inquire into the household affairs of a man who was both his friend and the governor of the colony. But faced with public questions as to why the church leaders were dragging their feet, Davenport and the church elders visited the Eaton household. What they found was worse than what they expected, and Davenport concluded that they would have to defer "treating with her any further about the error of her judgment [her views on baptism], till we might help forward by the will of God her repentance for these evils in life." They initially sought to admonish and deal with her privately, but after repeated efforts failed because of her "hardness of heart and impenitency," the elders informed her that the matter would have to be brought before the congregation.

In what was one of the most extraordinary events in the history of New England, on the Lord's Day, July 14, 1644, following the collection, John Davenport brought the misconduct of the wife of the colony's governor to the attention of the New Haven church. The first charge was that "Mrs. [Anne] Eaton, sitting at dinner with Mr. Eaton and old Mrs. Eaton, Mrs. Eaton struck old Mrs. Eaton twice on the face with the back of her hand, which [old] Mrs. Eaton said she felt three days after." On this occasion Theophilus was reported to have grasped his wife's hands as she cried out "I am afflicted! I am afflicted." One of those who was there thought that her shrieks were so loud that the Davenports must have heard her across the street. On another occasion, Anne quarreled with her step-daughter Mary, "grew outrageous, struck her, pinched her, . . . and knocked her head against the dresser, which made her nose bleed." On a separate occasion she falsely accused Mary of being pregnant, "saying her carriage was wanton." She also "charged Mary to be the cause of the ruin of the souls of many that came into the house." Anne was also charged with accusing Mary of spilling some milk which she (Anne) had actually dropped, and claiming that her step-daughter "wrought with the devil." When a keg tap wasn't where Anne expected it she attacked the servant girl Mary Launce when she fetched it. Pinching her servant's face, she then "struck her with the tap in the eye and made it swell, and made it black," and then grabbed her arms and pulled her by the nose. Other charges involved disputes and lies regarding the allocation of household servants between Anne and her mother-in-law. Anne was further accused of having claimed that the Eaton's black slave Anthony had bewitched the family beer. She "often charged" another servant, Mary Breck, with "lying and theft," having "worked with the devil in the house," and "whored too." She told all the maids that "God would send their souls to hell," and called them all "wicked wretches." During one of John Davenport's sermons against Anabaptism, "Mrs. Eaton said as she sat in her seat, 'it is not so,' and when Mr. Davenport said he would be brief, [she said] 'I would you would,' or 'I pray be so.'" When Davenport and his ministerial colleague William Hooke were meeting with her and Theophilus in the Eaton home, she quarreled with her husband before them and accused him of lying. One morning, when she was dissatisfied with one of the male ser-vants for not bringing water promptly into the house, she demanded that Theophilus reprimand the servant. Theophilus, "not seeing cause for it, did not reproach the man," at which point Anne yelled at her husband, told him to get out of the house along with the servant, and bragged that she could pay for her own bread and keep.

Each of the charges was supported by the testimony of two or more witnesses, and each was specifically referenced to the commandment she had broken. Davenport indicated that there were numerous other charges that were not brought before the church because of the lack of a second witness. When asked to respond to the charges, "she sat down and said nothing." The church proceeded to discuss whether her actions merited excommunication. Davenport suggested that, serious though they were, the offenses did not justify that sentence, and suggested that a formal admonition might be sufficient. With a show of hands the congregation agreed to this, and Davenport read out the sentence: "In the name of the Lord Jesus Christ, and with the consent of this Church, I do charge thee, Mrs. Eaton, to attend unto the several rules you have broken, and to judge yourself by them, and to hold forth your repentance according to God, as you will answer it at the great day of Jesus Christ."

Everyone expected that this would bring Anne to her senses, but they were surprised and disappointed to find that "she did continue offensive in her way" to her family and servants. When approached by the elders she often quibbled. The church had identified her physical attack on the old Mrs. Eaton as a breach of the Fifth Commandment, but she told the elders that "she was not convinced" because "she did not acknowledge her husband's mother to be her mother." Finally, on May 20, 1645, following the Sabbath services, she was called to appear before the church with her response. When the discussion went late, it was decided to postpone the conclusion till after the Thursday lecture. She still refused to repent and the church then proceeded to discuss whether she should be excommunicated for the original charges and also for lies that she had been caught in during discussions of her admonition. Given the seriousness of the case, Davenport had invited representatives of other churches in the region to attend and advise. The congregation and the visiting clergy, "with much grief of heart, and many tears," proceeded to excommunicate her. One of the visitors was heard to remark, "If this case had been in the churches up the river [Connecticut], it would not have been delayed so long."

Excommunication was a church censure intended to jolt the offender and bring about repentance. It did not carry with it the need to leave the community. In this case, Anne Eaton never bent to the will of the congregation and remained in the town and colony. Reports were that she ceased to share a bedroom with Theophilus and denied him "conjugal fellowship." Because she was no longer a member of the church in good standing, she had no stage on which to show her opposition to the congregation's baptism of infants. She seems not to have continued efforts to persuade others of that position, and in return formal efforts to persuade her she was in error appear to have ceased. This was in keeping with

New England practice, which allowed the private holding of errors and only challenged and punished public demonstrations of heresy.

Historians who have discussed the trial of Anne Eaton have generally used the event to criticize puritans for their attitudes toward women or their religious intolerance. Neither judgment seems appropriate. The fact that differences over doctrine were put aside to deal with more serious interpersonal violence is notable. And while some of the charges against the governor's wife could be considered within the range of master-servant disputes, her physical assaults on members of the household merited punishment in any society. The many attempts to wean her away from her bad behavior bespeak anything but rigidity and intolerance.

Anne was never called before the church to answer for her Anabaptist views because following her excommunication she was no longer a member of the congregation. She remained in the colony and was provided a place outside the church doors where she could listen to sermons should she so desire. On a number of occasions she urged her husband to return to England, but he was committed to the New Haven enterprise. Following his death in 1658 she did decide to return to England and was provided an honor guard to convey her to Boston for the voyage.

THE EMPHASIS puritans placed on the importance of each individual being able to access and interpret the scripture served to empower women. There is evidence that many women became thoughtful and active believers. Their beliefs led Anne Hutchinson, Mary Dyer, Lady Deborah Moody, and Anne Eaton to espouse positions that brought them into conflict with colonial authorities. But John Winthrop's mother, his sister Lucy Downing, and his wives Thomasine Clopton and Margaret Tyndal were all noted for their religious interests and piety. They, along with Anne Bradstreet and many other articulate women are less likely to attract our attention because their beliefs fell within the orthodox spectrum and they expressed themselves in support of that orthodoxy. There were many varieties of puritanism, and women were to be found along the entire spectrum.

THE TROUBLED KEAYNES

Of all the first-generation merchants whose efforts contributed to the prosperity of Massachusetts, the most famous is Robert Keayne. It might be more accurate to say that he is the most notorious, because his story has attracted historians largely due to his clashes with his fellow colonists, a number of whom accused him of shady business practices. His story is one that demonstrates the difficulties puritan merchants faced, caught between the puritan communal social ethic and emerging entrepreneurial principles. It is a tragic story because Keayne was himself torn between these conflicting values. A different type of notoriety was achieved by his daughter-in-law, Sarah Dudley Keayne, who became a sexually promiscuous street preacher in Civil War London. Their compelling stories point to yet other dimensions of puritanism in the Atlantic world.

ROBERT KEAYNE was the son of a butcher in Windsor, Berkshire, England. He was born in 1595 and when he was about ten his father apprenticed him to a member of the London Merchant Taylor's Company, one of the city's foremost guilds. After completing his apprenticeship Robert was admitted as a freeman of that company and set up his own business. By 1617 he had married Anne Mansfield, the daughter of a former master of mines and surveyor to Queen Elizabeth. The match attests to the fact that he had already achieved considerable prosperity. It also connected him to John Wilson, the future Boston minister, who was married to Anne's sister Elizabeth.

Keayne continued to prosper. He was admitted to the freedom of the City (meaning that he could vote), was being addressed as a gentleman, and in 1623 was admitted to the Honorable Artillery Company of London. This was a group that taught and exercised men who would command the London Trained Bands, the citizen militia who provided the backbone of the nation's military in time of war. Membership also signified one as a member of the elite, and enabled one to mingle with the city's mayor and civic leaders at public functions.

We don't know if Keayne was raised as a puritan or was influenced in that direction during his apprenticeship, but it is at least clear that he was a zealous puritan by the time he set himself up as a London merchant. The Cornhill district in which he lived had a reputation for clergy and laymen who promoted further reform of the church. Keayne purchased numerous religious treatises written in English. He travelled around the city to attend sermons delivered by prominent preachers, taking copious notes of the sermons for his later review. In a volume containing notes on sermons he heard between June 1627 and June 1628, he recorded over sixty sermons by a variety of London clergy that included Richard Sibbes, William Gouge, John Davenport, and Thomas Taylor, as well as visiting preachers such as his "brother Wilson" and John Cotton of Boston. It was common for him to hear two sermons on a Sunday—such as on July 15, 1627, when he heard Davenport at St. Stephen's and then walked to the Cornhill district to hear "Mr. Malthouse"—and on at least two occasions he found a way to hear and take notes on three sermons. Keayne also acquired numerous printed and manuscript religious writings, including a "little thin pocket book" that he copied, "a treatise on the sacrament of the Lord's Supper" by the Lincolnshire separatist Roger Brereley, which he claimed to "have read over, I think, 100 and 100 times." Brereley was one of those suspected of antinomian views to whom Thomas Shepard had briefly been drawn. It is likely during his years in London that Keayne also began to compile three large manuscript books in which he sought to copy down expositions of each chapter of the entire Bible. Later, in Boston, he would begin a similar volume in which he collected interpretations of the prophetic books of Daniel, Hosea, and Revelations.

Keayne's religious sentiments may have influenced his investment in the Pilgrim's migration in 1620. And it likely was why he invested in the Massachusetts Bay Company in the early 1630s. He also acted for that company in 1634 in the purchase of armaments for the colony. In July

1635 he, together with his wife and their son Benjamin, embarked for New England. He never explained what had led him to this decision. Certainly he would have recognized opportunities for economic success in America. And like other pious puritans he would have been disturbed by the actions of the newly elevated Archbishop of Canterbury, William Laud, to crack down on puritan preaching. It is likely that both considerations contributed to his decision.

In Boston, the Keaynes built a home in the center of the town (on the southwest corner of what is now Washington and State streets), one lot down from the meetinghouse of the Boston church and facing the market square. On his arrival he became one of the wealthiest colonists. Almost immediately he showed a concern for the community by contributing to the erection of defensive works on Fort Hill. All residents had to attend religious services, but only those admitted to membership by the congregation could receive the sacraments. In March 1636 Keayne was admitted to the Boston church. In that same year the Boston town meeting chose him to serve on a committee that dealt with land acquisitions and other business affairs. In 1638 he helped organize the Boston Ancient and Honorable Artillery Company, modeled after the London body of which he had been a member.

Keayne's arrival in Boston roughly coincided with the divisions in the Boston church that developed around the teachings of Anne Hutchinson, Henry Vane, and others who emphasized the spiritist dimension of puritanism. A number of scholars have argued that many of those found in that group were merchants, and Keayne's possession of one of Roger Brereley's tracts might suggest that he would have been found on that side of the divide. It is clear, however, that he did not support those individuals. He was not one of those who petitioned to overturn the General Court's condemnation of John Wheelwright, nor was he one of those whose position was inquired into by the General Court. Instead, he was one of the church minority who stood behind John Wilson, who was his kinsman. Keayne had kept his practice of taking extensive sermon notes, and he added to this the recording of other church business. The detailed account we have of Anne Hutchinson's church trial comes from one of Keayne's notebooks.

The fight in the Boston church left many scars that influenced the positions individuals took in later disputes, and Keayne may very well have made enemies at that time. He was particularly vulnerable to attack because of his position as a merchant. The seventeenth century saw a growing clash between an economic ethos that justified self-interest as a force that drove societal growth as well as individual profit and a traditional communal ethos that asserted that the common good was to dictate individual economic behavior. Puritans subscribed to the latter view, as was clearly demonstrated in John Winthrop's "Christian Charity" lay sermon, but they were by no means alone. This was an outlook that had permeated Christian culture all the way back to the days of the apostles.

Keayne's business practices were shaped in large part by the values of the Merchant Taylor's Company in which he had served his apprenticeship, and in the London environment in which he had practiced his trade. In a world in which fewer business transactions were conducted by individuals known to each other, contracts rather than trust dictated obligations. The lending of money increasingly became a business transaction rather than an act of charity—note the treatment of the subject in Shakespeare's *Merchant of Venice* (written when Keayne was a boy). Merchants argued that the price charged in any single transaction must allow a profit margin that would cover potential losses on other transactions. There was a dispute over whether employers needed to pay what we might call a living wage or could take advantage of a glutted labor market to pay less and maximize their own profits.

All of these practices were hotly debated in England in the decades surrounding the settlement of New England. The colonial situation made the debates more complex. Goods such as nails and tools that were in ample supply in England were scarce in the colonies—should merchants be allowed to charge what the market would bear? No one argued for that, but what was a fair price? Merchants pointed out that they bore the cost of transporting goods to the colonies, and before there was an insurance industry, they had to assume the risk of ships and their cargos being lost. But how were these costs to be factored into the price of commodities? The colonial magistrates tried to control prices and also the wages of those who would take advantage of the labor shortage that existed to demand unrealistically high wages. But too harsh an application of these restraints might jeopardize the economic growth on which the success of the colonies depended. In this situation it was easy to label merchants avaricious, and many were subjected to the scrutiny of their fellow colonists in court and church proceedings.

The most famous such case centered on Robert Keayne. In 1639 he was accused before the Boston church of having made an excessive profit in the sale of nails. The accusation was made by one of the magistrates—perhaps Richard Bellingham—who said that the merchant had charged him ten pence for nails that were valued at six pence. Keayne responded that Bellingham had brought back the original nails because they were too small and took delivery of nails normally valued at eight pence. Thus, the profit margin was two pence per nail, which was not outside the norms, but on the high side. During the deliberations others came forth with charges that Keayne had overcharged them for a bridle, buttons, and thread. None of these other charges were formally laid, and Keayne's explanation for his behavior was found to be true. But the General Court found Keayne guilty and fined him the extraordinary sum of £200, reducing it the next year to £80. Winthrop recorded in his journal that Keayne had a reputation in London for charging excessively, and that reputation had followed him to Massachusetts, which didn't help his cause. He was being held up as an example of bad practice as a warning to other merchants, but some of the animus against him might have derived from ill feelings stemming from the church controversy of a few years earlier.

More troubling to the merchant was the fact that the Boston church took up the question of how guilty he was of the "clamors and rumors" that had been brought against him. It is even more likely that the church proceedings drew on the divisions that remained in the congregation. John Cotton's consistent preaching against usury and unchristian business practices provided additional background to the church's deliberations. In the end, the congregation admonished Keayne "for selling his wares at excessive rates to the dishonor of God's name, the offense of the General Court, and the public scandal of the country." The admonition was lifted when he acknowledged his error and promised to mend his ways, but the stigma of the church action remained with him for the rest of his life, leading him to include a justification of his conduct in his lengthy last will and testament. Keayne is usually presented as the poster boy of merchant excess because of his never-ending effort to justify his behavior in this and other cases where he was charged with similar offenses. But the fact that he did obsess about his guilt also reveals that he wanted to behave in a godly manner. He was a man torn between what he had learned was acceptable and common behavior in the world of business and what some puritans insisted were the principles to be followed.

Trade of one sort or another was the life-blood of early New England. The fur trade had underwritten the survival of Plymouth. John Winthrop engaged in that trade in the 1630s, joining after a few years with William Pynchon, who became the most successful of the region's fur traders. The governor of the New Haven Colony (established in 1638) for much of its early history was Theophilus Eaton, perhaps the wealthiest English merchant to settle in New England. During the 1630s the regional economy was sustained by new arrivals who brought money and spent it on supplies they needed to establish themselves in their new homeland. When immigration dried to a trickle because of the English Civil Wars, colonists scrambled to find Atlantic markets from the West Indies to the Azores for the timber, grains, fish, and other products they could produce. John Winthrop's sons John, Stephen, and Samuel were all involved in this trade in one way or another. With commerce so central to the region's success, questions regarding business practices were frequently brought to the courts. During the first fifteen years of the Massachusetts Bay Company there were fifty cases involving fraud or violations of wage and price guidelines that came before the colony Court of Assistants. Additional cases were dealt with in the county courts once they were established after 1636.

Despite his embarrassment, Keayne's fellow colonists continued to entrust him with important responsibilities. In all he served as Boston selectman (a member of the town council) four times, was elected to represent the town in the colony's General Court seven times, and held various other positions.

Keayne's enemies found another opportunity to bring him down in 1642. Elizabeth Sherman accused him of illegally appropriating and slaughtering her prize sow. Six years earlier, when Keayne had only recently arrived in Boston, he came into possession of a stray sow. Many householders in the town had livestock that grazed on the common pasture, and some had smaller animals such as pigs which they kept on their home lots. Though there were regulations requiring such animals to be fenced in, the regulations were not uniformly enforced and strays were not uncommon. Keayne had his servants broadcast news of the stray sow around the town. A number of individuals came to see if it was their property, but found that it was not. A year later, after Keayne had killed what he contended was one of his own sows, the widow Sherman came to see if the stray he still held was hers. The markings were different, but she then accused the merchant of having killed the real stray, which was hers, and attempting to pass off one of his own as the stray.

There was already bad blood between the merchant and goodwife Sherman. Elizabeth's husband was absent in London and she had taken in a young lodger named George Story, a merchant newly arrived from London. Keayne had raised questions about the propriety of that situation, and although nothing came of his complaint, it embarrassed Sherman and angered Story, who throughout the following proceedings supported Sherman and urged her on. Sherman's accusations also came when the town was bitterly divided over the religious divisions in the church and when some residents were already raising concerns about Keayne's business practices, all of which meant that there were many who were eager to believe charges leveled against the merchant.

The dispute over the sow disrupted the community enough that the Boston church investigated, called various witnesses, and cleared Keayne. Mrs. Sherman responded by suing Keayne in the county court in 1640. Keayne was found not guilty and the Mrs. Sherman was ordered to pay

Keayne's court costs. If he had left the matter rest at this point, the issue
might have gone away. But Keayne promptly sued Sherman and Story for
having defamed him. Everything we know about Robert Keayne identifies him as extremely sensitive to any attacks on his reputation. Many puritans viewed their behavior as evidence of the state of their soul. Keayne
had heard many sermons in which clergy urged believers to examine their
lives, suggesting that sanctification (a good life) was evidence of their
having been transformed by God's grace. In his last testament Keayne
acknowledged himself to be by nature a sinner, and admitted that none
of his actions were sufficient to merit salvation. Like other puritans, he
believed that any goodness in his life was "good fruits and evidences of
justification." If he accepted the fact that he had engaged in sinful activities, he would have had to question his belief that he had been saved, that
he was one of God's elect. His self-justifications were as much an effort
to prove to himself that he was innocent of transgressions as they were to
prove his innocence to the community.

Keayne won his defamation suit against Sherman and Story, but Story
found a witness willing to attest that he had perjured himself on Keayne's
behalf and on this basis appealed the case to the colony's General Court.
That body divided over the issue, with most of the magistrates siding with
Keayne and a majority of the deputies (representatives of the towns) along
with two magistrates (one of whom was Keayne's old nemesis Richard
Bellingham) siding with Story and Sherman. The result was a constitutional crisis that led to the division of the General Court into two separate bodies—the Assistants or upper house, and the Deputies, or lower
house—in 1644. In the process the actual case that prompted that result
was decided, with the Court determining there was no reason to proceed
with Story's complaint. Far from a ringing endorsement of Keayne, this
meant that he could at least put the case behind him.

By 1644 Keayne had other matters to trouble him. In 1639 his son
Benjamin had married Sarah Dudley, the daughter of Thomas Dudley
and sister of Anne Dudley Bradstreet. Sarah was known as brilliant and
emotional, resembling her older sister in these respects, but more rebel-
lious than Anne. Her marriage to Benjamin Keayne came at the height
of the controversy over Robert's business practices and, perhaps it was

to escape that spotlight that in 1640 the couple moved to Lynn, where their daughter Anna was born. In 1642 Benjamin returned to England to represent his father's business interests. Having a family member at the other end of a trade connection was a common practice. There are hints, however, that problems in his marriage also contributed to Benjamin's move. Sarah did not originally accompany him, but followed separately. Various sources reported that her ship foundered, her goods were lost, and she barely escaped with her life. Once in London, Sarah began to behave in a fashion calculated to shock her family back in New England, as well as many Englishmen.

Civil war had erupted in England in 1642, with King Charles having raised his banner and called on loyal Englishmen to assist him in putting down a Parliament that had attempted to enact measures calculated to restrict royal authority and advance reforms in the church The Parliament, most of whose remaining members reflected a broad puritan outlook, organized its own army and the kingdom was thrown into a conflict that was to rage over the next seven years. During that period neither side proved capable of asserting control over the press and speech. Various individuals and groups sprang up advocating forms of religious, social, and political change that were radical for their time. Just as London had been the place where radical ideas circulated most freely underground in earlier decades, so now it was where such ideas were freely espoused in pamphlets and on street corners. Many women embraced this opportunity to draft petitions to Parliament and to advance their own religious views.

Sarah Keayne became immersed in this new culture of freedom. In March 1646 Stephen Winthrop wrote from London to his father, "My she cousin Keayne is grown a great preacher." Sarah had witnessed and possibly sympathized with the religious assertions of Anne Hutchinson and Mary Dyer. Though she did not achieve the fame of Katherine Chidley and other English female religious leaders, she clearly embraced the freedom to express herself on religious matters. She also crossed acceptable boundaries in her personal life. In a series of letters to John Wilson, John Cotton, and his father-in-law Thomas Dudley, Benjamin Keayne spelled out how Sarah had "run so fast from that height of error in judgment to . . . extremity of error in practice." The practice in question was sexual promiscuity, and, initially unaware of her "breach of the conjugal knot," Benjamin, in his efforts to "satisfy the insatiable desire & lust" of his wife, had contracted a venereal disease which "must needs come from her, I having never known any woman but herself." He lamented "that his body is too sad a testimony of the truth," and sought to have his marriage dissolved. He indicated that he could supply ample evidence of her sexual transgressions.

Benjamin remained in London and refused to support her, so that Sarah returned to New England at some point in 1646. In October 1647 she was formally excommunicated from the Boston church for "irregular prophesying in mixed assemblies," presumably her preaching in London; for "refusing to hear in the churches of Christ" and not responding to admonitions in this regard; and for "falling into odious, lewd, and scandalous unclean behavior." Adultery was a capital offense in the Bay colony, yet Sarah escaped civil prosecution, perhaps because the only witnesses were in England. Official influence is also likely to have played a part. Sarah's father, Thomas Dudley, sought to get the marriage dissolved. In March of 1647 Benjamin Keayne wrote letters to Dudley and to the ministers John Cotton and John Wilson, spelling out Sarah's transgressions. Dudley shared his letter with Robert Keayne and set about seeking to put an end to the marriage. Divorce was granted on limited grounds in Massachusetts at this time, but did not allow either party to remarry. Dudley, using his considerable political influence (perhaps aided by Robert Keayne) had the marriage dissolved by the General Court in a judgment that enabled Sarah to marry again. It helped to have kin (Thomas Dudley) in powerful places, even in the godly kingdom! The decision was unusual enough to prompt protests both in the colonies and from English correspondents.

No longer married, Sarah was accused of having illicit relations with a number of other men, including the excommunicated Taunton merchant Nicholas Hart, for which she was again admonished by the church authorities. She then married Thomas Pacey of Boston, whom Thomas Dudley provided with a generous allowance, clearly hoping that Pacey would be able to prevent further notorious activity. Benjamin remained in England for a time, though eventually returning to Boston. The humiliation of his son—who was seen as not having been able to properly govern his wife—was keenly felt by Robert Keayne. Robert left a legacy of £300 for his granddaughter Anna (Benjamin and Sarah's sole child), to be paid to her at the age of twenty-one or upon her marriage after age eighteen. Until she received the bequest the interest from the account was to be used for her "diet, clothes and learning." He expressed a hope that in addition to reading, she would learn "to write well and to cipher in a reasonable manner." The will also specified that Anna's mother "(sometimes the unnatural and unhappy wife of my son, that proud and disobedient daughter-in-law to myself and wife), Mrs. Sarah Dudley, now Sarah Pacey, may have no part nor benefit in or by what I have bestowed upon her daughter." He further explained that it was expressly against his will "that she who hath walked so unworthily (that I may give it no worse terms) to us all should have any relief or anything to maintain her pride and contempt from anything that ever was accounted mine."

It is possible that the embarrassment his daughter-in-law's conduct had caused him and the loneliness resulting from his son's continuing in England contributed to the final disgrace of Robert Keayne. In 1646 he failed to show up for an appointed meeting of the General Court, to which he had been selected as one of Boston's deputies. He was fined, and he apologized, but it suggests that he was distracted or worse. In 1651 he was appointed to sit on a judicial tribunal to hear minor civil cases. Soon after this, questions about his fitness were raised when reports circulated that the wealthy merchant was guilty of public drunkenness. One account had him staggering home from Charlestown on a cold and snowy night "full of beer or wine." Another witness recalled seeing him in a neighbor's house "to be much overcome with drink, for as he went towards the fire to take a coal to light a pipe of tobacco he reeled with his head so forward that she was afraid he would have fallen into the fire." Other reports followed, and in May 1652 the General Court declared that since he had been "proved to have been three times drunk, and to have drunk to excess two times" he was to be fined and removed from public office. He died within the year.

Despite his troubles, Keayne had not only achieved success as a public figure, but had prospered in business. He left a considerable estate, including three African slaves. Keayne's lengthy last will and testament is often referred to as his *Apologia* because much of it took the form of justifying himself against the charges that had been laid against him in his life. But what is most striking is the strong commitment to the common wealth that is revealed in it. He left funds to further build the colony's defenses. He left money for the Boston Church's fund for the relief of poor citizens. He bequeathed funds to pay for a schoolmaster to teach the town's poor children, and a substantial sum for Harvard College. He left money for the construction of a conduit to bring fresh water to Bostonians, and other funds to stock a granary in the marketplace. But most notable was the £300 he bequeathed the town to build a public market building or town house. The design he specified underlined his commitment to the business life that had brought him success but also to the spiritual life. The ground floor was to be an open market area in which goods could be bought and sold. The upper level was to include rooms that could be used for both civil and religious purposes. When completed in 1658 the floor above the market was a single large room that could be used for town meetings. On the third floor was a library (to which Keayne had willed his extensive collection with the exception of books his son chose to keep), two courtrooms, a council chamber, and a gathering place for clergy who assembled in the town for meetings of the General Court. He further left £40 to feed the clergy when they came together. In the Boston Town House would be found the harmonious blend of business, government, and the church that Keayne had struggled so hard to keep in balance throughout his life.

A POSTSCRIPT to the story of the troubled lives of Robert Keayne, his son and his daughter-in-law concerns Anna Keayne, Robert's granddaughter. Shortly after Keayne died in 1653 suitors began to gather around the wealthy heiress. One of these was Edward Lane, a prosperous merchant who arrived in the colony from London in 1656. Lane proceeded to woo not only Anna but her grandmother, Robert's widow, who was administering the Keayne estate. The couple were married in December 1657 by John Endecott (marriage was exclusively a civil ceremony in seventeenth-century Massachusetts). It soon appeared that Lane was impotent. After fifteen months of wrestling with this embarrassing circumstance, Anna petitioned the Court of Assistants for dissolution of the marriage, claiming that from first to last Edward had been "altogether deficient" in "the performance of a husband." Edward acknowledged the truth of the situation and the court granted the petition.

Edward had assumed many of the functions of administering Robert Keayne's estate from the merchant's widow. With his marriage dissolved, Lane sought to extricate himself from the responsibilities, at the same time claiming a substantial fee for his work that, when paid, diminished the inheritance owed Anna by two-thirds. Edward was also consulting doctors and soon was visiting Anna with reports that he had recovered from his malady. The couple approached John Endecott in December 1659 (nine months after their marriage had been dissolved) seeking to remarry! Endecott decided that if the reason for the dissolution had been removed, that judgment was void and that they might resume married life. Over the next few years Anna gave birth to two children. In 1664 Anna left Boston for England, leaving Edward behind. Soon after this he died. Anna didn't return to Boston for another two years, bringing with her a new husband, Nicholas Paige, another Boston merchant who had been in England. Richard Cooke, a friend of Edward Lane, who had been involved in various negotiations between his friend and the Keaynes from the beginning, charged that Anna had in fact married Paige before Lane had died. Furthermore, he produced a document signed by Lane that claimed the "second" marriage with Anna had been a sham to protect both of their interests in the Keayne estate, his impotency never having been cured. In fact, Cooke claimed that the two Lane children had in fact been fathered by Paige, who had a long sexual relationship with Anna before the two of them departed separately for England and were married there.

The magistrates were appalled by all of this, and found Anna "guilty of much wickedness." She readily repented and that was sufficient for the authorities to sweep all of the business under the carpet. Cooke had manipulated his friend so that it turned out that he now controlled much of the Keayne estate. After futile attempts to contest that control, Anna gave up and eventually she and her husband Nicholas Paige were accepted back into Boston society. The Keaynes were no longer to be a source of public gossip.

✳

STEPHEN WINTHROP

Soldier of the Lord

John Winthrop's son John is well known to those who study colonial America. He became an important political leader himself, serving as governor of the colony of Connecticut almost continually from 1657 till his death in 1676. He followed his father in working for a moderate, big-tent type of puritanism, which meant that Connecticut was less likely to persecute Quakers and convict witches than Massachusetts. When the Stuart monarchy was restored to power in England in 1660 he negotiated a political path that actually expanded Connecticut's boundaries and preserved its autonomy. But the younger John Winthrop was more than this. He was an industrial pioneer who initiated a number of projects to develop the resources of New England, including iron works in both Massachusetts and Connecticut. He was a key figure in the intersection of alchemy and science who was one of the early members of England's Royal Society, the world's leading scientific association. He corresponded with many of the leading scientists of his time. His curiosity about all aspects of the natural world made him knowledgeable in the treatment of diseases. John Winthrop Jr.'s story easily eclipses that of his brothers, two of whom, Stephen and Samuel, are the subjects of the following chapters. But their lives also reveal some of the unexpected sides of puritanism in the seventeenth-century Atlantic world.

S TEPHEN WAS the first child of John and Margaret Winthrop, born in Groton, England, on March 24, 1619, eleven months after their marriage. The delivery was difficult. Margaret was in labor for over forty hours, "so as it began to be doubted of her life." John, who had lost his previous wife in childbirth after barely a year of marriage, was fearful that he would be visited with a similar tragedy. Local clergy came to pray with Margaret, and John "humbled myself in fasting & mourning. I searched my heart for some sins & made up my peace with my God, & so getting a more large & melting heart to go unto the Lord, I set myself to prayer, & gave not over until God had sent her deliverance." Margaret's life was still in question, however, because the next day "she was taken with a burning fever." After eight days, Winthrop's cousin and physician John Duke "made little reckoning of her life, but . . . diverse godly ministers meeting together did in their prayer remember her case in particular, & that very day & hour (as near as might be guessed) she found a sensible release of her disease." Margaret's survival was still in question when the infant was baptized in Groton Church on March 31. He was named, as was customary, after one of his godparents, the clergyman Stephen Egerton, a kinsman of Margaret who was one of the leading puritan clergymen of the time.

John Winthrop recorded two instances in Stephen's childhood when he felt that God had shielded the youth from injury or even death. Once, when Stephen was two, he was drawn to the fire in one of the manor house hearths. He fell in but was rescued without harm. On another occasion, when he was nine, Stephen was standing by the stable with his younger brother Adam while his older brother Forth practiced his archery. An arrow went awry and barely missed the young spectator.

Two years after this incident Stephen accompanied his father to New England. Being raised in a godly household did not make one immune from sinful temptations. Though his father recalled that he had been "a dutiful child, and not given up to the lusts of youth," Stephen was unsure of God's love for him. As a young man of fourteen he was "buffeted by Satan," who subjected him to "blasphemous and wicked thoughts." "Mourning and languishing daily" in his anxiety, he nevertheless continued to attend to sermons, pray, and seek the counsel of godly members of the community, till he found "comfort in God's promise." The following year, 1634, he was admitted a member of the Boston church. Stephen would have been taught in his Groton home and then sent to grammar school while still in England, but his formal education ended when he came to New England. There was, as of yet, no college for New England's young men. Stephen struggled to find a calling and began to examine possibilities in commerce.

Stephen accompanied his brother John on a visit to Saybrook in 1636, and stayed on there for a short time conducting trade with the Pequots from a shallop anchored in the middle of the Connecticut River. On one such occasion he and his men were attacked by natives and escaped. This was one of the events that soon led to war with that tribe. It was his first taste of war, but not the last. In 1638 he journeyed to England, visiting aunts and uncles, carrying out some errands for his mother, Margaret, and establishing business connections. When he returned to Massachusetts at the end of that year, he set up in trade as a merchant. In 1639 Stephen journeyed to Bermuda to establish further trading connections, and on the way out and back stopped at New Haven, where he tried to develop some trading links in that new colony. On the voyage from Bermuda to New Haven he recorded yet another sign of God's protection of him, writing to his mother that the ship had been threatened by a severe storm but was saved by the hand of providence.

The young Winthrop's new status as a merchant (and likely his family's prominence) led in 1639 to his being appointed recorder for Massachusetts, a post in which he would keep official records of marriages, births, deaths, wills, sales, grants, and other legal documents. This was particularly important in New England because there were no church ceremonies marking the passages of life and thus no parish records of such events as were kept in England. In 1641 Stephen joined the Boston Artillery Company that Robert Keayne had helped found. In 1644 he was chosen as a deputy to the Massachusetts General Court representing the settlement at Strawberry Bank in modern New Hampshire. It was not necessary in England or the colonies to live in the community you represented.

Stephen had continued his business ventures while also serving the colony. In 1646 he found himself in straitened circumstances in an England that was at war. He had engaged in an early form of triangular trade, exchanging goods from Massachusetts to trade in Tenerife, and then seeking to sell goods acquired there in London, but an unexpectedly robust production of foodstuffs in the Canaries had depressed the price he could get for the goods he brought from New England, and the London market didn't allow him to recoup his costs. But his greatest difficulty was a suit brought against him by Alderman William Berkeley, a Londoner who had lost a judgment in the Massachusetts courts and who exaggerated Winthrop's role in that decision to hold him responsible in England's courts for his financial losses.

Berkeley was the owner of a ship that had been hired by a Madame LaTour, the wife of one of two Frenchmen contending for the control of French Acadia, who employed one of Berkeley's ships to bring her to her husband. When the outcome of the contest prevented Madame LaTour from joining her husband she sued Captain Bayley (the ship captain) and Isaac Berkeley (brother and factor of the Alderman) for not performing the charter to carry her to her husband's fort, blaming them for giving priority to their trading activities, and arguing that if they had taken her directly to Acadia it would have been possible to rejoin her husband. A special court was convened in Massachusetts and the jury awarded her £2,000. Captain Bayley and Isaac Berkeley were arrested and forced to deliver the cargo to gain their freedom, the value being set at £1,100. The remainder of the judgment would have required the unfurnishing of the ship.

Learning of this, and angered by the seizure of his cargo by the Massachusetts authorities, Alderman Berkeley first obtained a writ to seize a Massachusetts ship and its cargo. He relented and instead attached the persons of Stephen Winthrop and another colonist in London, Joseph Welde. Winthrop had been the recorder of the court when the case had been decided in Boston. Welde had been a member of the jury. The two were required to find sureties in the amount of £4,000 to answer the case against them in the Court of Admiralty. Berkeley lost his case there, was again defeated when he brought his complaint to the Chancery Court, but then petitioned the House of Lords. Eventually Winthrop and

Welde were found without fault, but while the case proceeded Stephen could not leave England. Needing to support himself while the legal maneuverings were unfolding, in 1646 Stephen accepted a commission in Parliament's New Model Army. He became a captain serving under his brother-in-law William Rainsborow in the cavalry regiment commanded by Colonel Thomas Harrison. Rainsborow had lived in Massachusetts for a short time, along with some of his sisters and a younger brother. Stephen had married one of the sisters, Judith, around 1644.

The New Model Army's decisive victory at Naseby had come the year before Stephen received his commission, and he saw little if any fighting before the First Civil War came to an end with the king's surrender. For a time the young officer was on garrison duty at Worcester. His father heard reports that Rainsborow's troop was likely to be dispatched to Ireland, but that didn't materialize. As negotiations with the king continued without resolution during 1647 and 1648, the campfires of the New Model Army became centers of political discussion that ranged over the nature of political authority, expansion of the franchise, and the responsibility of the state for religious reform, among other matters. This was a different army than people were used to. Early in the war, Oliver Cromwell had written that in choosing officers, "a few honest men are better than numbers," and that for himself, "I had rather have a plain russet-coated Captain that knows what he fights for and loves what he knows, than that which you call a 'Gentleman' and nothing else." The officers and soldiers of the New Model saw themselves as God's agents and believed they had a compelling interest in the final political and religious settlements.

In April 1647, objecting to some of the Parliament's plans to reduce the army without proper payment of arrears of pay, and to send some of the forces to Ireland, soldiers appointed representatives, termed "agitators," to present their grievances. When Parliament rejected their petitions and discussed disbanding the army, the troops called for a general rendezvous of the forces to discuss matters. Thomas Fairfax, the commander, along with Oliver Cromwell, seeking to maintain the unity of the army, acquiesced. They approved the formation of a General Council of the Army to include not only the commanders, but two officers and two elected representatives from each regiment. The first meeting of the General Council was held at Reading in July. There Henry Ireton, the army's commissary general and Oliver Cromwell's son-in-law, presented the Heads of Proposal, a comprehensive plan for the settlement of the kingdom that Ireton had crafted in conjunction with Lord Saye and Sele, Henry Vane, and other leaders of the Independent faction in Parliament. Among other things, the Heads of Proposal called for parliaments to be elected biennially, and to meet for a minimum of 120 days and a maximum of 240. The Privy Council would be replaced by a council of state whose members would have limited terms, and there would be no penalties for absenting oneself from religious worship. Neither the Long Parliament nor the king was willing to assent to the proposed reforms. In September the army camped at Putney (outside of London) and the General Council began weekly Thursday meetings in the parish church.

Stephen Winthrop was engaged in discussions of these matters with his fellow officers as well as with the troops in Harrison's regiment, and his experience of a godly political order in New England would have seemed relevant to the discussions. In the summer of 1647 Stephen appears to have shared some of the concerns that the army's leaders had about the king's failure to agree on a political settlement, but he expressed his general confidence, saying, "God is doing some great work." By 1648, and perhaps earlier, he was one of the regimental representatives to the General Council of the Army, listening to and debating with generals Fairfax, Cromwell, Ireton, and others. His own regiment included many who would later be seen as radical. Harrison in particular had a reputation as a religious zealot—the clergyman Richard Baxter recalled standing next to Harrison at the battle of Langport and hearing him "with a loud voice break forth into the praises of God with fluent expressions, as if he had been in a rapture." Over the following years Harrison would be one of the strongest advocates of removing the king, whom he referred to as "a man of blood." He became one of the leading Fifth Monarchists, believing in the impending reign of King Jesus and that "the saints . . . shall take the kingdom." Stephen's brothers-in-law, Thomas and William Rainsborow, were among those army officers who were perceived to be among the most radical.

Stephen Winthrop
Courtesy of the Massachusetts Historical Society

As the stalemate between Parliament and the king continued, some of the troops began to espouse more radical views. John Lillburne and his supporters in the army and the countryside, who came to be called Levellers, called for more extensive reform, setting forth their views in the Agreement of the People. They asserted that sovereignty rested with the people, rather than king or Parliament. They called for the dissolution of the existing Parliament, proposed regular biennial elections for the legislature, and called for members to be allocated proportional to the size of constituencies. They also called for a degree of religious freedom and government on behalf of the common good. For almost two weeks at the end of October and into November of 1647 the small church at Putney became the scene of heated debates between the more radical elements of the army and its more conservative leaders. During the debates Thomas Rainsborow asserted "I think that the poorest he that is in England hath a life to live as the greatest he; and therefore truly, Sir, I think it's clear, that every man that is to live under a Government ought first by his own consent to put himself under that Government; and . . . I should doubt whether he was an Englishman or no that should doubt of these things." The goal of Oliver Cromwell was to keep the army united—"let us be doing, but let us be united in our doing" he said—but the debates broke up acrimoniously and the generals had to use the threat of force to control the more radical elements in the ranks. Hugh Peter was there, and so was Stephen Winthrop.

Late in 1647, King Charles, who had rejected all of the Parliament's proposals for a political settlement, escaped from custody and signed an engagement with the Scots whereby he hoped to regain his authority. In the spring of 1648 the Second Civil War began as uprisings on behalf of the king occurred in various parts of the kingdom. Insurgents in Kent under the Earl of Holland attempted to capture Reigate Castle, where Stephen was based, but his troops beat them off. While focused on the task at hand, Stephen had reasons to be concerned about his family. His wife Judith, along with his children, had been staying at Deal (on the southeastern coast) with her brother, Thomas Rainsborow, who had been appointed vice-admiral of the fleet. In May the crew of Rainsborow's flagship mutinied, triggering a general uprising in the fleet. Judith and the Winthrop children "were turned out of doors, so as the Vice Admiral was forced to put them aboard a small boat . . . and run over to Harwich with them." From Harwich, at the mouth of the Stour River, they moved on to Ipswich, where they likely stayed for a time with Winthrop kin or friends. But by the summer they were safe in London.

As the conflict continued, Parliament's General Fairfax focused on reducing Colchester, the center of an Essex uprising, while Cromwell besieged Pembroke Castle. This left Major-General Lambert's army to confront a 9,000-man Scottish force that entered England. Harrison's regiment had been sent to join Lambert, and so Stephen was moving north. In July the regiment held off an attack by Sir Marmaduke Langdale at Appleby, just south of the Humber River. Harrison personally captured the enemy's colors, though he was seriously wounded in the battle. But the troops were buoyed by what they saw as a providential sign. The Scots outnumbered the English on the field, and threatened to cross the river and overwhelm Harrison's men. But in a short time the river had unexpectedly risen so high that the English had "no ford to maintain, but only the bridge," where they held their own and killed large numbers of the enemy.

The regiment rejoined Cromwell's forces as those troops reached the north in mid-August, and it is likely that Stephen Winthrop's responsibilities were greater in the absence of Harrison. He played an active role in the ensuing campaign and "was in the van" when Cromwell's forces crushed their enemy at the battle of Preston in August. Following Preston the campaign became one of mopping up isolated strongholds of royalist sentiment. John Winthrop, Stephen's proud father, reported to the younger John Winthrop: "Sowlby was taken by a stratagem by your brother (who hath done very good service through the Lord's assistance, to whom he ascribes all)." But for the family these good tidings were eclipsed by news that Stephen and Judith's two young sons had died in August of smallpox, and that their kinsman Colonel Thomas Rainsborow had been killed at Doncaster by four royalists who were trying to abduct him.

Cromwell's victory at Preston had been decisive in bringing the Second Civil War to an end, and once again the king was in the custody of the Parliament. Yet the way to a settlement was no clearer than it had been a year earlier. Agitation for popular rights came to the fore again. Those in the army and outside it who were in sympathy with the Agreement of the People continued to agitate for its adoption. In November Cromwell's son-in-law, General Henry Ireton, drafted a remonstrance calling for the purging of Parliament and the trial of the king. Shortly thereafter, Harrison, Hugh Peter, and Ireton met with some of the Leveller leaders in an attempt to develop a united front. When Parliament rejected the army program, in early December the military purged the most recalcitrant members from that body in what became known as Pride's Purge. As Stephen Winthrop explained it in a letter to his brother, the army "set guards about the house, & withheld all those from coming to sit in the house who were for a treaty of the king."

The remaining members of Parliament, the Rump as the body came to be known, "voted the trial of the king." On the 27th of January 1649 the specially appointed High Court of Justice passed sentence against Charles I. Among the fifty-nine men who signed the sentence were Cromwell, Ireton, and Harrison. Three days later Charles was beheaded. Over these months the General Council of the Army continued to debate how the nation should be settled. Stephen Winthrop was involved in the discussions at Whitehall on December 14 and 26, and on February 22. The focus on those days was the provision of the Second Agreement of the People that called for prohibiting the punishment of anyone for professing "his faith, or exercise of religion according to his conscience in any house or place." On May 19 Parliament declared England a republican Commonwealth and free state. But dissension continued among the now triumphant puritans.

Stephen Winthrop reported the news of "the trial of the king, who is since beheaded," and how the Rump had "voted the kingly government down, & likewise the House of Lords," and that "the House of Commons [is] to be supreme." Writing in March, he indicated, "All is quiet, but I know not how long it will last." At that time, the king's son had been proclaimed Charles II in Scotland, and Winthrop would soon be engaged in fighting once again. But in the meantime, agitation for further political reform had continued to build in the army. Adding to the soldiers' discontent was the continuing failure of Parliament to settle with the troops over arrears in pay, and resistance of some troops to renewed plans to send them to Ireland, where a revolt had continued to drag on since October 1641. In May 1649 soldiers in the regiments of Ireton, Scrope, Reynolds, Harrison, and Skippon mutinied. Fairfax and Cromwell were able to crush the rising, and three of the ringleaders were executed. Winthrop's troop was among those which mutinied, but he was exonerated of any responsibility. He was soon restored to command and promoted to major as the army prepared for an expected invasion from Scotland.

STEPHEN WINTHROP's engagement in England's wars demonstrates colonial support of the Parliament and the puritan attempt to reform England, but that is not the only significance of his story. New Englanders in general were welcomed in England during the years of this struggle. Shortly after settling there, the clergyman Nathaniel Mather wrote to a friend in Massachusetts that "'tis a notion of mighty great and high respect to have been a New-English man, 'tis enough to gain a man very much respect, yea almost any preferment." The experience that such men had had in shaping new political and religious institutions gave them an authority that many Englishmen hoped to learn from—especially those who rejected Scottish models of reform.

But just as Stephen Winthrop and others helped to shape the course of events in England, so too did their experience there give them new insights that they drew on to advise their friends and family in the colonies. In particular, their involvement in discussions about the limits of religious toleration moved most—but not all—of them toward a more liberal stance. This was certainly true in the case of Hugh Peter, but also in the case of Stephen Winthrop. Fighting in the army alongside Baptists and other sectaries gave him an appreciation of the commitment such men had for the common cause. The fact that his father and his brother John were noted for their efforts to define the perimeter fence of orthodoxy generously, and to accommodate those on the fringe, may have predisposed Stephen to accept the need for a broad toleration. He was sensitive to the ways in which New England actions might divide the colonists from their English allies, and warned there "is great complaint against us for our severity against Anabaptists. It doth discourage any people from coming to us for fear they should be banished if they dissent from us in opinion."

Having achieved prominence in the New Model Army in the 1640s, Stephen continued to serve the puritan cause in England and to share his insights with his colonial correspondents. Following the execution of King Charles and the declaration of the Commonwealth, in July 1649 Stephen wrote to his brother John, "General Cromwell is made Lord Lieutenant for Ireland and is this week to take shipping for Ireland." His own regiment was not part of the army that crossed the Irish Sea. While his wife stayed with Winthrop kin in Groton, Stephen and his troop went into quarters in Wales, where he reported that he was "left with some horse to keep quiet these parts." It was at this time that he began to be entrusted with responsibilities outside of the army. Along with other officers of the regiment he was named to the Commission for Assessments for the County of Herefordshire, and also appointed to the Commission for the Propagation of the Bible in Wales. Acting as one of the Hereford Commissioners of the Militia, in August 1650 Stephen summoned Sir Edward Harley on information that he was disaffected from the government. Harley's papers were searched and he was sent to London, where he was detained for a time.

In that same summer of 1650 Stephen was able to report that Ireland had been reduced to submission by Cromwell; that Fairfax had resigned his commission; and Cromwell, who had returned from Ireland, had been made "Lord General of all the forces." Following the execution of Charles I, his son Charles had been proclaimed King of Scotland. Following his return from Ireland, Cromwell and his forces marched north to confront the army seeking to assert Charles II's claim to the thrones of the three kingdoms. Cromwell decisively defeated the Scots at Dunbar in September, and soon thereafter entered Edinburgh. But the war continued.

In March of 1651, Harrison's regiment was moved north. The troops were stationed for a time at Edinburgh. A number of officers are reported to have preached to the citizens and, given his father's record as an occasional lay preacher, it is possible that Stephen was one of them. In August Cromwell placed Harrison in command of three thousand horse to pursue a Scottish army that was moving south with the objective of raising support in England and marching on London. Winthrop was involved in battles at Newcastle and Rippon, and then, after Harrison joined forces with Lambert, was unsuccessful at Warrington in attempting to prevent the enemy's occupation of Worcester. Harrison's forces fought on the eastern side of the Severn River in Cromwell's defeat of Charles II's army at Worcester on September 3 that brought the war to an end. Following the conclusion of the campaign, the regiment returned to its post in south Wales.

During this period Stephen became more outspoken in his opposition to religious intolerance. In a letter to his brother John in 1651 he reported, "God hath done great things here in England, Scotland, and Ireland,"

and commented, "What God will bring out of all this is the thing in expectation. Powers fall down apace, and not any persecuting spirit, either in nation or person, doth stand when discovered. God declares so particularly against that spirit that it breaks any man to pieces that is found in it." He prayed that "the Lord in mercy keep it from New England." When in London he visited with Hugh Peter (who referred to him as "son Winthrop"), Henry Vane, and other New Englanders. He met with Roger Williams, who was in England at this time, and who wrote to John Winthrop Jr., "Your brother Stephen is a great man for soul liberty." Stephen also encountered Sarah Dudley Keayne, whom he had known in Boston, noting her presence in London and her public preaching.

Hugh Peter wrote that Stephen lived "very well." He had purchased a fine home on James Street in the Marylebone district of Westminster and built additional houses on adjoining property. But service in the army had taken its toll. He had been separated frequently from his family and had suffered the death of six children. The campaigning itself, with "much lying in the wet fields upon the ground" had weakened his health and left him "extremely troubled with the sciatica." In August 1653 he travelled to Bath to find relief in the therapeutic waters there, but any benefit appears to have been short lived.

The Rump Parliament had failed to deal with the pressing issues before the nation, and had failed to fulfill its promise to hold new parliamentary elections. In April 1653 Cromwell expelled the members. The Council of the Army chose 140 men from individuals nominated by England's puritan congregations to sit as a Parliament. Disturbed by some of the ideas put forth by some of its more radical members, the moderate majority of this Nominated Parliament dissolved itself in December. The Army Council, led by General Lambert, devised an Instrument of Government, which created the Protectorate, with Oliver Cromwell designated as Lord Protector of England, holding many of the powers of a traditional monarch. Many of those who had fought the king were disturbed by what they saw as a turn backward toward monarchy. Major General Harrison, Stephen's commander and one of the radical members of the Nominated Parliament, resigned his commission as a protest against the Protectorate.

These divisions were taken advantage of by opponents of the puritan regime, who organized various uprisings, including one in Scotland led by the Earl of Glencairn. Winthrop's troop was one of those dispatched to deal with the troubles in Scotland, though the resignation of Harrison and others left the regiment's command structure in disorder. Henry Cromwell was being considered to replace Harrison, and General Lambert wrote to Cromwell that he needed more officers for the unit, "major [Winthrop] being weak, and never a captain to assist him, not so much as a captain lieutenant." General George Monck, who was appointed to command the army in Scotland, reported in May of 1654 that Winthrop "being ill, and unfit to endure the field, I have given him liberty to go to England, and I think he will hardly return again." Yet when it was decided that Henry Cromwell should be sent to administer Ireland rather than take over Harrison's command, Winthrop was named colonel of the regiment.

The uprising had been put down by then, and there was no urgency in Winthrop assuming his command, though he did make periodic journeys to the northern kingdom. He was in London in the summer of 1654, when Roger Williams sought him out and reported that Stephen "flourisheth in good esteem, and is eminent for maintaining the freedom of conscience as to matters of belief, religion, and worship." Stephen's colonial background and his experience trading in the West Indies made him a valuable resource as Cromwell pursued what became known as the Western Design, an effort to dislodge Catholic Spain from its possessions in the West Indies. After the establishment of the Protectorate, John Cotton, praised Cromwell for having "fought the Lord's battles," saying, "The Lord hath owned you, and honored himself in you." He then shared with the English leader his belief that the "Euphrates [in the Book of Revelation] was the West Indies," an interpretation that Roger Williams believed had helped shape the Lord Protector's plan. Stephen Winthrop is likely to have advised the Protector on the planning of the campaign and had confidence in the outcome, writing that "it is not the manner of the Lord Protector to do things by halves. He will tug with Spain for it, cost what will." In December 1654 an English expedition of 38 ships and over 6,000 men sailed for the Caribbean.

New Englanders were actively involved in the Western Design. Cromwell named Plymouth's Edward Winslow, who had been serving as an agent of Massachusetts in England, as the chief of three civil commissioners to govern new conquests. The expeditionary force failed in its attempt to capture Hispaniola in April, 1655, but did capture the island of Jamaica in the following month. While at sea Winslow contracted a fever and died, his body being committed to the sea with a forty-two-gun salute. Robert Sedgwick, another New Englander, was sent with reinforcements to Jamaica and served as co-commander of the English forces on the island, where he later died. In July 1656 the Council of State appointed Stephen Winthrop to the Committee for Managing Affairs in Jamaica and the West Indies, which advised the Council on matters pertaining to that region.

Following a 1654 ordinance that united England and Scotland, Stephen Winthrop was selected to represent Banff and Aberdeen in the Second Protectorate Parliament, which convened in September 1656. During the remainder of that year he served on five committees, including one for the relief of debtors and creditors, an issue that his constituents had brought to his attention. He was also appointed to be one of the Commissioners for the Security of the Protector for Scotland, empowering him to investigate and determine charges against those whose activities threatened the peace of the Protectorate. By this time it was clear to Stephen that he would likely never return to his colonial home. Writing in 1655, he expressed his wish that he and his brother John might be reunited at some time, in England or New England. But he accepted that it might not be: "We must be disposed of according to the good pleasure of the Eternal Being. . . . It is best to be where we may be most serviceable in our generations, & doing things tending to the best & utmost ends, which always brings comfort with it."

Stephen Winthrop, was "very sick, being forced to keep to my chamber & house most part of this winter [1656–57]," but was able to resume his work in Parliament by the spring. He noted in a letter in April that "the great business at hand is the desire of the Parliament that his Highness [Cromwell] would take upon him the title of king. He hath refused it once & twice, & the Parliament still insist." Stephen didn't share his own view on this, though it is clear that he had long admired Cromwell. Ultimately, Cromwell turned down the crown but accepted the Humble Petition and Advice, which gave him the right to name his successor as Lord Protector. Despite continuing to be plagued by "rheums and coughs," which he attributed to the fact that "the air is too moist for me," Stephen remained active in the Parliament. He served as a teller for votes on various issues, as a member of different committees, and as a participant in some of the debates. Interestingly, on a debate over whether to impose oaths on members of Parliament, he voiced a view that was reminiscent of a position long advocated by his friend Roger Williams. Stephen stated, "It seems unuseful, incongruous, and unreasonable that a people that are not trusted with anything, should be under any obligation to perform a trust to themselves."

The Second Protectorate Parliament was dissolved in February 1658. Stephen's health continued to decline. Around this time a certain Captain Bernard was convicted and sentenced to death for robbing Winthrop's home. Bernard had led a group of thieves that had broken into Winthrop's London residence "all having their faces covered with their handkerchiefs, but this captain's cover fell off from one side of his face, whereby . . . 2 servants knew him." Bernard appealed to Cromwell but the Protector rejected it and Bernard was hanged.

Stephen made his will in May 1658 and died that summer. Among his bequests he left £100 for the poor of Boston on condition that the town erect a monument of at least £50 value over the grave of his parents, John and Margaret Winthrop. Stephen himself was buried at Groton, where he had spent his earliest years.

STEPHEN WINTHROP's life illustrates the engagement of New England's puritans in an Atlantic community. A colonial merchant engaged in trade between the Old World and the New, he became a military and governmental leader who helped shape the course of events of England's puritan revolution and experiment in godly government. Like Oliver Cromwell, a man he came to know well and admire, his puritanism was evident in the sense he had that his life was guided by divine providence. He saw the hand of God in events such as his escape from youthful dangers, the circumstances that forced him to stay in England and accept a commission in the army, and the rising of the river Humber that saved his regiment at Appleby. He willingly submitted to God's will. His life also demonstrates the ability of some puritans to see the essence of godliness in men and women who disagreed with them. Sharing the rigors of campaign life with Baptists and other sectaries made him more aware of the error of intolerance, and prompted him not only to speak out for a measure of religious liberty in England, but to urge the same tolerant spirit upon his friends and family in New England.

＊

HUGH PETER

Regicide

Previous chapters have mentioned the outbreak of war in England in the 1640s and some of the ways in which that conflict impacted New England. Having come to New England to create an exemplary society that, coupled with the colonists' prayers, might move England to the reforms that puritans had long advocated, the colonists embraced the possibilities posed by the English struggle, supported the forces of Parliament, and distanced themselves from the king's cause. Many clergy wrote tracts designed to promote the New England Way in their mother country. Other clergy returned to England to personally lend a hand to the task of reform. Still other colonists, including Stephen Winthrop and John Leverett, returned and served in the Parliamentary armies and the puritan regimes that followed the defeat and execution of Charles I. But the New Englander who became most identified with England's Puritan Revolution was Hugh Peter.

HUGH PETER was born in Cornwall, in the far southwest of England, in 1598. His father's family had emigrated from Antwerp much earlier in the century. Hugh matriculated at Trinity College, Cambridge, in 1613 and graduated with his BA in 1618. He moved to London where for a few years he taught school. He had been drawn to the city, as he later explained it "to ripen my studies, not intending to preach at all, where I attended Dr. [William] Gouge, Richard Sibbes, and John Davenport's ministry, with others; and I hope with some profit." He became close to Davenport, on whose recommendation the Earl of Warwick appointed him to the parish of Raleigh, in Essex in 1623.

Peter left this Essex parish around 1626 and settled again in London. He assisted the Feoffees for Impropriations (a group organized by Davenport and other puritan leaders to place zealous clergy in the nation's parishes), helped raise funds for Protestant refugees from the Thirty Years War, and developed contacts with the leaders of some of the churches of foreign Protestants in the city. Peter was frequently found as a visiting preacher in various London churches, and on one such occasion was heard to pray that the queen might forsake her "idolatry and superstition," a reference to King Charles I's French Catholic wife and the tolerance of Catholic religious services in her household. He was arrested and imprisoned. The Earl of Warwick paid his bail, but his license to preach was suspended in August 1627.

Despite his license being suspended, Peter continued to preach on occasion in Raleigh. He also journeyed back and forth to the Netherlands, and he accepted a position as proctor of Friesland University, where the distinguished English puritan émigré William Ames was the rector. Late in 1629 he accepted a position ministering to the congregation of English merchants in Rotterdam.

From his earliest days in London Peter had shown an interest in international Protestantism and support for the Protestant interests in the Thirty Years War raging on the Continent. His position in Rotterdam gave him an opportunity to follow that struggle closely, and in 1631 he took a leave from his congregation to accept a position as chaplain to an English regiment commanded by Sir Edward Harwood that was fighting with the Dutch forces in the conflict. Harwood was the brother of a London merchant who was one of the Feofees for Impropriations, and his connection with that group likely led to Peter making the colonel's acquaintance. Serving as chaplain, Peter came to admire the colonel's character and abilities, writing that "religion, fidelity, and prowess met in him." The regiment, along with other English forces, was serving under the Dutch prince Frederick Henry in defending Bergen Op Zoom against Spanish attacks. Among the English officers engaged in the battle with whom Peter would later have connections were Thomas Fairfax, Philip Skippon, George Monck, Lion Gardiner, and John Underhill. Based on his experiences, Peter penned an account of the struggle, *Digi-*

tus Dei, or Good Newes from Holland (1631). The following spring Peter accompanied Harwood when the colonel was dispatched to prepare for the siege of Maastricht. While the siege progressed he took a leave and accompanied another English clergyman, John Forbes, on a visit to the encampment of the Swedish king Gustavus Adolphus, who was leading the Protestant forces in Germany. Peter returned to Rotterdam with a heightened commitment to international reform and a familiarity with battlefields that he would draw upon later in his life.

In Rotterdam over the following years Peter would play an important role in shaping the nature of puritan congregationalism. At the time when Peter was there Rotterdam was the second largest city in the Netherlands, eclipsed only by Amsterdam. In 1634 the Englishman William Brereton visited the city and was impressed with what he saw. In the harbor he saw "an infinite number of tall and gallant ships," including thirty Dutch men of war, docked in channels fifty or sixty yards broad that divided the streets of the port. Bridges and drawbridges spanned the channels. On one of the bridges, "seventy or eighty yards broad" and with "a fair market-place upon it," he found "the portraiture of Erasmus, of very large stature, with a book in his hand." He found "windmills here in the tops of houses." Brereton was concerned, however, that he found among the Dutch "little respect had to sanctify the Sabbath." He learned from Hugh Peter that "a religious burgomaster, two years ago, [had] attempted to reform the profanation of the Sabbath" and imposed and collected a fine from all who worked on that day. The brewers, however, had "in a mutinous manner told the burgomaster that they would not be subject to his new laws" and the effort collapsed.

English and Scottish merchants had settled in Rotterdam as trade between that city and British ports grew. In 1611 the municipal authorities had granted the English settlers permission to hold occasional religious services. Eight years later they approved the creation of a church to serve the English community and a preacher to be paid by the provincial States of Holland. Rather than affiliating with the Classis of Rotterdam, the church remained independent until it joined a classis of English congregations headed by John Forbes. In 1632 the city magistrates donated to the congregation a building known as the "Acadmie" on the

Glasshaven quay. It was, according to a member of the congregation, "a large house of wood well finished with studs and a fair pulpit and table." The Glasshaven was a new part of the port that had been built during an expansion of the harbor in 1614. The Academy had been the home of a group of rhetoricians who had performed plays there. The English congregation cleared out all of the theatrical props and converted the structure for church services.

More significant than the transformation of the Academy was the transformation of the congregation. Early in 1633 Hugh Peter, disdaining (in the words of Stephen Goffe, an anti-puritan informant to the English authorities) to "be called by the vulgar English of Rotterdam," insisted on his call to the congregation's ministry by "the Godly, and so he framed a new covenant in paper to which all must put their hands, and none but those which were of that covenant should have any vote to call him." There were fifteen articles to the covenant. The first agreed that all who sought membership in the church should undergo a "meet trial for our fitness to be members." The second pledged the members to seek the "true and pure worship of God and to oppose all way of innovation and corruption." The third stipulated that the scriptures would be the congregation's guide in any controversies. In the following articles, the members pledged to "labor for growth of knowledge and to that end to confer, pray, hear, and meditate"; to "submit to brotherly admonition and conference without envy or anger"; and to "be thoroughly reconciled one to another even in judgment before we begin this work." They pledged to be exact in their commitment to live godly lives and to reject earthly vanities, committing themselves instead to "labor to get a great measure of humility and meekness and to banish pride and highness of spirit." They committed themselves to "furthering of the gospel at home and abroad as well in our persons, as with our purses." Concern for communal harmony continued in articles that pledged the members to "take nearly to heart our brethren's condition and to conform ourselves to these troublesome times both in dress and apparel that they be without excess," to "deal with all kinds of wisdom and gentleness toward those that are without," to "study unity and brotherly love," and "to put one another in mind of this covenant and as occasion is offered to take an account of what is done in the promises." The final article affirmed the need "diligently to instruct children and servants" for "the furthering of the kingdom of Christ."

The Rotterdam congregation having been re-formed by those who took the covenant, John Forbes, representing the English Classis, called upon the members to approve Peter as their pastor. Looking out at the congregation Forbes (again, according to Goffe's account) said, "'I see the men choose him, but what do the women do?' . . . Hereupon the women lift up their hands too." This is one of the few descriptions of congregational formation in England, the Netherlands, or New England that explicitly documents the vote of women in choosing their pastor. Brereton, on his visit to Rotterdam in 1634, attended services in the church and referred to Peter as "a right zealous and worthy man."

The typical churches in England that Peter had been familiar with were the parish churches established by higher authorities in the distant past. Governance—from prescribing rituals to approving clergy for pastoral posts—was from the top down. The only churches that were actually formed and governed by believers were separatist, or, in the case of a church formed by Henry Jacobs in London, semi-separatist. Traditional English parishes did not exist for Englishmen abroad who wished to worship, forcing them to organize their religious communities with little or no hierarchical supervision. Queen Elizabeth's archbishop, Edmund Grindal, had extended permission to the clergy of merchant chapels abroad to adapt to their local religious environment. One of the most significant of these churches was that of the English Merchant Adventurers based in Antwerp. In the 1570s, the Antwerp merchants, supported by the English ambassador William Davison and Sir Francis Walsingham, had taken steps to transform what had been a chapel into a formal church. The puritan Walter Travers was engaged as the congregation's first minister (1578–1580), and was followed by another noted English puritan, Thomas Cartwright. A tradition was established whereby that church would maintain a Reformed outlook and an internal governance in which the members of the congregation selected elders and deacons. From the beginning the English Prayer Book played a minor part, if any, in the worship service. As different from the organization and forms of worship of the English church as this was, the Antwerp church, established by the Company of Merchant Adventurers with the cooperation of local civil authorities, was still considered part of the English national church. The Rotterdam church had similarly been formed out of the desire of members of the Merchant Adventurers in that city to worship in English.

Having taken up his own residence in the Netherlands, William Ames had developed views on church government that emphasized congregational authority. He had argued that "the essential form of a visible church is the covenant of God, or true faith made visible by profession. . . . The integral constituting form is that . . . relation or reference which a congregation of such professors have to one another by virtue of their settled combination." His views were said to have influenced the English congregation gathered at Middleburg in 1623, which was organized by "'a solemn and explicit covenant with God, and one another.'" Ames included a strong assertion of the importance of covenant-based congregations in the 1627 edition of his *Medulla Theologica*. Peter, whose Dutch career owed much to Ames's assistance, would have been very familiar with this.

Aside from its covenant, Peter's Rotterdam congregation was also innovative in the way it accepted individuals to membership. In 1636, after Peter had left, but reflecting the practice he had established and that was carried on by John Davenport, a new arrival described how he came to be admitted to the church. Daniel Bradford and his wife left Norwich in 1636, settled in Rotterdam, and sought to join the church. They were given a copy of the covenant to study and, after a period of instruction, appeared before the congregation "for trial of our fitness to be members. We did each give an account of the work of God's grace in our souls. Then Mr. Davenport asked if we were willing to join with them in the covenant. We said we were. They did then vote to receive us members of the church. Afterwards we turned to prayer." Later that same year, the English clergyman Sidrach Simpson desired admission to the Rotterdam church following the afternoon Sunday service. According to a contemporary account, "two things were required of him, a profession of his faith, and a confession of his experience of the grace of God wrought in him. Both of which he did so excellently perform, that the hearts of all there present were much affected, professing that this had been the fruit of prayers and tears, and many were upon the wing for heaven, saying, Now, Lord, lettest thou thy servants depart in peace, the glory of church-communion being so brightly discovered, and the state of godly souls so graciously anatomized. . . . For a whole hour he poured out his soul into our bosoms, and we as heartily embraced him in the beauty of the church." These two accounts indicate that some form of relation of the experience of grace was given by at least some individuals admitted to the Rotterdam church at that time. This may well have been the first use of such relations in a puritan church.

IN THE EARLY 1630s English authorities who were seeking to turn back puritanism in England sought to also curtail its expression in Ireland and in the Netherlands. Prompted by William Laud, initially as Bishop of London and then as Archbishop of Canterbury, the English Privy Council ordered that all services in English congregations in the Netherlands be conducted according to the forms of the English Church. While this effort would not be as successful as Laud hoped for, it pointed to a significant change in the viability of the Netherlands for English puritan exiles. At the same time, the situation of English puritans at home was also worsening, with bishops such as Matthew Wren cracking down more forcefully on nonconformity in traditional reform strongholds. Redress of such grievances through parliamentary action was precluded by the king's determination to rule without that body. Increasingly, more puritans began to consider immigration to New England, where Massachusetts was firmly established.

Hugh Peter was among those who decided to immigrate. In 1628 he had invested in the Massachusetts Bay Company, and attended meetings of the company when in London. The company leadership had considered sending him to Salem in 1629, but his commitments at Franeker complicated matters, and Samuel Skelton and Francis Higginson were sent instead. In 1632, Peter's friend and patron, the Earl of Warwick, was involved in plans for another puritan settlement in New England. Serving as president of the Council for New England, Warwick sold a patent he held to the lands that would later be known as Connecticut to William Fiennes, 1st Viscount Saye and Sele, the 2nd Lord Brooke, and nine others, including Sir Nathaniel Rich, Sir Richard Saltonstall, John Hampden, John Humfry, and John Pym. The patentees came to be known as the Saybrook Company. John Winthrop was well known to these men and well aware of their plans for southern New England. Though not in power as governor of Massachusetts at the time, he remained engaged in planning the future of the region. He helped plan a visit to the British Isles by his son, John Winthrop Jr., and the clergyman John Wilson, one purpose of which was to meet with some of the men involved in the new colonizing plans. The younger Winthrop met with a variety of individuals who were involved in the enterprise. In July 1635 the leaders of the Saybrook Company met in London and appointed Winthrop Jr. as "governor of the River Connecticut in New England and of the harbors and places adjoining." Hugh Peter and John Davenport, who was then co-pastor of the Rotterdam church, had close connections with the Saybrook proprietors and followed their plans. In the summer of 1635 the two clergymen assisted the proprietors in identifying and engaging Lion Gardiner, an engineer and master of works of fortification whom Peter had met at the siege of Bergen Op Zoom, to be the commander of the fort that Winthrop Jr. was to establish at the mouth of the Connecticut River. A number of proprietors, including Arthur Heselrige and George Fenwick, asked Winthrop Jr. to have homes prepared for them in the new colony. Oliver Cromwell, who was the tenant of another proprietor, Henry Lawrence, may well have been planning to immigrate to the new colony at this time.

Peter, who had toyed with the idea of immigration in the early years of the decade, accepted an offer from the Saybrook proprietors to journey to the region along with Sir Henry Vane to assist Winthrop Jr. in asserting their rights to the region against groups of colonists who had moved into the Connecticut River Valley from Massachusetts. Peter left Rotterdam in the summer of 1635. While he did briefly visit Saybrook, he decided to accept a call to be pastor of the church in Salem, Massachusetts, that Roger Williams had been considered for prior to his banishment. One of Peter's first steps there was to draw up a new church covenant

Hugh Peter, frontispiece from his *Dying
Father's Last Legacy to an Only Child*

and require all to subscribe to it. He was credited with doing much to
heal the divisions that had threatened Salem in the aftermath of Williams's challenge to the colony officials. He soon became immersed in
the controversy that swirled around Anne Hutchinson, siding with the
majority of the clergy against what he saw were potentially subversive
religious ideas.

Following the failure of King Charles I to suppress a rebellion in
Scotland caused by his efforts to impose English church forms on that
Presbyterian kingdom, and the refusal of the so-called Short Parliament
to grant him needed funds before he dismissed it, a new Parliament, to
be known as the Long Parliament, had forced the king to agree that
it, and not the king, would decide when its business was done. By 1641
that Parliament had begun to pressure the king to redress long-standing

grievances, including illegal monetary assessments and unpopular religious measures. The Massachusetts authorities chose Peter, along with the clergyman Thomas Welde and the merchant William Hibbins, to travel to England as agents to further the cause of reformation there and to gain economic support for the colony from Parliament and private investors. Shortly after the agents arrived in England the political situation became more complex with the outbreak of a rebellion in Ireland. Thousands of the English settlers there were killed and reports of atrocities flooded the English press. Relations between king and Parliament worsened as the two sides could not agree on who would be entrusted to control an expedition to suppress the uprising.

Despite the political turmoil, the Massachusetts agents achieved considerable success. They succeeded in gaining financial support for the colony and persuaded Parliament to do away with measures that hampered New England's trade. The colonies were suffering from a labor shortage that was largely attributable to a decline in immigration as English puritans waited to see the outcome of the struggle between king and Parliament. Peter raised funds to facilitate the transport to the colonies of poor children, many of them English orphans of the Irish rebellion. In New England the youth could be apprenticed or serve as servants until reaching maturity. Peter and Welde also facilitated the publication of writings by colonial clergy that set forth the advantages of the New England Way.

In August 1642, Charles I, who had reached an impasse with the Parliament and previously had departed from London, raised his standard and declared Parliament in rebellion. This was the start of England's Civil Wars, sometimes referred to as the Puritan Revolution. Even before the formal outbreak of hostilities, Parliament had authorized an expedition to suppress the Irish revolt. Peter accepted a position as chaplain to the expedition. Once again he would contribute to advancing the Protestant interest on the battlefield. The expedition was a failure, but Peter put the best possible interpretation on the events in *A True Relation of the Passages of God's Providences in a Voyage for Ireland* (1642).

Back in London, Peter emerged as one of the more outspoken promoters of the Parliamentary cause. He joined with fellow puritan clergy in petitioning the Parliament not to compromise the rights of the people in any agreement with the king. Parliament had convened an assembly of clergy to recommend changes in the English church, and Peter lent his efforts to writing for and lobbying on behalf of the Congregational Way which he had helped shape in the Netherlands and advanced in New England. He travelled through the counties of Kent and Surrey urging residents to volunteer for service in the army and to donate funds for its support. He proved to be an effective propagandist for the cause, attracting the attention of both parliamentary leaders and the royal court. Because of his connections in the Netherlands he was sent there in September 1643 to lobby Dutch leaders against lending their support to the king. Returning to London, he became an interested observer at the trial of Archbishop Laud, and on one occasion accosted the bishop and angrily berated him for his previous actions against puritan reformers.

Peter's ability to identify with and offer support to men in uniform led to close associations with Sir Thomas Fairfax, Oliver Cromwell, and other military leaders, but also with common soldiers. He accompanied the troops on various campaigns, becoming one of the most famous of the army preachers. On one occasion he accompanied his old friend the Earl of Warwick on a naval expedition to relieve the siege of the port of Lyme. His commanders often delegated him to carry news of the campaigns back to Parliament and to lobby for the army's needs.

In the effort to reform the English Church, those who supported a national Presbyterian settlement had triumphed in the clerical gathering called by Parliament to propose ecclesiastical reform (the Westminster Assembly) and presented a plan for such reorganization to Parliament. Supporters of congregationalism sought permission for their own congregations to remain independent of such a system, and had been joined by various sectaries, including Baptists, in opposing a Presbyterian settlement. These "Independents" had a strong presence in the army, and in the end Parliament was unable to successfully impose any particular church system. During the 1640s, the lack of clear authority allowed various self-proclaimed religious leaders to emerge, and a proliferation of various religious groups. Street preachers such as Sarah Keayne were common. Figures like George Fox began to draw large crowds; his

Society of Friends (stigmatized as Quakers by their critics) would attract followers such as Mary Dyer, and emerge as one of the most significant religious movement of the 1650s. Peter remained an outspoken defender of congregationalism, but his exposure to the diversity of religious views in the army led him to appreciate the zeal of many of the sectaries. It soon became evident that Peter had come to embrace a broader definition of acceptable views than he had considered proper when in New England. In 1647 he explained to John Winthrop, "I am no tolerator, but a peacemaker I would be."

The king had been effectively defeated in 1646 and was taken into custody by Parliament, which sought to negotiate a settlement with him. But the king was unwilling to concede much and escaped confinement late in 1647. Rallying supporters, he renewed the conflict, but this Second Civil War lasted less than a year, with the royalist forces crushed and Charles once again at the mercy of his enemies. During these years, Peter's engagement with the soldiers of Parliament's New Model Army led him to adopt more radical political views than he had previously expressed. He sympathized with those, including the Levellers, who advocated abolishing the monarchy and establishing a broad-based constitutional republic. He was present when the army officers and representatives of the regiments discussed such issues at Putney during September and October 1647. In his writings and sermons Peter became one of the most vociferous advocates of bringing the king to justice, and it was widely reported that in the aftermath of the Second Civil War he played a key role in persuading Oliver Cromwell that the king must be brought to justice. When Charles actually went on trial Peter was energetic in lobbying members of the tribunal to stand to their principles, and preached public sermons to justify the action. When Charles was executed in January 1649 his supporters placed much of the blame on Peter.

Hugh Peter served the puritan regime in various capacities in the aftermath of the regicide. He was appointed an army colonel to make it easier for him to assume responsibility for the transport of supplies for Cromwell's expedition to finally suppress the Irish Rebellion. He was granted property formerly belonging to William Laud, which he made his London residence. He was a friend and supporter of Cromwell, who became Lord Protector of England in 1653. He supported Cromwell's tolerance of diverse opinions, and in a sermon at St. Paul's he stated, "The Protector sleeps upon no easy pillow. If 'twas such a matter for King Charles to be Defender of the Faith, the Protector has a thousand faiths to protect." Peter was appointed to be a member of the Council of State and advised the committee that considered the New England law codes in its deliberations over English legal reforms. He was a member of the committee of triers appointed by Cromwell to supervise the appointment of clergymen to church livings. When Cromwell died in 1658 Peter preached a sermon on the text of Joshua 1:2 — "Moses my servant is dead." While he tried to shape the events that followed the death of his friend, he was largely ineffectual.

When invited to assume the throne in 1660, Charles II promised to forgive those who had rebelled against his father. But the vengeful Parliament that brought about the Restoration of the monarchy was not so generous, and various men were excluded from the act of indemnity. One of these was Hugh Peter, who along with other "regicides" was tried for his role in the events of the previous decades.

As a young man Hugh Peter had come to London to hear the word of God preached and to embark on his own ministry. On October 16, 1660, his pilgrimage came to an end when he was executed in London. Peter had been accused of having devoted himself to the "stirring up of this war and driving it on." He was charged with having been an agitator among the troops and with being a key figure behind the prosecution of his enemy Archbishop Laud, whose death he was said to have witnessed. He was charged with having been more than a chaplain to the troops, taking up arms himself to fight at various battles in England and Ireland. He was said to have participated in and given thanks for the fall of Drogheda. The third day after his trial and conviction, Peter, along with the solicitor John Cooke, was dragged on hurdles to Charing Cross, the appointed place of their execution. Cooke was the first to suffer. Hanged by the neck, he was cut down while still alive, his body cut open, and his bowels burned in his sight. He was then beheaded, following which the body was quartered for display. Peter was forced to watch what he would next endure, but if the intent was to break his spirit, it failed. Claiming

that God had allowed him to see his fate "for my support and encouragement," he suffered the same penalty. His head was later set on a pole on
London Bridge to warn others of the price traitors paid.

WHILE AWAITING his execution, Peter penned *A Dying Father's Last
Legacy to an Only Child* (1662), a lengthy epistle of advice to his daughter, Elizabeth, who was then nineteen. Elizabeth had been born and
baptized in Salem, shortly before her father had departed on his mission to England. While she was still very young, her mother had shown
signs of mental instability and was judged by many to be insane. Elizabeth had therefore been raised in the household of Thomas Shepard.
In 1649, following Shepard's death, colonial friends sent Mrs. Peter and
her daughter to join Hugh in England, a decision Hugh was very upset
with. According to Roger Williams, who spent a good deal of time with
Peter during his trips to England, Mrs. Peter was "not wholly, but much
distracted."

A Dying Father's Legacy was one of Peter's most effective and affecting works. Published shortly after his death, it quickly went through six
editions. Addressed to his daughter, its message was applicable to any as-
piring Christian. He urged her to "hear the best men, keep the best company, read the best books," and throughout the epistle he recommended
specific works by puritan authors such as Gouge, Hooker, and Sibbes.
He anticipated that she might marry (though acknowledging that the
name Peter was not going to enhance her prospects), and emphasized
that marriage required "conjugateness (like a yoke) [which] must still be
lined with more love to make the draught easy." When troubled, husband and wife "need to pray out, not quarrel out their first brablings." He
warned her of embracing the world too closely, for "it will kiss you, and
kill you," a lesson he had learned the hard way, having been "vain in a
vain world." He urged her to find a true Christian friend, "a soul friend,
which you will never find among children, fools, or profane." Above all
she should trust in Christ, who would always comfort her, as "in the
night, the waking child is quiet at the nurse's coming to it, because there
is more of comfort in the nurse, than fear in the dark."

Peter also reflected on the troubles of the times. He regretted that "many more polemics and disputes are printed than profitable, every party striving [for] their own advancement," and he wished that more men and women would be content to rest in the fundamentals of faith. Too many people had been misled into changing their beliefs, while he at least could rest content knowing that it was "my very great mercy that temptation never led me from that honest, old, godly, puritan professing of the everlasting truths of the Gospel." He expressed his belief that true religion, as taught by Luther, and preached by Hugh Peter, meant "to believe things incredible, to hope things delayed, and to love God when he seems angry." He reviewed his own understanding of the process of salvation, which started when "the spirit of humiliation first wakens a miserable lost sinner, and that by the Law, [which, however] can only bring him to the gate. Then vocation opens the door. Then justification puts on Christ's righteousness. Sanctification teaches him how to walk, taking away the power of sin. Adoption makes him a brother, and gives him his privileges. And glory, begun here [on Earth] in part, by sanctifying, shows him his estate."

Preparing to meet his last day, he shared his understanding of heaven, something not often discussed in print by puritans. Heaven was universal, "whereas all things here below are but partial." Happiness there was continuous — "the good things are not like cherries drawn by the lips, or comforts tasted and gone, but they stay and are good forever." In heaven "evil knows no place, there sin cannot dwell with that holiness, sorrow cannot mingle itself with that joy; no more fading riches, dying friends, changing honors, perishing beauties; no more aching heads, languishing diseases; no more hearing the chain of the prisoner, nor anger of the oppressor." In heaven one lacked nothing: "every bottle is full, and every bed easy . . . ; every room is paved with love." It was a place "where wisdom, power, mercy, and grace have combined to make all glorious and pleasant."

At the conclusion of his *Last Legacy* Peter reviewed some of his own life. He talked of how as a young graduate he had been moved by the "love and labors" of Thomas Hooker in Essex, how he had attended on the ministry of Davenport, Sibbes, and Gouge in London, and then later immigrated first to the Netherlands and then to New England. He continued to express a fondness for New England, claimed that he had always hoped to return there, and expressed the belief that Elizabeth might find happiness there. He recalled the New England Way as a "tender presbytery" where he learned to hear and gain experience from other Christians rather than judge them. The fact that he had never returned to "that people I was engaged to in New England . . . cuts deeply; I look upon it as a root evil." He argued that he had never been motivated by anger in his dealings with the king and bishops in England, but had labored for "a good government, where men may be as good as they can, not as bad as they would," a view of a godly kingdom that his friends John Winthrop and John Cotton would have appreciated.

John Davenport and the Middle Advent

Hugh Peter's friend John Davenport has often been portrayed as one of the most conservative of the first generation of New England clergy, and the town and colony he founded as the most rigid of all the Bible Commonwealths. New research has called these judgments into question, and raises further questions about how we understand early New England. There are a few things that make his story worth telling. It sheds light on the question of what made an individual a puritan. Davenport was a well-respected member of the English religious establishment until circumstances turned him to nonconformity. He was one of the most international of all the puritan clergy of the seventeenth century, making contributions to the religious history of England, the Netherlands, and New England. At a time when many puritans were becoming interested in the role New England was to play in the coming of the promised millennial rule of the saints, Davenport engaged with that subject more than any of his contemporaries and his ideas on the millennium shaped the society he helped craft. Equally important, his career reveals a strong commitment to congregational principles. In the last decades of his life he was the foremost opponent of the movement to expand the authority of ministers within congregations and of church councils over congregations.

JOHN DAVENPORT was born in the city of Coventry in the midlands of England in 1597. His father and uncle were both prominent citizens and each would serve as mayor of the city. His uncle Christopher, who played a large role in John's life, was a noted benefactor who founded a free school for the town's poor as well as supporting other charities. Coventry had a reputation for harboring radical religious elements going back to the time of the Lollards, and its citizens had been quick to embrace the Reformation. During John's early years clergymen such as Richard Eaton, Humphrey Fenn, and Thomas Cooper railed against Catholic threats and urged the citizens to live godly lives and care for others as for themselves.

John was educated in the town grammar school until he left to study at Oxford in 1613. He started his studies at Merton College but after a year transferred to Magdalen Hall. Though students of puritanism frequently point to the roots that the movement established at Cambridge, during the sixteenth century Oxford's Laurence Humphrey was recognized as one of the nation's foremost Reformed theologians. Magdalen Hall was one of the colleges recognized as having a puritan orientation in Davenport's time. But John's story is one that should make us cautious about placing too much emphasis on environment in shaping religious outlook. He was accompanied to Oxford by his nephew Christopher, who was actually a few years older than he was. Christopher had also been raised in Coventry. The two shared a room at Merton and both moved to Magdalen Hall. Yet while John would become one of the leading puritan divines of his age, Christopher converted to Roman Catholicism, took the name Franciscus a Sancta Clara, and became one of the leading proponents of bringing Catholicism back to England.

After only a few years at Oxford, John left the university. His uncle, who had paid for his education, evidently was no longer willing or able to do so. John had determined on a career in the ministry, but was too young to be ordained. Despite this, he was offered a position as chaplain to the Hilton family at Hilton Castle, outside Sunderland in County Durham. He was not able to administer sacraments, but he could preach. He left a notebook in which he recorded forty-three sermons that he delivered between November 1615 and March 1616. The North of England was still a stronghold of Catholicism, and anti-Catholic rhetoric featured significantly in his sermons. For the most part, he espoused a standard Calvinist theology. He commented both on the shortcomings of those clergy who failed to educate their flocks and those lay men and women who gave themselves "to pleasures on the Lord's Day, and neglected the house of God," leaving themselves in a miserable condition, "perishing for want of knowledge." He strongly urged those in the pews to embrace every opportunity to come to God.

Davenport left Hilton Castle in 1616 and in October of that year was ordained deacon and priest by John Overall, the Bishop of Coventry and Litchfield. In March 1617 he married Elizabeth Whalley in the small town of Eaton Socon, Bedfordshire. The couple soon moved to London, where young clergymen were most likely to find opportunities to make a mark. Davenport first served as a lecturer in the parish of St. Mary Aldermanbury, stepping in for the ill curate. The attention he drew there led to an appointment as curate and lecturer in the parish of St. Michael Huggen Lane in January 1618. John earned a reputation as a powerful preacher and this led the lay vestry of the more prestigious parish of St. Lawrence Jewry to call him to be their curate and lecturer in June 1619. St. Lawrence was near the Guildhall, the civic center of the city, and John was soon making contacts with prominent business leaders and members of the king's court. As a result of these connections he was invited to preach to the members of the Virginia Company in 1621, following which he was admitted to membership in that colonial enterprise.

In October 1624 the vestry of St. Stephen's Colman Street elected Davenport as vicar of the parish. This was one of the parishes that had the right to choose its clergy, subject to the willingness of the bishop to induct the individual chosen. The bishop of London hesitated to approve Davenport, in part because his popularity in the city led to suspicions that he might be a puritan, a charge John vehemently denied. By enlisting the aid of friends such as Lady Mary Vere and Sir Edward Conway, he was able to overcome the opposition. Hard on the heels of his induction, Davenport was faced with the consequences of a city ravaged by the plague. "Death walks in every street," wrote one observer, and during its course over 35,000 men, women and children perished in London,

350 in St. Stephen's parish alone. While many clergy fled the city for their own safety, Davenport stayed in his post, earning the gratitude of his new parishioners.

Over the following years Davenport emerged as one of the city's leading clergymen. His prominence was signaled by his selection, along with Richard Sibbes, to edit the works of John Preston following that eminent clergyman's death in 1628. Together with three other clergymen and eight laymen, Davenport organized the Feoffees for Impropriation, a trust that raised funds for the placement of godly clergy in pulpits that were without an adequate preaching ministry. Numerous other clergy, including Hugh Peter, helped the Feoffees.

His interest in the international Protestant cause was signaled when Davenport joined with his fellow clergymen Richard Sibbes, Thomas Taylor, and William Gouge in penning a circular letter seeking contributions for the relief of Protestants displaced by the Thirty Years War. That conflict, which had begun in 1618, was viewed by most Europeans as the climactic struggle between Protestantism and Rome. Many Englishmen were distressed that King James I and his successor Charles I refused to come to the aid of the Protestant cause, despite the fact that the first champion of the cause was James's son-in-law, Frederick, the elector of the Palatinate. Davenport not only raised funds for distressed refugees but took the son of one of the displaced ministers into his own home.

Davenport's efforts on behalf of Continental Protestants brought him into contact with two men with whom he formed lasting friendships. Samuel Hartlib, an émigré from Poland, moved into the parish of St. Stephen's and assisted Davenport and his associates in distributing funds. Hartlib would become the center of a network of correspondents dedicated to advancing scientific discovery, religious reform, and educational innovations. Through Hartlib, Davenport came to know John Dury, the son of an exiled Scottish preacher who devoted his life to seeking to unite Protestant Christendom. Dury recognized Davenport as "earnest and judicious" in this ecumenical work, which included an effort to translate English works of practical divinity for the use of Continental divines. Another member of the Hartlib circle whose ideas Davenport became interested in was Jan Amos Comenius, whose plans for educational reform became a part of the utopian aspirations of all of these men.

For most of the 1620s, Davenport's support of efforts to unify the Protestant cause made him willing to accept practices in the Church of England that he had reservations about. Despite concerns about practices such as kneeling at communion, he had asked, was it "not better to unite our forces against those who oppose us in fundamentals than to be divided among ourselves about ceremonials?" He preached against the establishment of Henry Jacob's semi-separatist congregation in London. But much of this changed when William Laud became Bishop of London in 1628. Laud viewed the Feoffees as an attempt to subvert the character of the established church, and saw efforts to promote the Protestant cause in the Thirty Years War as criticism of the king's authority to shape foreign policy. Furthermore, Laud was part of a group of English bishops who not only were determined to enforce conformity to existing ceremonies, but sought to advance the "beauty of holiness" by introducing new practices that struck reformers as leading the English church back toward Rome. Puritans such as John Cotton who had skillfully negotiated a position of semi-conformity found that compromise was no longer negotiable. In the early 1630s, many were forced from their livings or saw the handwriting on the wall and left to seek new ministries elsewhere. Some journeyed to the Netherlands, others to New England.

Laud censured the authors of the circular letter to support Protestant refugees, had the Feoffees prosecuted and shut down, and called upon Davenport to answer various charges about how he conducted his ministry at St. Stephen's. Faced with the Laudian initiatives, discussions with friends such as John Cotton, Philip Nye, and Thomas Goodwin as well as an exchange with some of the imprisoned members of the Jacobs church made him reconsider and abandon his use of various ceremonies. In the fall of 1633 Davenport left London and journeyed to the Netherlands. He hoped that the Laudian tide would ebb and that he would be able to return to St. Stephen's. In the meantime he answered a call from the English merchant church in Amsterdam to join John Paget (who had been ill) in the ministry of that congregation. The call originated from a strong faction of lay members in the church, but ran into opposition from Paget himself. Paget had earlier blocked efforts to call Hugh Peter and Thomas Hooker to be his assistants. His opposition to Davenport was based on John's refusal to agree to the indiscriminate baptizing of any child brought to the church. Dutch practice allowed any adult—whether a member of a particular church or even, potentially, a non-Christian—to present a child for the sacrament and required the clergy to administer baptism. Davenport insisted that only adults who were members of the church or who could satisfy him that they were knowledgeable Christians should have that right. While Davenport was popular with the members of the congregation, his installation was blocked, through Paget's efforts, by the Dutch classis to which the congregation belonged.

Just as his experiences of the Laudian thrust for the beauty of holiness had led him to take a more advanced position on liturgical ceremonies, so his experiences in Amsterdam made him reconsider the source of authority in the church. Predisposed perhaps by his experience in St. Stephen's, he came to believe that it was the lay congregation of believers that should determine affairs that affected each particular church. This understanding was reinforced when he joined his friend Hugh Peter in ministering to the English merchant church in Rotterdam from 1634 to 1637. That church had been reformed with a written covenant that vested power in the lay members of the congregation. While there, Davenport responded in print to attacks from Paget, presenting his beliefs in congregational church governance as opposed to the presbyterian forms that Paget advocated, in which councils of clergy supervised individual churches.

Davenport's initial hope that he would be able to return to his ministry died with reports that Laud was still eager to prosecute him, and on a visit to England he resigned his living at St. Stephens. Inspired by letters from John Cotton and others in which New England was described as "the New Heaven and the New Earth, wherein dwells righteousness," he decided to immigrate to America. Together with his friend Theophilus Eaton, other members of St. Stephen's parish, and some others, he embarked for the New World. Arriving in Boston in the midst of the Free Grace controversy, he participated in the synod of 1637 that defined which religious views were too dangerous to be tolerable, worked with Winthrop and others in rejecting those on both extremes and building a middle way, and briefly persuaded Anne Hutchinson to reconsider some of her positions during her church trial. But the Davenport-Eaton group had intended from the start to settle along the southern New England coast in territory that had been granted to Davenport's friend Lord Saye and Sele. Two things would distinguish Davenport's New England career—his struggle to create the closest approximation to a godly kingdom that was possible, and his unceasing defense of congregational principles against encroachments by those who sought to elevate ministerial authority.

ON SUNDAY, April 25, 1638, the ships bearing John Davenport and his fellow adventurers sailed into the four-mile-broad estuary on the northern shore of Long Island Sound that was Quinnipiac harbor. Before them was a plain situated between a rampart of hills to the west, north, and east. The plain itself was cut by three rivers—the West, Mill, and Quinnipiac as they would become known—that flowed into the estuary. This was the site for a new colony chosen by Eaton and other members of the enterprise on an exploratory journey the previous year.

The new settlement was largely shaped by Davenport and influenced by his understanding of the course of history God laid out and set forth in the scriptures. While many historians have quoted later New England statements about a puritan "errand into the wilderness" and argued that the first settlers of the region saw themselves as the New Israelites crossing the oceanic wilderness to establish a new Canaan, few such references can be found in the writings of the first generation. Similarly, claims that the settlers were embarked on a millennial quest and that they believed that their enterprise would usher in the New Jerusalem foretold in the Book of Revelation are an exaggeration at best. Yet if, as Cotton Mather later judged, thoughts of the millennium were "hardly apprehended by many divines" of the first generation, Davenport clearly believed it was coming. According to Mather, he "both preached and wrote those very things about the future state, and coming of the Lord, the calling of the Jews, and the first and second resurrection for the dead."

The Thirty Years War and the possibility that it might be the apocalyptic struggle foretold in Revelations sparked interest in the millennium in some Protestant quarters. Davenport's views were influenced by the writings of the English clergyman Thomas Brightman and discussions with members of the large Jewish community in Amsterdam. But Davenport's millenarianism differed from that of those who used their belief in the imminence of the Second Coming to justify a revolutionary social or political agenda. Nor did Davenport believe that New Haven, or even New England, would be the location for the dawn of the kingdom of the saints. It would not be the ultimate center of the kingdom, but might provide a step toward that goal. Davenport's focus was not on the Second Coming but on what Brightman identified as the intermediate Middle Advent, an explosion of supernatural power that would enable men to restore the institutions and practices that God had established in the Israel of the Old Testament and that were found in the apostolic church. The Old Testament Israel and Jerusalem were examples for the reformation of the church, examples for spiritual inspiration.

To make that inspiration visible, Davenport laid out the town of New Haven in a pattern of nine squares, an arrangement that evoked the design not only of the encampment of the Israelites in the wilderness, but of Solomon's Temple, Ezekiel's vision of the Temple, and the New Jerusalem seen by John in Revelation. Equally distinctive was the institutional foundation of the town. Shortly after their arrival, following "a day of extraordinary humiliation" and fast, "the whole assembly of free planters" agreed to a "plantation covenant" that committed them to the establishment of a theocracy as defined by Davenport. The settlers pledged, "In matters that concern the gathering and ordering of a church, so likewise in all public offices which concern civil order, as choice of magistrates and officers, making and repealing of laws, dividing allotments of inheritance, and all things of like nature, we would all of us be ordered by those rules which the scripture holds forth to us." The commitment to use scriptural guidelines for the administration of justice would be one of the most distinctive aspects of New Haven's polity, though in practice the result was not that different from what English law dictated.

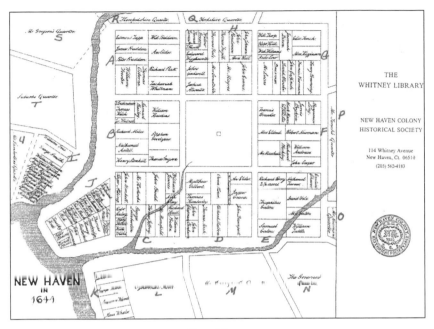

New Haven
Courtesy of the New Haven museum

On June 4, 1639, all of the settlers assembled at a large barn owned by Robert Newman to begin the process of formalizing the organization of the church and civil government. Davenport took the lead in directing the meeting. Having opened the session with prayer and invoking the guidance of the Holy Spirit, he propounded a series of questions that the settlers were asked to vote on. The first question was "whether the scriptures do hold forth a perfect rule for the direction and government of all men in all duties which they are to perform to God and men, as well as in the government of families and commonwealths as in matters of the church." In a show of hands, the gathering unanimously agreed. Next Davenport asked the settlers if they held themselves still bound by the plantation covenant they had taken earlier, pledging to direct all their affairs by the rules of scripture. Again everyone, including some who had arrived since the plantation covenant had been sworn to, raised their hand to show their assent. The third question was whether everyone had a "purpose, resolution, and desire that they may be admitted into church

fellowship according to Christ as soon as God shall fit them thereunto."
Everyone "did express this to be their desire and purpose."

Davenport next asked them if "they held themselves bound to establish such civil order as might best conduce to the securing of the purity
and peace of the ordinances to themselves and to their posterity." After
everyone had again assented, "Mr. Davenport declared unto them by
the scripture what kind of persons might best be trusted with matters
of government," and elaborated on the texts of Exodus 18:2, Deuteronomy 1:13, Deuteronomy 17:15, and 1 Corinthians 6:1–7 in discussing
what this would mean. The texts demanded that "wise men, of understanding, and known among your tribes" be chosen as rulers whom God
would empower, and that believers be judged by those who were of the
faith community. All agreed with this. The final question Davenport
posed was "whether free burgesses"—those who would have the right
to vote—should be church members. After a brief discussion, this too
was agreed to unanimously. Significantly, all those who had settled in
New Haven agreed to this, including some who would not be admitted
to the church. This was a remarkable event. The government of the town
was established with the participation and free consent of all the male
inhabitants. It epitomized the commitment to popular participation in
governance that puritanism was moving toward and that Davenport already embraced.

Before the settlers concluded their meeting, Davenport asked them
to nominate twelve men who were considered fit to advance the work of
church formation. The settlers as a whole then subjected those nominated
to scrutiny and approved them. By August the twelve men so charged
had selected seven of their number to be the pillars of the church. Those
seven then made a church covenant, and drew up a confession of faith.
It is likely that the document published as *The Profession of the Faith of
that Reverend and Worthy Divine Mr. J. D., sometimes Preacher of Stevens
Coleman-street, London Made Publiquely before the Congregation at his Admission into one of the Churches of God in New England* (1642) demonstrates
the knowledge of faith that Davenport and the faithful expected those
seeking membership to express. The church having been formed, other
planters could present themselves for membership, making their own

professions of faith, with the ever-increasing membership determining the qualifications of each candidate. While at least a few churches in New England asked candidates to share a statement of how they had been born again as evidence of their sainthood, the New Haven puritans believed that sainthood could be discerned from observation of an individual's life and assessment of the spiritual knowledge displayed in a profession of beliefs.

Over the following years the New Haven Colony grew as new communities such as Guilford, Southold, and Milford joined the town of New Haven. Sunday church services in New Haven were much as previously described for the Boston church. Regular lay meetings were encouraged for sharing religious experiences and discussing difficult points of belief. The colony's legal structure differed from that of other New England colonies in that scriptural law was the explicit basis for decisions, and magistrates rather than juries determined guilt or innocence. Despite this the history of the colony was more a variation on common New England themes rather than a dramatic alternative to that of the other Bible Commonwealths. One of the first steps taken in the colony was to establish a school. Davenport worked hard to create a college in the colony, but was unsuccessful.

Contributing to the failure to establish a college was the fact that New Haven failed to achieve the economic success its founders had anticipated. Geography prevented the town from becoming the key port of southern New England. The dream of launching a viable trade with England collapsed with the loss of a large ship that the colonists had acquired to open that trade. Efforts to establish a far-flung fur trading enterprise were thwarted by the Dutch.

Despite his concern over these setbacks, Davenport kept one eye on the events beyond the colony's borders. From the first days of his ministry in London, John had demonstrated a commitment to advancing God's cause throughout the world. Following his settlement in New England he continued to maintain contact with former allies in that effort such as Samuel Hartlib and John Dury. He followed the events in Britain that led to the outbreak of the Bishops Wars between Charles I and the Scots in 1638, and, like many New Englanders, saw the early efforts of the Long Parliament as offering a chance of the type of renewal he had long prayed and labored for. When Charles I rejected the parliamentary agenda and plunged England into Civil War in 1642, Davenport and his fellow colonists supported the Parliament and sought to do whatever was in their power to contribute to the triumph of their godly friends. Davenport declined an invitation to be a member of the Westminster Assembly, charged by Parliament with reforming the English church, but he did contribute to the cause of reform through his writings. William Hooke, who shared the New Haven pulpit for a time, returned to England and was close to Oliver Cromwell, who was his wife's kinsman. Hooke kept Davenport posted on the flow of events in England and interceded with the Lord Protector on behalf of New Haven.

The collapse of the puritan regime and the Restoration of the monarchy was a blow to the hopes of all New England and threatened the futures of the Bible Commonwealths. Working to advance the Middle Advent, Davenport had not been deluded into thinking that the thousand-year rule of the saints was close at hand, and so he was better able than many puritans to absorb these blows and to help his congregation make sense of them. In a series of sermons later published as *The Saints Anchor-Hold in All Storms and Tempests* (1661), he began by acknowledging the "frustration and disappointment" of many colonists "when they have given up their names unto Christ, looked for peace, prosperity, and good days, but find troubles, crosses, and afflictions of various kinds." He counseled them that "God's deferring of the rule of the saints is no empty space but a time of fitting his church and people for the good things promised." The trials the colonists faced were like a physic, and "when the sick humor is purged out, then comes health." He told his congregation to "withhold not countenance, entertainment, and protection from such [persecuted people], if they come to us from France, Germany, England, or any other place."

Davenport himself acted as he had urged others to do when two of those exempted from the king's pardon—Edward Whalley and his son-in-law William Goffe—made their way to New Haven. Both had held command in the New Model Army, had been members of the court that tried and condemned Charles I, and had served as major-generals in Cromwell's experiment in governing the English counties. The two regicides had fled to New England, spent a brief time in Boston, and then moved on when they recognized that they would be aggressively pursued. Following a seven-week journey through the winter landscape of New England, Whalley and Goffe arrived at New Haven on March 7, 1661, and took up lodging in the Davenport home. A cave on top of West Rock was prepared as a haven for the two regicides to use when their pursuers came close, though they were offered homes to spend very bad weather in, and on at least one occasion they were seen in the town, even attending services in the church. In August they took up residence with Michael Tomkins in Milford, where they stayed for two years. Davenport then assisted them to move to Hadley, a newly formed town north of Hartford where Davenport's friend John Russell was the clergyman.

New Haven suffered under the dual disadvantage of having no recognized charter and having been energetic in its support of the revolution and the Protectorate. The colony's sheltering of the regicides, though not proven, added to the case that could be made against it, and when John Winthrop Jr. managed to secure a royal charter for Connecticut in 1662, the crown included the smaller New Haven Colony in its jurisdiction. Though most in New Haven protested, it was to no avail, and the Jerusalem on the Quinnipiac ceased to exist.

IN ADDITION to his support of international Protestantism, Davenport stood out in his time for his strong defense of congregationalism. Davenport had never been a member of the sort of informal clerical associations in England in which ministers such as Thomas Hooker, Thomas Shepard, and Thomas Welde gathered to seek agreement on matters of faith and practice. At St. Lawrence Jewry and St. Stephen's he had been associated with parishes that jealously protected the rights they had to choose their own ministers. His experience in the Netherlands, where a Dutch classis had prevented his call to the English church in Amsterdam, had helped shape his commitment to congregational autonomy, and his years with the Rotterdam church strengthened that position. When he arrived in New England he found himself in the midst of a struggle in which the majority of clergy claimed the right to criticize what was happening in the Boston church and to question the teachings of his friend John Cotton. While he did evidently accept the listing of heretical views adopted by the synod of 1637, his concern about the exercise of such collective ministerial authority may have contributed to his decision to turn down invitations to settle in Massachusetts.

In May 1646 the Massachusetts General Court, prompted by Thomas Shepard, among others, invited the churches of New England to send delegates to a synod or assembly at Cambridge that would produce a definition of orthodox faith and practice in the colonial godly kingdoms. The Court was particularly focused on the need to better define the qualifications for baptism and membership. Some churches hesitated to send representatives, fearing that the gathering itself was an infringement on congregational authority. After the Assembly had met on and off for over two years, it accepted as a statement of doctrine the Confession of Faith that had been crafted by the Westminster Assembly and supported by both English Presbyterians and Congregationalists. It also drew up its own statement of the New England Way. Clergy from Connecticut and New Haven were represented at the Assembly. It is doubtful that Davenport was there for all the sessions, but he did leave a mark on the proceedings. At a meeting of the commissioners of the United Colonies held in New Haven shortly after the Assembly was convened, he prompted a resolution that the colonies guard the doors to God's house by holding to their original rules and practices. The *Platform of Church Discipline* adopted by the Assembly was printed by the infant press in Cambridge, Massachusetts, in 1649, commended to the churches of New England by the Massachusetts General Court, and dispatched to England for the consideration of those still debating the reform of the nation's church.

The Cambridge Platform asserted the principle that each congregation was an autonomous entity that chose its own ministers and lay elders, and determined its own policies. Assemblies or synods (which were authoritative in a presbyterian church order) were merely advisory. Yet despite the general approval for the document, many colonists continued to be concerned about what they saw as a move toward establishing an authority (if only advisory) above the individual congregation. Davenport was one who had reservations. Years later he reported that he "was present and observed with grief that the tempter was then tempting, . . . and that an hour of temptation was then beginning upon these churches." In the end, he had a strong influence on the way the *Platform* addressed the issues of baptism and church governance. On the issue of baptism, Davenport and his supporters prevented a redefinition of church membership that would have allowed the admission of any adults who had been baptized as children whether or not they demonstrated any evidence of grace in their own souls. This was a matter that would continue to stir controversy. On the issue of church governance, many of the delegates to the Assembly were inclined to argue for a higher concept of the power of the ministry, including that an ordained minister could preach and administer sacraments in neighboring churches as well as in the congregation that called him. Davenport maintained a stricter form of congregationalism than many of his fellow clergy, arguing that a clergyman was empowered by a congregation to minister to that particular congregation and to no other. Due to his advocacy, the most that the *Platform* allowed was that clergy might minister to other congregations if specifically called to do so by that church. Davenport consistently maintained that it was the members of the church who received the power of the keys from Christ (and this was one of the reasons why he defended a restricted membership), though they had to choose officers through whom they formally exercised that authority.

Davenport continued to assert congregational rights in the following decades. Though he tried to avoid becoming embroiled in a controversy that racked the Hartford church in the 1650s, he ended up supporting the lay members against their pastor Samuel Stone's assertion of his right to overrule the membership in the choice of a second minister. In 1657, when the Massachusetts General Court invited all the churches of New England to send delegates to a synod to resolve the still troubling issue of baptism and church membership, New Haven declined to send anyone, Davenport expressing the fear about "a synod or any such meeting, which in such times may prove dangerous to the purity and peace of these churches and colonies." The synod of 1657 recommended the extension of what came to be called Half-Way membership to all baptized children when they reached adulthood, but few churches accepted the practice at that time.

In December 1661 the Massachusetts General Court called yet another synod to meet in March 1662 "for settling the peace" of the churches." Only Massachusetts churches responded to this call, with most of the eighty-plus delegates being laymen. In the new synod Richard Mather led the push for the Half-Way Covenant, ably supported by Boston's John Norton (chosen as the synod's moderator) and Cambridge's Jonathan Mitchell. Charles Chauncy joined Increase and Eleazar Mather in opposition to the proposed changes, all of them in close contact with Davenport, who provided them with his critique of the proposed changes in church practice. The synod proceeded to adopt the Half-Way Covenant and sent its report to the Massachusetts General Court, which this time recommended that the churches of the Bay accept the proposal. Davenport's opposition was widely circulated in print and manuscript.

Davenport and his supporters made the argument that it had always been the policy of New Englanders to insist that individuals who were baptized as infants had to step forward on their own when they reached maturity if they were to have membership. He cited Cotton and Hooker in this regard. As befit his concern for international Protestantism, Davenport also argued that the policy he was defending was that of the church in Bohemia as described by Comenius, that practiced in Martin Bucer's Strassburg, and elsewhere. Increase Mather identified their position with the Savoy Declaration recently approved by England's congregationalists, marshaled the writings of the English puritan John Beverly in his support, and quoted from a letter written to him by an English clergyman who raised concerns about the Half-Way Covenant.

Davenport and his allies believed that the broadening of membership anticipated by the Half-Way Covenant would bring the churches closer to a geographically inclusive system that New Englanders had previously rejected. It would, in short, move the colonies toward presbyterianism. As Increase Mather explained, "one practical difference between Congregational men and Presbyterians (whom the Lord unite in truth) is that the Congregational men would baptize children of none but such whose parents were fit for the Lord's Supper, whereas the Presbyterians would baptize the children of such whose parents were not fit for the Lord's Supper."

Davenport was also concerned with what he saw as a drift toward presbyterianism in New England. If one element of that system was a broader membership, another was the establishment of a governing authority superior to that of the individual congregation. Davenport was strongly opposed to the synod's call for a consociation of churches, something that he believed would impinge on the independence of individual congregations. He accepted the legitimacy of congregations refusing the right hand of fellowship to a neighboring church that persisted in error, but rejected the proposal that a synod or council could pronounce a judgment of non-communion on an erring congregation, thus in effect excommunicating it. This was "to establish a new form of church [in New England], having power of church government, and exercising it over particular churches in classical or synodical assemblies — [in short,] a Presbyterian church." Davenport asserted that "particular churches are sisters to one another . . . and there is a brotherhood of visible saints throughout the world." But "the manner of their communion must be *social*, as between equals, none exercising jurisdiction and authority over another." He reminded his readers that another quest for uniformity had "brought great persecution under the prelacy upon the godly part in our native country, whereby sundry of us were driven into this wilderness."

Davenport may have been particularly alert to this danger since the churches of Connecticut were moving toward the type of "consociationalism" or "presbyterialism" that blended presbyterian elements with congregational traditions, a system that would later be formalized in the Saybrook Platform of 1708. This Connecticut trend involved a more inclusive form of church membership, a shift in the balance of power within a congregation from the laity to the clergy (such as Samuel Stone had articulated), and regular clerical associations. The idea of such clerical associations would also become popular in western Massachusetts after the death of Northampton's Eleazar Mather in 1669.

IN SEPTEMBER 1667, following the death of John Wilson in the previous month, a majority of the First Church Boston voted to invite John

Davenport to be their new pastor. With the New Haven Colony ab-
sorbed into Connecticut and the town of New Haven reduced to a relatively unimportant backwater as a result, Davenport saw the opportunity to preach from the foremost pulpit in New England as an act of
providence. Believing in the authority of the individual congregation,
Davenport needed the approval of the New Haven church to leave, and
that approval was given, though grudgingly (some said it was never given
explicitly enough) because many in that church did not want to lose him.
His call was also controversial in Boston. A clear majority of the First
Church, led by men such as John Leverett and Edward Hutchinson,
wanted Davenport, admiring the moderate stand he took on Baptist
and Quaker dissenters, agreeing with him on rejecting the Half-Way
Covenant, and seeing him both as a defender of the church's tradition
of asserting congregational autonomy and of the need to resist royal en-
croachment on the colony's privileges. But those were positions opposed
by a minority of the church, who consequently objected to Davenport's
call. Their stand precipitated a highly public debate on the rights of
individual church members, the authority of a particular congregation,
and the role of clerical associations and councils.

When the call was extended to Davenport the First Boston minority
wished to secede to join another church. Davenport sought to reconcile
his opponents to the decision, but failed. The church majority refused to
dismiss the minority, who appealed to the other churches in the region.
A council consisting of representatives from the churches of Dorchester,
Dedham, Roxbury, and Cambridge met to address the issue in August
1668. The delegates were clergymen and laity who had supported the
Half-Way Covenant and took a larger view of ministerial authority and
the importance of councils than Davenport believed in. The council
recommended that if the dissenters could not be reconciled they should
be dismissed to form another church, pointing out that a new church in
Boston was probably needed anyway, since the town's "two places of their
public assembling to worship God cannot entertain" all the residents of
the town. The First Church majority rejected this advice and discussed
censuring the minority for its obstruction and criticisms of the majority.

The dispute escalated following Davenport's ordination in September 1668. The minority claimed that the August 1668 council's advice should be authoritative. At their request another council met in Boston on April 13, 1669, with fifteen churches represented. Davenport's son John wrote to John Winthrop Jr. that the council was "contrary to the express mind of the church." The gathered clergy determined that the First Church minority should be dismissed to form a new church, and justified their intervention on the basis of the synod of 1662's definition of the role of such gatherings. Davenport, who had disputed that definition, responded saying, "I do not see that you are an orderly council. . . . We cannot meet and act with you in matters that concern this church against the expressed mind of this church."

In the end the First Church minority simply withdrew from the church. With the support of virtually all of the other churches in the area they formed a new congregation, Third Church, which would become known as Old South. The dispute spilled out into politics. By Massachusetts law, the formation of a new church required the approbation of local congregations *and* of the colony magistrates. While First Church refused to recognize the legitimacy of the proposed new congregation, the dissenters asserted that the council's permission was sufficient ecclesiastical approval. The colony magistrates proved divided. Six of them, one of whom had been a lay representative at the first church council, and two of whom were representatives at the second, approved the decision to form a new church. But Governor Richard Bellingham, a member of First Church, and five other magistrates, including First Church members John Leverett and Edward Tyng, signed a statement judging the decision of "several persons of the first church of Boston . . . to gather into a church by themselves . . . to be greatly inconsistent with and contrary to the said order of the Gospel." They concluded, "We approve not of the said transaction." The objections were pushed aside, however, and the Third Church was formed on May 12, 1669.

Davenport welcomed an invitation from the deputies of the Massachusetts General Court to deliver the annual election sermon one week after the formation of Third Church. The elderly clergyman minced no words. Having first elaborated on the need for the people to choose godly magistrates, and for the magistrates to honor God, he told the magistrates gathered before him, "When they that are called to ruling power cease to exert it in subservience to the kingdom of Christ, there will be an end of New England's glory, and happiness, and safety." Davenport evoked his authority as one who was involved from "the first beginning of this colony of Massachusetts." He told them of his role in the Massachusetts Bay Company when it was first organized. He went on to describe how the first churches "were gathered in a Congregational way, and walked therein, according to the rules of the Gospel, with much peace and content among themselves," so that his friend John Cotton wrote that in New England "the order of the churches and of the Commonwealth was so settled, by common consent, that it brought to his mind the New Heaven and New Earth wherein dwells righteousness."

This order, he charged, was now threatened by "two extremes: misguided zeal and formality." In words that clearly referred to the magistrates' interference in the affairs of his congregation, he warned that they "deprive not any instituted Christian church, walking according to Gospel rules, of the power and privileges which Christ hath purchased for them by his precious blood." He indirectly criticized the council of churches which had endorsed Third Church, and directly criticized the magistrates, who had "countenance[d] and upheld others to exercise power over the churches in such things, to whom Christ never gave such power." He acknowledged the need for occasional synods or councils, but reminded his hearers that Cotton had taught, "concerning the power of councils, that the question is carried to the council, but the cause still remaineth in and with the church." He denied the need for standing councils—which was the direction the authoritarian elements in the region were moving toward—warning that such bodies, "under a pretence of helping the church with their light, bereave them of their powers." Should the magistrates and deputies fail to correct their behavior, they would feel "God's punishing justice," and the Lord would "remove the golden candlesticks and the burning and shining lights in them."

This was as stinging a public attack on the civil leaders of Massachusetts as had ever been delivered by a respected clergyman. The deputies, who sided with Davenport, voted their thanks. The magistrates declined to do so. It was in this highly charged atmosphere that supporters of the Third Church accused Davenport of having behaved improperly in the events leading to his assumption of the First Church pastorate. The normal procedure for a clergyman to assume another post required that the congregation he was currently ministering to release him. The Third Church faction charged that Davenport, along with First Church elder Thomas Penn, had first concealed a letter from the New Haven church that denied Davenport the dismissal he had requested, and that they had then forged the letter read to the Boston congregation purporting to be a New Haven dismissal.

The impetus for this attack was undoubtedly Davenport's election day sermon. Adding further fuel to the fire was First Church's criticism of new steps the colony had taken against the Baptists. The regional clergy, who supported the new measures, jumped in again to attack Davenport Declaring themselves "the Lord's watchmen," the clergy expressed their amazement that the First Church elders were so insensible of how they had offended others by their action, and stated that in what they had done the elders had blasphemed against the name of God. While Davenport and First Church vindicated their actions, the broader controversy continued, even after Davenport died in March 1670.

The divisions over the synod of 1662 and the formation of Third Church were evident in the May 1670 session of the colony's legislature The magistrates, members of the Council (upper house), passed a vote calling for the colony clergy to be called together with the members of both houses to confer on healing the differences in the colony. The deputies (the lower house) rejected the suggestion because they shared Davenport's opposition to anything that suggested an authoritative gathering of clergy. The deputies appointed their own committee, which listed many ways that God had shown his displeasure with New England in recent years, and identified twelve causes, among which was "declension from the primitive foundation work, innovation in doctrine and worship, . . . an invasion of the rights, liberties and privileges of churches, an usurpation of a lordly and prelatical power over God's heritage, . . . turning the pleasant gardens of Christ into a wilderness, and the inevi-

table and total extirpation of the principles and pillars of the congregational way." They stipulated that the formation of Third Church Boston
was irregular, illegal, and disorderly.

Fifteen clergy angrily responded to the General Court at its following
session in 1671. Ten of the fifteen had been involved in the council that
authorized Third Church and had also signed the report that accused
Davenport and First Church of gross misconduct and forgery. The group
complained that by the action of the deputies "an antiministerial spirit
had . . . been strengthened and emboldened." The General Court that
they addressed was different from that which had produced the deputies'
report of the preceding year. Thirty of the fifty deputies who had sat in
the lower house in May 1670 had been replaced through the electioneering of those who supported the Half-Way Covenant, consociation
of churches, and the formation of Third Church. This new court embraced the ministers' complaint. The Boston First Church and its leaders continued to resist the Half-Way Covenant and to sympathize with
Baptists, and John Leverett would exert himself to preserve Davenport's
legacy. But the struggle for a pure congregationalism and a restricted role
for the clergy was essentially lost. The future of New England would see
an expansion of baptism and a growing consociation of churches.

SAMUEL WINTHROP

From Puritan to Quaker

Like his brother Stephen, Samuel Winthrop sought his future in trade. He eventually combined that pursuit with ownership of a sugar plantation in Antigua. He employed slaves on the plantation and became one of the leading citizens and political leaders in the colony. Obviously his career opens questions about the attitudes of puritans towards slavery. But there is another dimension of his life that illustrates the variation of puritanism. A pious man, Samuel was distressed by the lack of godly clergy in Antigua. Like his father and brothers, Samuel's puritanism was more open than that of some to recognizing godliness in different places. Seeking religious sustenance, he listened to and was convinced by one of the early Quaker missionaries to the region. He became a Quaker and opened his home as a meeting place for fellow members of the Society of Friends. Despite this, he retained close ties with his New England kin and friends.

SAMUEL WAS born to John and Margaret Winthrop in Groton, England, and baptized in the parish church there on August 27, 1627. Because of his youth he remained with Margaret when John left for New England in 1630, travelling with his mother to rejoin the rest of their family a year later. He learned to read and write at home and then likely studied at the Boston Latin School. In 1643 he entered Harvard College as part of the class of 1646. His father may well have hoped that Samuel would use his college training to enter the ministry, a career John had once been drawn to and that Samuel's older brother Forth Winthrop had been poised for when he died young in November of 1630. Certainly

Samuel would display throughout his life the piety that may have suited him for a clerical career.

In October 1645, Samuel joined his brother Stephen on a transatlantic trading voyage. England's Civil Wars had led to a decline of immigration that had plunged New England into a prolonged period of economic distress. Increasingly, enterprising colonists were looking to rebuild the region's economy on trade, looking to supply foodstuffs and timber to European outposts in the Atlantic where land was more profitably used for the production of valuable cash crops. Stephen was carrying a cargo of grain, dried fish, and other commodities to the Canary Islands, planning to exchange them for wine that he could then take to and sell in England.

It is possible that a change in his family's finances had something to do with Samuel's departure from Harvard. It is equally likely, however, that the young man had developed doubts about a ministerial career, or perhaps he merely wished to test his vocation. In a letter he wrote to his father in March 1645 he seemed to be continuing a conversation with John as to what he should do with his life. He wrote that he felt he had "no fixed calling, not knowing what profession I should embrace." He asked his father, "Remember me in your daily prayers to the Omnipotent, who alone can direct us in the right path." It is unlikely that John had tried to direct Samuel's path, since Samuel concluded his letter by writing, "I know not how what I have done will please you. If I had been aware of your wishes, I should have followed them implicitly. I hope nothing will annoy you." Samuel still felt a strong connection with Harvard. Before leaving he had joined with one of his classmates and two of the Harvard tutors (one of whom was his cousin, George Downing) to purchase a plot of land in Cambridge that they donated to the college. It was planted with apple trees and came to be known as the Fellows' Orchard. In his letter to his father he asked that he be "remembered as courteously as you can to all the Elders who shall ask after me, and to our most esteemed President, Henry Dunster."

Samuel's original plan was to accompany his brother Stephen to London, where he may have been apprenticed to a merchant. Instead he decided to take advantage of an opportunity that presented itself in

Tenerife, the largest of the Canary Islands. A local merchant, Ferdinando Bodge, was looking to develop trade with New England and had an opening for an assistant. An energetic young man with impeccable connections in New England was just what Bodge needed. The fact that the merchant had recently lost the services of two clerks was seen as providential. Bodge was, Samuel told his father, a man of "shining honesty, the uprightness of whose life, the blamelessness of whose morals, and the sweetness of whose disposition are so surpassing that I, your son obedient to you in all things, greatly desire to take up my abode with him." Stephen agreed with his younger brother's decision, believing it offered Samuel a chance to be like others who had "got in a short time great estates who had nothing but their own diligence and faithfulness to prefer them."

The Canary Islands were a Spanish possession, and Stephen Winthrop acknowledged that while it was "a place of greatest liberty to Protestants of any part in Spain," public worship was not tolerated so that "men's private devotions [were] their chief help." Samuel himself confided to his father his lack of "the precious means of grace, which God knows, to my helpless grief, I am deprived of." Yet, he wrote, in "what spare time I have, which in the summer time is indifferent, I spend in reading God's word and in other good studies." The lack of spiritual sustenance was of growing concern for Samuel and in the spring of 1647, following his father's advice, he moved to Barbados. During his last days in the Canary Islands he witnessed a major volcanic eruption on the Island of La Palma, visible from Tenerife, which was sixty miles away. He collected some ash that blew as far as his location and sent it to his brother John, whose fascination with science was well known to him.

Henry Winthrop, one of Samuel's older brothers, had been the first of the Winthrops to be involved in the New World, settling on Barbados in 1627, at which time, as he had written to his father, there were only "three score of Christians and forty slaves of Negroes and Indians." But Henry's attempts to grow tobacco were a dismal failure and he returned to England after running up large debts owed to his father and other kin. He had joined his father in the immigration to New England, only to drown a few days after his arrival when he attempted to swim the North

River in Salem. Samuel hardly knew Henry, having been born when his brother was in Barbados and being only three when Henry sailed for Massachusetts. But he would have heard of Henry's efforts in Barbados and perhaps encountered planters there who had known his brother.

Samuel stayed on the island, a well-established colony with its own supply of merchants dealing with New England, for only a few months. In August 1647 he wrote to his father that he had settled on St. Christopher in the Leeward Islands. There he was befriended by Sir Thomas Warner, the governor of the island, who had been born and raised in Suffolk and knew the Winthrop family. Warner was eager to help the young man when he discovered his relationship to the Massachusetts governor, offering Samuel "advice and assistance," and treating him with "fatherly care." It was while he was on St. Christopher that Samuel heard of the death of his mother, Margaret Winthrop, who died in June 1647. He prayed that "out of this greatest affliction I may receive greatest benefit," and found that "grief cuts me off, so that I cannot write."

While still mourning the loss of his mother, Samuel himself came close to death. Yellow fever swept the colony, killing, according to one contemporary estimate, almost 6,000 residents. One of those was a merchant with whom Samuel was engaged in trade. The day after that merchant was buried, Samuel "fell sick of the same disease, which was so extreme then in the island that scarce a young man escaped it. For the most part those that survived the high fever for three days recovered." In Samuel's case, his fever "continued ten days in such extremity" that everyone not only despaired of his health, but expected that he "should depart to another world." "Extreme bleeding," which was a common treatment for fever in those days, surprisingly led to his recovery.

The epidemic had left the island's economy in shambles, as all sorts of transactions had failed to be completed. Surviving merchants found themselves engaged in numerous lawsuits. Governor Warner and Clement Everett, a local justice of the peace who may have been a grandson of John Winthrop's father-in-law, John Forth, assisted Samuel in negotiating the legal processes. In return, Samuel agreed to serve as executor to the estates of some of the deceased merchants, and this took him, late in 1647, to the Portuguese island of Faial in the Azores. From Faial he journeyed to the Netherlands. There he married Elizabeth Hodgkel in Rotterdam. Aside from the fact that John Winthrop referred to her as being Dutch, little is known about her background and how Samuel met her. He wrote to his New England kin telling them of the marriage and indicating plans for visiting them before again trying to establish himself in Barbados, where he believed he could "live better than in other places."

Samuel had received little material assistance from his father, and stated, "If I never do I am contented." But this meant that his greatest challenge would be at his initial settling, his "stock being very small." Everything he had was, as he said, "gotten by the sweat of my brows, and so I must live." He hoped that New England friends and kin would be willing to engage in trade with him. But his plans to settle in Barbados were put on hold, perhaps because Elizabeth had become pregnant. Their first child, Henry, was born in Rotterdam early in 1649. In June of that year Samuel was reported to be representing the interests of a London merchant on St. Christopher, indicating that he had again settled in the Leeward Islands. He was also said to have property on Antigua, an island a little over fifty miles away. Like St. Christopher, Antigua was an island settled largely by small planters, so colonists with few resources had a better chance of success there than they would have in Barbados, where a wealthy landed elite had already emerged.

Englishmen had been active in the Caribbean as early as the reign of Queen Elizabeth, when privateers such as John Hawkins and Francis Drake had raided and plundered Spanish settlements in the region. Such raids remained a source of wealth during Samuel Winthrop's lifetime, with Henry Morgan being the most famous of the pirates who were often encouraged by English authorities. Ordinary settlers in the early English colonies such as Barbados sought to make their fortunes through tobacco cultivation. During the mid-century the Caribbean was beginning to play a larger part in the Atlantic economy. As tobacco production ceased to be profitable, sugar was emerging as the new route to great wealth. Planters on Barbados and other colonies turning to the new crop relied on food imports so that they could devote most of their land to sugar production, and this offered an important opportunity for New England exporters of foodstuffs. Men like Samuel Winthrop served as middlemen, negotiating the movement of cargoes between the islands and New England as well as trade with England.

The Leeward Islands, in the southeastern Caribbean, were first colonized by Englishmen when Sir Thomas Warner established a settlement on St. Christopher in 1623. Warner discovered that there were also French settlers on the island, and the two groups agreed to a division of the island in 1627, with certain features such as salt flats and a sulfur mine open to use by both. Cooperation was deemed wise, as both sides feared the larger influence of Spain in the region. Yet another colonial presence from the 1620s was the Dutch, who focused on establishing trading centers rather than plantation economies. The English expanded slowly to colonize Nevis, Montserrat, Antigua, and Barbuda, all of which, along with St. Christopher, were under the jurisdiction of the governor of Barbados during their early history. In addition to their share of St. Christopher, the French controlled Guadeloupe, St. Lucia, and Martinique. The Dutch presence was primarily at St. Martin and St. Eustatius, with an important colony on the South American mainland in what became Guyana. Over the course of Samuel Winthrop's years in the region these various parties would come into conflict.

Winthrop established himself as a merchant trading primarily from St. Christopher, with his profits largely going into a plantation he established in nearby Antigua. All of the Leeward Islands, including St. Christopher and Antigua, suffered from earthquakes, floods, and especially hurricanes. Most of the islands had been shaped by volcanic activity and their mountainous terrain limited the amount of land that was suitable to agriculture (though the quality of the soil on St. Christopher made the sugar grown there most desirable). All of the islands lacked sources of fresh water, making them susceptible to drought. Antigua, the largest of the four islands at 108 square miles, was also the flattest, and it had three excellent natural harbors. Winthrop's land on Antigua was in the northeast part of the island. His presence left its mark on the map with the names of Winthorpe Bay and Winthorpe Creek.

There are few sources that provide information of Samuel's first five years on the island, or his reaction to the death of his father in 1649, but by 1654 he had established communication links that enabled him to correspond somewhat regularly with his brother John in Connecticut. Most of his opportunities to write came when he was at St. Christopher's, which attracted more Atlantic shipping than Antigua. Family was very important to him, and his letters are filled with laments about his inability to see his kin in England and New England. On one occasion he wrote that reading about gatherings of this kin bred in him "a two day melancholy." He was not totally isolated, however. His cousin Margaret Gostlin Heathcote settled on Antigua about seven miles distant from Winthrop's plantation. His "cousin Dudley"—possibly Paul Dudley, son of Thomas Dudley—was a merchant who spent some time with Samuel, who considered leaving Dudley in charge of his affairs on an occasion when he thought he might be able to return at least for a time to New England.

Samuel and Elizabeth had their own family—Henry, Joseph, Elizabeth, Sarah, John, Samuel, Thomas, Rebecca, and Stephen. In 1657 Samuel sent the two oldest boys, Henry and Joseph, to be educated in New England. As he explained to his brother John, "I do not find this country good for children, and [with] God's blessing, desire to provide the best I can for them." He entrusted their care to Watertown's Deacon Ephraim Child and his wife, Elizabeth. Elizabeth Child had been Samuel's nurse when he was young. He had mentioned her often in his letters and now would rely on her to mother his own young children. Ephraim Child died in 1663, but Samuel affirmed a "great engagement to my nurse, Mother Child." Acknowledging her great love, he told his brother John that he had no reason "to desire any other body's care of them." He did ask John to advise her in the care of his boys, and also hoped that the youngsters might soon be suited for Harvard, asking John to make the case for their admission to the college president when the time came.

Samuel was one of first Antiguans to engage in sugar production, which proved the means to considerable wealth. When he died he had accumulated over 1,000 acres of land on that island. He named his plantation home Groton Hall, after the English manor house in which he had been born. The plantation would have contained what he referred

A sugar mill that survives on what was
Samuel Winthrop's Antigua plantation
Photo by Francis J. Bremer

to as his "sugar works"—mills to extract juice from the harvested sugar
cane, a boiling house to clarify and extract sugar crystals from the juice,
a separate facility for drying the crystals and draining the molasses, and
a distillery for turning the molasses into rum. Some of the conical mills
are all that remain of the plantation, which was in the northeast of the
island on land now occupied by the United States Naval Air Base and the
island's international airport. Samuel indicated that he produced brown
sugar, slightly easier to produce and of less value than white sugar, which
was often refined in England. He took great pride in the quality of the
rum he produced, complaining at one point that one of his shipments
had been sold along with a cargo of Barbados rum, which, he said, "was

the cause it was sold at such undervalue, for mine was not rum of that price."

The process of producing sugar and rum was a demanding one, involving hard labor, close supervision, and careful planning, since it took sugar cane fourteen to eighteen months to ripen. The processing of the cane took place in the spring and early summer; after July, he indicated, there was no manufacturing of sugar. On Antigua, as throughout the Caribbean, African slaves performed the labor. In the 1660s Samuel owned over fifty slaves, which made him one of the leading slave owners on the island. Most slaves brought to the island at this time probably came either from the Niger Delta region of southeast Nigeria, or the Allada coast, which would be today's Republic of Benin. Some also came from Gambia and surrounding areas. If they were carried in British vessels, they would have been shipped from Africa to Barbados and then moved to Antigua. But because of the presence of the Dutch in the region it is also possible that they came from Africa as part of the Dutch slave trade, much of which originated on the Guinea coast.

It should not be a surprise that Samuel employed slaves. Slavery was to be found in every one of the English colonies on the mainland and in the islands. When his brother Henry had been a planter on Barbados in 1627 slaves were a part of the labor force. The first Africans were brought to Massachusetts in 1638. Deane Winthrop, Samuel's brother, employed some African slaves on his farm at Pullen Point in Massachusetts. Samuel's uncle Emmanuel Downing had sought (unsuccessfully) to persuade John Winthrop that the economic future of New England required slave labor, arguing that one could maintain thirty African slaves for the cost of paying one English servant. Despite this, slaves were a very small part of the New England population when Samuel was growing up there.

There is no evidence that would enable us to understand the composition (male/female, adult/children) of Samuel's slave labor force, nor how he treated them. In New England the evidence is that slaves were treated similarly to white servants. They were to be taught to read and required to attend church services. John Winthrop recorded with satisfaction the admission of a black female slave to membership in the Dorchester, Massachusetts, church in 1641, commenting on her "sound knowledge and true godliness." But the slave population in Antigua in the 1670s was equal to that of the white settlers, and the practices of slave owners throughout the Caribbean were noted for being harsh.

It is certainly possible that Samuel's treatment of his slaves may have been influenced by his religious faith. From his earliest surviving letters, written from Tenerife, Samuel had demonstrated a strong religious sensibility, reporting how he had spent much of his private time in reading scripture and religious works. He consistently referred to God's will in shaping his life and that of his family, and offered prayers for the good fortune of his friends and kin. He prayed that his sons would receive God's "blessing, that they may grow up and increase in the knowledge of him and his son Jesus Christ, whom to know is life eternal."

In February 1660 Samuel wrote to his brother John lamenting that he and his fellow colonists lacked "the chief good, a powerful ministry," a situation of which they had been made "more sensible, in regard of some great scandals in life discovered" in their "parson of Middle Island parish [in St. Christopher], for which he is put out of office." Samuel wrote that the now vacant benefice was the best on the island and "might content a reasonable minister." The people, he stated, were desirous of a New England minister and he urged John to encourage any likely candidate to accept at least a trial of the position. The candidate should, Samuel believed, be a young man "that must deal with this people, nor any that will seem to wink at their madness," a "severe reprover of their vices," and "one that will teach them by his example to walk soberly as in the day." The need for such a minister was emphasized by a letter Margaret Heathcote, a cousin of both the Winthrop brothers, sent to John from Antigua, where she and her husband had settled. She praised Samuel, writing that he was "a real Winthrop and truly noble to all." But she was not as complimentary in writing of the other colonists — "they all be a company of sodomites that live here."

Such complaints were not unusual in the islands of the Caribbean. Drunkenness was a common complaint of visitors to the region, one clergyman on Barbados complaining that "the inhabitants had pissed out 15,000 [pounds sterling] . . . against the wall by their excessive drinking."

A visitor to that same island in 1655 was so offended by the behavior of the colonists that he concluded that "this island is the dunghill whereon England does cast forth its rubbish." To counter this, Barbados was able to attract at least ten Church of England clergy by 1641, and that number slowly increased. But the quality of the clergy left much to be desired and the settlers on the islands more recently settled had an even harder time finding men to minister to their spiritual needs. One governor of the Leeward Islands complained to the authorities back in England that the 10,000 colonists were ministered to by only two clergy, "both scandalous livers." Another found that the clergy available on Antigua in the early 1670s amounted to "one drunken orthodox priest, one drunken sectary priest, and one drunken parson who had no [holy] orders."

Men like Winthrop were left to lead their families in prayer and scripture reading themselves and to personally catechize their children and servants. Such household exercises were expected as a supplement to puritan faith, and Samuel had considered the ministry himself, but this evidently didn't provide all of the religious structure he desired. At some time in the 1660s Winthrop met a visiting Quaker missionary, perhaps Jonas Langford, who came to the island in 1660 and settled there, and he was convinced to become a member of the Religious Society of Friends. The Quaker chronicler Joseph Besse identified him as one of four heads of households on the island who were Quakers in 1664. The first time Samuel used the distinctive Quaker form of "thee" in writing to his brother John was in 1667. In 1671 the Quaker missionary William Edmundson visited the Caribbean and spent time with Winthrop, who, he reported, had previously "received the Truth [and had] several large, heavenly meetings in his house." "Several justices of the peace, officers, and chief men" came to the meetings at Groton Hall, "and confessed the truth which we declared in the power of God."

Quakers believed that the light of Christ's spirit dwelled within all men and women who came into the world. They sought to hone the meditative skills needed to allow that inner light to guide them to an understanding of how God wished them to lead their lives. Quakers needed no ordained ministers to tell them God's will—God spoke directly to them. They needed no external sacraments such as baptism and the Lord's Supper to connect with God's grace, for that grace was already in them. In many ways the movement had developed from the spiritist wing of puritanism that had produced Anne Hutchinson and Mary Dyer. Just as his puritan parents had believed that each individual could be guided by the Spirit, so Samuel came to rely on this. But such ideas could lead to religious anarchy, even to antinomianism. This is what led most puritans to test their own religious understanding against the teachings of a ministry trained to discern God's will. Quakers rejected such guides but called upon Friends to share their sense of God's light in meetings with other friends. At meetings such as those Samuel Winthrop hosted in his Antigua Groton Hall, individuals were moved at times by the Spirit to shake and quake and shout, and they shared what they believed God had revealed to them. Among the early testimonies they could agree on were injunctions to live simply and treat all men equally.

In 1671 Samuel used his own ship to take Edmundson and other Quakers to Barbados to meet with the English Quaker leader George Fox, who was there to spread his message. Edmundson wrote that there they "had many large, precious meetings, [where] the Lord's power and presence accompanied his testimony, . . . and many were brought into the way of life and peace with God." One of those who participated in these meetings was Lewis Morris, a prominent member of the Barbadian Assembly who had become a Quaker. Like Winthrop, Morris had a puritan background, having been an indentured servant in the puritan Providence Island colony and then fought with the puritan privateer William Jackson against the Spanish. Morris and Winthrop became good friends. In the 1670s Morris began to spend more time in New York, where his family became one of the leading forces in the colony's politics.

When Fox continued his journey to New England, he told Rhode Island's William Coddington of his encounter with Samuel. Coddington had left Massachusetts with Anne Hutchinson and later became one of those whom he described as "the people of God which are in scorn called Quakers." As a prominent merchant and one of the leaders of the colony of Rhode Island, Coddington had contacts with Samuel's brother John Winthrop. He wrote to John that Fox had told him of Samuel's visit to see him in Barbados and that Fox had expressed the hope that John Winthrop Jr. was like Samuel, and that John "wouldst stave off persecution in thy day, in thy jurisdiction." In fact, John had little of the persecuting temper found in some New Englanders. Like his father, who had sympathized with Baptists and tired of signing orders of banishment in his last days, and like his brother Stephen, John Jr. was noted for a tolerant spirit. Certainly he continued to correspond with and assist Samuel after the latter's conversion.

SAMUEL'S QUAKER FAITH did not prevent him from owning slaves. It was not until the next century that crusaders such as Anthony Benezet and John Woolman led the Society to agree in testifying against slaveholding. Some individual Quakers had spoken out against the practice late in the seventeenth century (just as Samuel Sewall and a few other New England puritans would come to denounce the institution). But in Samuel Winthrop's lifetime, when slavery was legal in all the British colonies, the furthest that any Quakers went was to demand the good treatment of slaves. On his 1671 trip to Barbados, George Fox had urged Quaker slaveholders to regard blacks and Indians as members of God's universal family, telling them, "Christ died for the tawneys [Indians] and for the Blacks, as well as for those of you who are called whites." Winthrop, who had sailed to Barbados to attend the meetings Fox held, would have heard these words. The Quaker leader encouraged Friends to consider freeing slaves who had served them well for a long time. He urged them to treat their slaves with kindness and love, and to exhort them and lead them to an understanding of God's truth. Slaves were to be included in family meetings.

Winthrop's friend Lewis Morris, who had hosted Fox on his Barbadian estate, was a major slave owner. Morris subsequently became a leader in efforts to promote godly ideals for those who owned slaves. Unfortunately there are few surviving records that describe how Samuel Winthrop or any other Caribbean Quakers treated their slaves, or whether many in fact included them in family meetings. That some did is suggested by William Edmundson, who on a second voyage to the islands did record that on Barbados, at least, "many of the Blacks are convinced and several of them confess to truth." And the records do show that after a 1676 Barbadian law that prohibited including slaves in meetings, Morris persisted in doing so despite being heavily fined for the practice. Though such efforts were intended to spread the faith, they also established a religious basis for slave acceptance of their status. Whereas visitors to the islands commented on the generally harsh treatment of the slave population, there is some evidence that the life of slaves owned by Quakers was less onerous.

SAMUEL'S CONVERSION to Quakerism was remarkable because he was not merely a wealthy planter, but an important figure in the governance of Antigua. The first indication that he held office in the colony comes in a letter he wrote to his brother John in October 1660, in which he indicates that he had recently "laid down my secretary's place." To understand why he would have done this it is necessary to review the complex history of the region, and particularly the struggles to control the colonies during the period of Civil War and puritan rule in England.

Following his success in colonizing St. Christopher in 1623, Sir Thomas Warner had been appointed governor of the Leeward Islands by Charles I in 1625. In 1627 the king granted a patent to the lands of Barbados and the Leeward Islands to the Earl of Carlisle, and Carlisle allowed Warner to serve as governor. Then in 1632 Sir Thomas sent his son Edward to colonize and govern Antigua. During the English Civil Wars Parliament named Robert Rich, the Earl of Warwick, governor-in-chief of England's North American and Caribbean colonies and named a commission to assist him. Warwick appointed Sir Thomas Warner lieutenant-general of the Caribbean islands, and governors were named or confirmed for the islands that were covered by the Carlisle patent. An attempt in 1645 by James Ley, third earl of Marlborough, to control the islands for Charles I failed. Carlisle, who still had proprietary rights to the lands, supported the royalist cause in the Civil Wars. In 1647, fearing that he might lose his patent, he leased it to Sir Francis Willoughby for a term of twenty-one years. Shortly thereafter Willoughby, who had been a moderate presbyterian, fell out of favor with England's puritan leadership and fled to the Netherlands, where he proclaimed his loyalty to the king. Following the execution of Charles I in 1649, the exiled Charles Stuart (now Charles II to his supporters) reconfirmed Willoughby's lease of the Carlisle patent and sent Willoughby to the West Indies as lieutenant-general.

Willoughby established himself on Barbados as governor in 1650 and the island assembly proclaimed Charles II king, a step the planters on Antigua and Bermuda also took. Reacting to this, the puritan Parliament prohibited trade with all colonies that had proclaimed Charles II king and dispatched a fleet under Sir George Ayscue to reassert control over the region. Willoughby surrendered in January 1652. Ayscue, who had been named governor by Parliament, put Barbados under the control of Daniel Searle as acting governor.

Thomas Warner had remained as governor of St. Christopher until his death in 1649. Antigua's governor Edward Warner died soon after Carib Indians captured his wife and child in 1639 and presumably killed them. From late 1640 the new governor of Antigua was Henry Ashton. It is perhaps Ashton's rule that gave Antigua a reputation as a royalist colony during the 1640s, but his prime objective seemed to be to keep the island from the controversies of the times. Ayscue, having established Parliament's authority over Barbados, moved on to the other islands, confirming Clemens Everard as governor of St. Christopher and replacing Ashton as governor of Antigua with Christopher Keynall, a former parliamentary officer who had served under Philip Skippon. Keynall settled on the island, acquiring a large plantation that became known as Betty's Hope. Late in 1652 Prince Rupert, a nephew of the executed Charles I, led a fleet to the Caribbean in an attempt to restore the region for the king. He expected a warm welcome, and some Antiguans did offer support. Keynall, however, was able to rally enough support to force the prince to abandon his efforts.

Samuel Winthrop presumably was first appointed to office under Keynall. Though he had arrived in the region five years earlier, his family's reputation for puritan leadership would have made him an unlikely candidate for patronage from royalist governors. It is also likely that only in the early years of the 1650s was he achieving a level of prosperity that would have justified holding office. The position he mentioned to his brother was likely secretary to the Antigua council.

Under Keynall the island maintained its loyalty to the puritan regime in England. The expedition under Robert Venables and Admiral William Penn that Cromwell dispatched late in 1654 to effect the conquest of Hispaniola from Spain stopped at various English-held islands to recruit volunteers. Antigua supported the venture but was exempted from providing troops because of its relatively small population and the continuing attacks on the colony by Carib Indians from neighboring islands. In fact, in 1655 the plantation of a Captain Lee was attacked; many Englishmen were killed, and the captain's wife was kidnapped and held by the natives for three years. Cromwell's Western Design failed in its primary objective of wresting control of the islands from the Spanish, but the fleet did capture Jamaica, and some Antiguans, along with residents of other island colonies, were induced to settle there. In 1656 Keynall petitioned the English Committee for Trade and Navigation on behalf of the colony, stressing its strategic importance and the need for assistance if it was to grow. Among the things he sought was the transportation of prisoners of war to the island where they could be employed as indentured servants (Scots prisoners had been sent to New England in previous years after Cromwell's victories at Dunbar and Worcester).

The death of Oliver Cromwell in 1658 and the Restoration of the monarchy in 1660 raised concerns in all of the colonies who had recently at least given their allegiance to the puritan regime. Identifying himself in a letter to his brother as one "that holds lands from Oliver's governor," Samuel was fearful of what the change of regime might mean. Resigning his official position was a way to disassociate himself somewhat from his support of the previous governor. Charles II appointed John Bunkley as the new governor of Antigua. One of Bunkley's first acts was to crack down on Quakers. Jonas Langford and two other Quakers were imprisoned, and Bunkley pursued a law that would have made Quaker meetings illegal. Before he could achieve that objective Bunkley was replaced as governor by Robert Carden. Meanwhile King Charles II assumed the proprietorship of the islands, making them a royal colony. Sir Francis Willoughby had his lease of the lands validated by the king on revised terms, and in 1663 Charles II named Willoughby royal governor of Barbados and the Leeward Islands. Men such as Carden, though referred to as governors, were in effect lieutenant-governors under Willoughby's overall authority. When Willoughby finally visited Antigua, in 1664, Samuel was pleasantly surprised. The governor validated existing land claims in return for the colonists' approval of a modest customs duty on exports. Moreover, Samuel wrote that he had "received favors from him more than I did expect." Starting in 1674 Samuel regularly served as a member of the Antigua Council.

The Caribbean was a cockpit for war throughout the mid-seventeenth century. The first Anglo-Dutch War (1652–1654) had seen minor actions in the region. Cromwell's Western Design had colonists at St. Christopher, Barbados, and (to a lesser extent) Antigua play a role in the conquest of Jamaica. During the Second Anglo-Dutch War (1665–1667), the Dutch admiral Michiel De Ruyter sailed a fleet of thirteen vessels into Carlisle Bay on Barbados and destroyed a number of English ships. One of the ships he captured was carrying a valuable cargo of choice sugar being shipped by Winthrop, who wrote that De Ruyter then captured "a great many ships at Monserat and Nevis," after which he sailed north toward New York. Winthrop also conveyed reports of the war in Europe, where, he wrote, there were "mighty preparations on both sides, as if they meant to plant the sea with pines before they begin, and turn it into a forest." The Dutch did not directly attack Antigua, but the conflict disrupted the trade that men such as Winthrop depended on.

Antigua experienced worse than an interruption of trade in 1666. France was an ally of the Netherlands at this time, and in 1666 the Anglo-Dutch conflict expanded, with France entering the fray. As Samuel Winthrop put it, "The differences in Europe between our countrymen and the Dutch gave the French the opportunity of molesting us here in the Caribbean islands." Conflict first broke out on St. Christopher, where English and French colonists had divided the island. In

April the French repulsed an English attack on their portion of the island and followed up by conquering the English settlements. Hearing
of this, Willoughby raised a force to reclaim St. Christopher. Before
reaching the island the fleet encountered a hurricane. Eighteen English
vessels sank with all crew, including the governor-general. Only two vessels survived to limp into Antigua. In September eight French infantry
companies arrived at Martinique, followed the next month by a new
French lieutenant-general for the region, Seigneur Le Barre. Antigua
had recently been subject to attacks by native tribes in the area, and there
were also fears of a slave revolt. It was against this background that, on
October 25, Le Barre led a force to effect the conquest of Antigua.

The story of the attack on Antigua was related in considerable detail
by Samuel Winthrop himself when the end of the war made it possible
for him to reestablish communications with his brother in New England.
He wrote that the attack on the island began at Five Island Harbor, on
the west coast. A cannonade from the French ships silenced the English
batteries that defended the harbor. The French then landed troops and
advanced toward St. John's Bay, burning all the houses in their path,
including the stone residence of the governor (probably Carden, though
Bunkley was still on the island). Carden attempted to block the advance, but he was captured, his home burned, and his troops routed. The
situation looked bleak, so Samuel sent his wife and children to Nevis,
dispatching them in a shallop from the landing place on his plantation. On the third day of the invasion two hundred Antiguan troops
under Lt. Colonel Bastiaen Bayer defended Bayer's fortified home at
St. John's harbor against a French force of about six hundred men. The
stone home was surrounded by a strong palisade, and "the contention
was very smart for about half an hour," wrote Winthrop. He added, "Our
men withstood them very resolutely, but, being overpowered with men,
were put to flight." Although "many were slain on both sides," the English casualties were greater, with fifty or sixty killed. The French "took
many prisoners, plundered the house, fired all that was combustible," and
prepared to complete the conquest of the island the next day.

At this point Winthrop's Groton Hall was the only defendable structure remaining on the island, and the available English troops retreated

there. At noon on the following day the French forces appeared. They demanded that the English surrender, offering generous terms and threatening to destroy the colony "by fire and sword, and give no quarter" if they did not. Adding to the colonists' difficulties was that the "cruel Indians" had taken advantage of the situation and were "burning and massacring on the windward" side of the island. After two days of negotiations, a treaty was agreed to between the French and English, who met along St. John's Bay. Those who swore fealty to the French king could keep all their lands. Those who refused had six months to sell their property and leave. A levy of 200,000 pounds of sugar was to be paid in six months. The colonists were to swear not to take up arms again.

After the terms were agreed to, but before the treaty was signed, the French left to suppress an uprising elsewhere. Before they returned, Daniel Fitch arrived from Nevis to take over the governorship of the island. He rejected the treaty that the colonists had agreed to, and, when the French did return, Fitch called the English colonists to arms near Pope's Head, along the north side of the island. However, "seeing [the French] to be stronger than he thought, . . . he ran away from the companies, got into a little boat, and made his escape." Their commander having fled, the English force fell apart. The French commander came to an agreement with Lieutenant Colonel Bayer and Samuel Winthrop that if the islanders laid down their arms they would be well treated. Following this surrender, the French commander made Groton Hall his headquarters for the following week. During that time 100 French soldiers were stationed there. On their departure they pillaged the house. According to Winthrop, the French commander "possessed 24 of my slaves (the rest escaped) and most of the slaves in the island, [and] destroyed most of my stock, his soldiers plundering the country round about." He did not, however, destroy Winthrop's sugar works, and burned only the homes of those settlers who had fled the island.

It is clear that Winthrop was already a Quaker by this time, because when the French commander demanded that the English take an oath not to take up arms against the French, Winthrop, Jonas Langford, and two others refused, oath-taking being opposed on religious principles by Friends. Despite the urgings of some of their fellow settlers, they indicated that "they could not swear, what suffering soever should follow." Eventually the French commander told them that he regarded them as "honest men, and if you will promise not to fight against the King, my master, during this war, I will take your words." The Friends agreed.

While Winthrop clearly adhered to the Quaker testimony against taking oaths, it is not clear that he took a stand against fighting. The peace testimony had not been a Quaker testimony in the earliest years of the movement, when many Friends had fought in the parliamentary army. Fox had even argued that one Quaker soldier was worth seven non-Quakers! And Fox had urged that the government should have an aggressive policy, such as Cromwell's Western Design, against Catholic powers. Pacifism became more widespread among Friends after 1661, but the policy was not subscribed to by all. The challenge of the peace testimony was greater in the West Indies and in North America, where Quakers lived in colonies under a constant threat of warfare. In New England there were Quakers who did not feel called upon to refuse military service, and Samuel probably knew this. The limitations of the peace testimony in that region were most evident during King Philip's War (1675–1676), the devastating conflict with the native population. Rhode Island was governed by Quakers—Governor William Coddington and Deputy Governor John Easton—and yet joined the other colonies in waging war. The colony's Quaker leaders led the defense of the colony, blockading the Mount Hope peninsula, and coordinating military efforts with the governor of the Plymouth colony.

In the islands the possibility of slave insurrection also called for military preparedness. Lack of evidence makes it difficult to assess the situation in Barbados, Nevis, and Antigua. Clearly many Quakers did refuse to bear arms or serve in the colonial militias, and some suffered imprisonment for their refusal. During William Edmundson's visit to the islands, Samuel Winthrop conveyed Edmundson to Nevis. When they arrived, Winthrop and Edmundson were not allowed to disembark because of fears that they would spread their faith. Colonel Edmund Stapleton complained that, since the coming of the Quakers to the region, "there are seven hundred of our militia turned Quakers; and the Quakers will not fight, and we have need of men to fight, being surrounded with enemies." Yet some Quakers pursued a middle way. Barbadian Quakers, led by the prominent planter Lewis Morris, sought to reach an accommodation with the government that excused Quakers from bearing arms in return for a commitment that they would take their turns in standing watch and patrolling the coast. Nevis Quakers sought the views of George Fox on pursuing a similar policy, and in 1675 Fox told them that it would be "a great mercy of the Lord" if the governor of the island "will permit you to watch in your own way, without carrying arms, which is a very civil thing." The Quaker leader also pointed out that a similar dispensation from a rigorous application of the peace testimony was employed in Rhode Island. Fox pointed out that even the most rigorous Quakers stood watch against threats to their homes and families.

There is no evidence that a peace testimony was formally adopted by any Quaker meetings in the islands at this time. Samuel Winthrop, like his Rhode Island contemporaries, appears to have taken a very liberal interpretation of what was called for. In 1668 George Heathcote wrote to John Winthrop Jr. that he had heard from his parents in Antigua that "thy brother Samuel was Commander-in-Chief." Heathcote also wrote that Samuel "did intend to give up his commission, for it was, I think, as it were in manner forced upon him." This would suggest that Samuel was not committed to an interpretation of the peace testimony that precluded defensive measures at that time. It is likely that he had taken an active role in the defense of the colony during the French invasion.

The treatment of Quakers on Antigua seemed to depend very heavily on the views of individual English officers and governors. Governor Bunkley had imprisoned Jonas Langford and two other Quakers and sought to make their meetings illegal; Governor Carden released them and did not pursue the legislation. Fourteen files of men were appointed to guard duty each night (and doubled just before and after the full moon) to warn against Indian attacks. In 1673 four Quakers were committed to prison for nine days when they refused to bear arms while patrolling. Major Thomas Mallet was one of the island's militia commanders at least as early as 1673. In command of forces in the northern part of the island, which included Groton Hall, his hostility to the Quakers may have been tempered by Winthrop's prominence in government circles, but was given freer rein after Samuel's death. On one occasion he singled out two Quakers who refused to drill with his company, whipping them with "many sore and grievous stripes over their faces, backs, and heads, to the shedding of their blood and bruising the flesh upon their bones." When some of his own troops reproved him he "called the Quakers infidels and said it was no harm to kill them." On another occasion he inflicted fifty stripes on John Haydon for failing to drill with the troops. Mallet also seized property from Jonas Langford and other Quakers for their refusal to arm themselves and their servants. Informed of these actions, the governor "reproved Mallet for what he had done," ordered the seized property to be returned, and "ordered the said Mallet not to strike them any more."

Mallet, however, continued to strike out against Quakers when he could. Some governors, such as James Vaughan (1678–1680), sought to rigorously enforce the militia acts and punish Quakers, and encouraged Mallet and similar officers. Other issues in addition to those centering on their opposition to using arms led to penalties against Quakers. On one occasion Quakers were cited for working on a colony-appointed day of fast. Yet other governors, such as Philip Warner and Paul Lee, exercised more moderation. After his death, Samuel's wife and surviving children thus continued to live an uncertain existence as they practiced their faith.

THE HOSTILITY of men such as Thomas Mallet to the Quakers on Antigua makes Samuel's emergence as a key figure in the colony following the French invasion remarkable. Any property he had held on St. Christopher was gone, since the French had not only captured the entirety of that island but for many years refused to return English lands as called for in the Treaty of Breda, which had brought the conflict to an end in 1667. Samuel's economic setbacks forced him to abandon the dream of sending his elder sons to Harvard, and he soon brought them back to Antigua. But over the remaining years of his life he rebuilt his fortune so that when he died he had over 1,100 acres of land and sixty-four slaves. Along with three associates he was granted the small neighboring island of Barbuda for a period of thirty-two years. The four used the island to breed cattle and horses, building a small blockhouse to help their servants defend their property.

Winthrop also rose to become one of Antigua's civic leaders. The end of the war had led to a restoration of English control of Antigua. Under the 1663 reorganization of the Leeward Islands a governor-general oversaw the group of colonies, with power to appoint a separate governor (sometimes referred to as a lieutenant governor) for each individual colony. Winthrop appears to have served as governor of Antigua from 1667 till 1671. During that time the colony records indicate that he made numerous land grants as settlement once again expanded. He was governor when the legislature passed a law providing for public compensation to masters whose slaves were executed for crimes, a measure evidently designed to discourage owners from hiding crimes to protect their property. When the new governor-general, William, Lord Willoughby, voided all land titles and required the Antigua colonists to record their titles anew, Winthrop was chosen as the registrar of deeds.

In 1671 Sir Charles Wheeler was appointed governor-general of Barbados and the Leeward islands. He reported that he "found a Quaker President of the Council, who refus[ed] the oaths of allegiance and supremacy." He thus removed him and bestowed the post on Colonel Philip Warner, one of the sons of Sir Thomas Warner. Winthrop was also replaced as registrar. Wheeler was highly unpopular with the local planters, who successfully petitioned the king for his removal. The king divided the government, with Lord Willoughby being returned as governor-general of Barbados and the Windward Islands while William Stapleton was appointed governor of the Leeward Islands as a whole. Willoughby, who had remained in touch with Winthrop, summoned Samuel to Barbados early in 1673, but any opportunities that were discussed came to an end when Willoughby died in April of that year. In Antigua, Wheeler's removal and Winthrop's friendship with Antigua's Governor Warner might explain the fact that Samuel seems to have retained his seat on the Council. That body continued to meet occasionally at his home, and in April 1672 he was mentioned as president of the Council.

These latter years were difficult ones for Winthrop personally. In addition to the losses he suffered from the French invasion, his family was afflicted with disease. He and his son John were both stricken early in 1671. Three days after becoming ill John died. Samuel "very narrowly escaped." He saw his personal and political reverses as a "trial whether I will stand in the counsel of the Lord and be obedient to the commands and dictates of his blessed light, which leads out of darkness and death, and guides and directs us to light and life eternal." He drew consolation from his faith, hoping that he and his kin "might live before the Lord, that the drawings of the father might bring them to the Son, for he only that hath the Son hath true freedom and life." Samuel was well aware of the fact that Quakers were severely persecuted, and even executed, in some parts of New England. His own circumstances became an occasion for telling his brother John that he was "much comforted to hear and read of" John's "tenderness to persecuted friends in New England, who have taken up the cross and despised the shame, to give their testimony of the light and to reprove that which is evil, to declare against all buildings that are not set upon the Rock, and have lost their lives for the testimony of Jesus." He commended his brother for his moderation, and commented, in words that might have been uttered by their father, "It is great wisdom to be cautious in these matters, lest a man be found to fight against God."

SAMUEL WINTHROP died some time in 1674. His will (which does not survive) is said to have been dated December 12, 1672. In it he evidently divided his estate so as to provide for his wife and to offer a legacy for all his seven surviving children. His oldest son, Henry, who had been educated in New England, became a militia captain and a planter holding about 250 acres. Joseph, the other son educated in New England, also was a militia captain and owned a plantation of 300 acres. A younger Samuel married a daughter of Governor Philip Warner; his daughter would inherit Groton Hall. Stephen was in his early teens when Samuel died, and did not long survive his father. Three surviving daughters—Elizabeth, Sarah, and Rebecca—married into the planter elite.

Samuel's wife, Elizabeth, died in 1675. Her will testified to her continuing Quaker faith. She left a legacy, including her "great Bible" to Jonas Langford and named that prominent Quaker one of the overseers of her estate and guardian of her young children. She stipulated that they should continue to entertain "the true ministers of the gospel whom the world in scorn calls Quakers" at Groton Hall, and that those Quakers be "accommodated freely and assisted in what business or occasions that [they] have from time to time." The will ended with an exhortation —"Lastly, my dear children, I commend you all to the true fear of the Lord and the instruction and guidance of Christ, the Light, who alone is God's salvation to the ends of the earth. Farewell."

THOUGH HE ENDED in a different religious affiliation, the piety of Samuel Winthrop had much in common with his father and the Harvard tutors whom he held in high regard. He was, as his cousin Margaret Heathcote expressed it, "a real Winthrop, and truly noble to all." Like his father and his brothers Stephen and John, his puritanism made him humble, which led him away from the dogmatic certainties of colonists such as Thomas Dudley. But for all of the ways in which he reflected the puritan values of New England, he also clearly diverged from what we tend to think puritans were like. He was a plantation owner and a slave owner. He was a Quaker. His life and writings reinforce the point that there was no one set puritan character in the Atlantic world of the seventeenth century.

✳

John Sassamon

A Puritan between Two Cultures

Puritans acknowledged that the elect were to be found in all places. God's saints were female as well as male, and black as well as white. Nowhere was this better demonstrated than when the Dorchester congregation admitted a female slave to membership in the church. Native Americans were called as well as Englishmen. This belief underlay the effort to convert the native population. But cultural prejudice shaped the colonists' understanding of what was required of Native American converts religious transformation must be accompanied by the adoption of English norms of civility. Some natives met this threshold but found that even this was not necessarily enough. Could an Englishman ever see a Native American or an African as a fellow citizen of their city upon a hill? John Sassamon represents the transition from aboriginal culture to puritanism and his story tells how conversion left him isolated, trusted by neither the people of his birth nor the faith community he aspired to join.

JOHN SASSAMON was born a Wampanoag near modern Canton, Massachusetts, around 1620. His parents moved soon thereafter and seem to have been living near the Massachusetts town of Dorchester when they succumbed to the smallpox epidemic of 1633. They had embraced Christianity, but whether on their deathbed or earlier than that is unclear. Just as John Wilson took in and raised the son of Sagamore John at about this time, Richard Callicot of Dorchester brought the young native into his home and taught him to read and write English. It is likely that the youth attended the school in Dorchester at this time. John Eliot, the minister of Roxbury who had taken an interest in converting and civilizing the natives, often visited the town and taught at that school. He came to know Sassamon at this time and was impressed with his ability.

During the Pequot War Sassamon joined Callicot as a member of John Underhill's expedition, serving as both interpreter and soldier. Underhill noted his bravery in confronting and firing on some Pequot scouts. When the war was over many of the defeated natives were enslaved by the English, and others were distributed to their Mohegan and Narragansett allies. Callicot and Sassamon accompanied some of these captives back to Massachusetts, stopping briefly to meet with Roger Williams, who negotiated with them for some of the prisoners. Callicot himself claimed two of the captives to be servants in his household, one of whom, Cockenoe, became an interpreter for John Eliot. Sassamon himself received a young Pequot woman who may have later become his wife. Little is known of Sassamon's activities over the next few years, though he seems to have remained connected with Callicot and did serve the English as an interpreter on a number of occasions. A contemporary record noted the presence of Callicot and "an Indian, his man," at a treaty signing in Boston in 1645.

Though the conversion of the natives had been one of the stated objectives of the puritan errand into the wilderness, the colonists had largely neglected that mission during the first decade of settlement. The settlers' struggle for survival was a partial explanation, as was the difficulty of organizing missionary activities within the congregational church system that had been developed. There had, however, been a few attempts to convert and civilize the natives in the early years of colonization. John Wilson's efforts with Sagamore John were typical of the limited nature of most such endeavors. Roger Williams had demonstrated an interest in the native language and culture, but his suspicions of organized churches made him disinclined to attempt native conversion. Thomas Mayhew, and particularly his son Thomas Jr., would have some success on Martha's Vineyard in the 1640s.

In the aftermath of the Pequot War much more energy was devoted to the effort. In the early 1640s English critics of New England used the colonial failure to live up to the evangelical goal as one of the ways to attack the colonies. Thomas Welde and Hugh Peter did their best to claim success for missionary outreach in *New England's First Fruits* (1643), but the tale they had to tell was not very impressive. The key figure who emerged as New England's "Apostle to the Indians" was Roxbury's John Eliot. His involvement with young natives such as John Sassamon and Cockenoe in Dorchester may have triggered his interest, and by the 1640s he envisioned a program of bringing both faith and civility to all the native peoples of New England. Eliot became convinced that this was an obligation that must be assumed, writing of the natives, "I trust, in God's time, they shall learn Christ." But Eliot also saw the task in a larger context.

Like many others, Eliot came to believe that the American natives were the lost tribes of Israel, who had journeyed eastward from their biblical homeland until finally migrating to North America from Asia. Strange as this identification might seem to us, it was a belief shared by many at the time. The English clergyman Thomas Thorowgood had exchanged letters on the subject with Roger Williams in the 1630s and later gathered these and other reports from the Americas in *Jewes in America, or Probabilities that the Americans are of that Race* (1650). The clergyman John Dury had encountered a similar theory when living in The Hague in the 1620s, and came to believe that the American Indians were the "dry bones" referred to in Ezekiel 37. Dury discussed these ideas with the prominent Jewish scholar Menasseh ben Israel, who also came to believe that the American Indians may have been the descendants of the lost tribes. Other members of the Hartlib circle likewise subscribed to the belief. John Davenport, who was a friend of Dury and familiar with ben Israel, accepted it. Plymouth's Edward Winslow endorsed the idea in his *The Glorious Progress of the Gospel amongst the Indians* (1649). Supporters of the belief drew on their readings of scripture, but also pointed to what they saw as similarities between native speech and the Hebrew language, as well as to shared customs of the two peoples. If the identification was true, the implications were significant, for the conversion of the Jews was one of the signs laid out in scripture for the coming of the millennium. For Eliot and many others, converting the Indians was thus a key to the advancement of God's ultimate kingdom. This is similar to the reasons why many American evangelicals today engage with the state of Israel.

Puritans saw the missionary effort as evolving through a series of stages. They believed that the first step was to raise the natives from their state of "savagery" to "civility." Next they had to instruct them in the true faith of Christianity. With God's help this would lead to the conversion of individuals, and the process would culminate in the formation of congregations of native saints. The submission of a number of local sachems to the authority of the Bay colony in 1643 and 1644 underlined the urgency of moving this process ahead. John Winthrop expressed the "hope that the Lord's time was at hand for opening a door of light and grace to those Indians." In June 1644 the General Court stipulated that natives "who have submitted themselves to this government" were to receive religious instruction on Sundays, and in November of that year the magistrates asked the county courts to make arrangements for such instruction. Shortly thereafter the Bay authorities empowered Edward Winslow to act as their agent in England and designated one of his tasks to be the raising of funds for an American Indian mission.

We don't know who or how many clergy may have responded to the call to provide religious instruction to natives in their vicinity, but we do know that John Eliot's first recorded sermon to the Indians was preached in September 1646 to a group residing in the vicinity of Dorchester. Though he acknowledged it was unsuccessful—the natives "gave no heed to it," Eliot admitted—he preached again the following month to Indians at Nonantum, near Cambridge. This time he and Thomas Shepard, the local minister who accompanied him, were pleased with the response. They believed that questions asked by some of the natives indicated an engagement and interest. Following this success the General Court entrusted Eliot, Shepard, and John Allin with the task of advancing the work of civilizing the Nonantum natives by securing for them a place to live and developing a code of behavior.

Though assisted by Shepard, Allin, John Wilson, and others, John Eliot would dominate the New England missionary thrust over the following decades. He would be assisted financially by the English Society for the Propagation of the Gospel in New England (generally referred to as the New England Company), which, at Winslow's urging, Parliament chartered in 1649. In 1651 the Massachusetts authorities awarded a 2,000-acre tract outside of Dedham to be the site for a settlement of Indians willing to embrace the missionary agenda. That settlement, Natick, became the first of many. By 1674 there were fourteen such towns in Massachusetts with a total population of over 1,100. In Plymouth there were additional towns with about 500 residents.

Eliot believed that in the millennium men would return to the forms of government of God's original chosen people, and drew upon the scriptures to organize the civil polity of Natick and the other towns according to that pattern. Natives chose leaders of tens, fifties, and hundreds. Residents were urged to wear English-style clothes, to abandon their "heathen" hairstyles, and to deport themselves in other ways as Englishmen. Because Eliot firmly believed that true knowledge of God required the ability to read the scriptures, he emphasized the need for schools in the various towns, where the inhabitants could learn to read their own language. He worked with native converts such as John Sassamon to prepare a written form of the native tongue. He also composed a short catechism for use in the schools, organized the translation of the Old and New Testaments as well as various tracts, and wrote two original religious works in the native language. In all, sixteen works were published between 1654 and 1672.

Religious instruction took place in each town's own meetinghouse, with two sermons on the Sabbath and an additional weekday lecture. Eliot preached regularly at Natick and occasionally at other settlements. After an initial false start, eight Natick Indians offered acceptable conversion narratives to the members of Eliot's Roxbury congregation and the visiting ministers John Wilson and John Allin. One scholar who has compared these narratives to English statements of faith has found patterns that speak to the cultural differences between the two peoples, arguing that the affective elements of Indian faith were not as pronounced as those typically found in English conversion narratives. The Indians apparently did not experience the depth of despair expressed by many puritans, and consequently also did not experience the intense joy that puritans felt with their experience of God's caress. Nevertheless, the accounts did demonstrate a satisfactory knowledge of the faith and a certainty on the part of the speakers that they had closed with Christ, which led to their acceptance as church members. In 1660 an Indian church was formally organized in Natick itself.

Eliot, though he studied and learned the native tongue, relied heavily on Indian assistants such as Sassamon to interpret his words and to help translate the Bible and religious works into the Massachusetts dialect of the Algonquian language. The work of translation was particularly challenging for those who were both simultaneously learning the written forms of their native tongue and mastering the nuances of the English text they were translating. Another Christian native, known as James Printer, set the type and corrected the proofs at the Cambridge press.

The work of teaching the residents of the "praying towns" to read was largely undertaken by native converts. According to Daniel Gookin, the Massachusetts superintendent for Indian affairs, one of the reasons for this was that few Englishmen were interested in learning the native tongue. Eliot himself wrote that it was "a blessing of God" that a number of natives proved competent to teach their countrymen, since he found "few English students willing to engage in so dim a work as this is." Much of the preaching was also undertaken by natives.

Initially, Cockenoe was Eliot's principal assistant, but when Cockenoe returned to his own people on Long Island, John Sassamon replaced him. Sassamon was involved in the organization of the community at Natick and became the town's first schoolmaster. In 1653 Eliot arranged for Sassamon to study for a time at Harvard, where his classmates included the young Increase Mather, the sons of Simon and Anne Bradstreet, and Thomas Shepard Jr. Sassamon was no more immune from the temptations of the world than other puritans, and in 1654 he appears to have been one of a number of Eliot's promising native protégés who became drunk and forced liquor on one of their young peers. Though this cost Sassamon Eliot's favor for a time and may have had something to do with his departure from Harvard, he was eventually forgiven.

By the early 1660s Sassamon had left Natick and settled among the Wampanoags. Massasoit, the leader of that tribe who had signed a

peace treaty with the Pilgrims in the 1620s, died in 1660 and was succeeded initially by his son (or grandson) Wamsutta, and then, following
Wamsutta's death two years later, by Wamsutta's brother Metacom. As
a token of their alliance with the Plymouth authorities, the two Wampanoag brothers asked to be given new titles. The English authorities chose
two names from the classical past—Wamsutta became Alexander, and
Metacom became Philip. Sassamon served all three leaders as a scribe
and interpreter and instructed them and their people how to read. Surviving documents show him as a witness to various Wampanoag land
transactions. He married Metacom's favorite niece and was granted land
along Assawompsett Neck. Some have argued that Sassamon's decision
to settle among the Wampanoags indicated a break with Christianity.
Cotton Mather started this interpretation, writing that Sassamon "apos-
tatized from Christianity and lived like a heathen in the quality of a
secretary to King Philip." But most contemporary evidence undermines
this view. It is clear that Sassamon remained in contact with Eliot and
did what he could to steer the Wampanoags toward Christianity. By the
late 1660s Sassamon had returned to Natick, and entered into the ministry in a more formal fashion. Then in 1671 he settled as the minister to
the praying town of Namasket, not far from Metacom's home at Mount
Hope.

By this time the general relationship between the two peoples of New
England was heading for a crisis. Disputes between different native
peoples, which had existed prior to the arrival of the Europeans, had
continued following the Pequot War. The English trusted and allied
themselves strongly to the Mohegan sachem Uncas, who had supported
them in that earlier conflict. The English were suspicious of the Narragansetts, simply because they were the largest and most powerful tribe
in the region. Uncas, who had for a time been forced to suppress his
people's traditional enmity toward the Narragansetts, did everything
he could to spread rumors that would feed English fears and suspicions
toward his enemy. Believing the rumors of planned Narragansett treach-
ery, the English authorities attacked the Narragansetts in 1643. The Narragansett sachem Miantonomo was captured by Uncas's warriors and

turned over to the English authorities, who returned him to Uncas and instructed him to execute his rival. Uncas was glad to carry out the execution, which not only rid him of a rival, but demonstrated to everyone the strength of his alliance with the English. Relations between the Narragansetts and the English continued to deteriorate through the 1650s and 1660s.

While some tribes submitted themselves to the authority of Massachusetts, the Narragansetts benefitted from the arrival of a royal commission sent to New England in the early 1660s, through which they directly pledged themselves as subjects to the king. The commissioners, in return, removed Narragansett territory from the jurisdiction of the colonies, a decision that threatened the colonies' territorial claims and stoked their hostility to the commission. At the same time, as the Narragansetts drew closer to the neighboring Niantics, the English were drawn closer to the Wampanoags, who were traditional foes of the Niantics.

While various tribes sought to use the Europeans to gain advantage against their native enemies, the way of life of all of the region's natives was being eroded. The Indians had embraced European manufactured goods that made traditional pursuits easier and more effective, but as time went on they found that the only resource they had to trade for such goods was their land. And while land transactions generally allowed the natives to hunt, fish, gather, and even plant on the land they sold, the fact that the English cleared the land, planted much of it, and used the rest to graze cattle, made these rights meaningless. As Miantonomo stated it in 1641, "Our fathers had plenty of deer and skins, our plains [and woods] were full of deer . . . and of turkeys, and our coves full of fish and fowl." But the English had "with scythes cut down the grass, and with axes fell the trees; their cows and horses eat the grass, and their hogs spoil our clam banks, and we shall all be starved."

The extension of English law over those who had submitted to colonial authority was also cause for tension. By their standards, the English saw themselves as applying equal protection of the world's best legal system to the natives. Colonial courts in general treated Indians as they did Englishmen. Procedures were applied equitably, Indian testimony in court cases was accepted as meaningful, and English offenders suffered no greater and no less penalties than those imposed on natives found guilty of the same crime. In all of this, Indians in New England were provided legal protection that exceeded that which could be found in any other English colonies existing at the time. What the puritans failed to appreciate, however, was that there were fundamental differences between their legal culture and that of the natives, and that what stood for justice among the colonists might seem very different in the eyes of the Indians.

The success of the English missionary initiatives itself became a source of conflict. While the first residents of praying towns continued to pay tribute to their sachems, this eventually ceased to be the case. Each Indian who settled in a praying town meant a loss of important resources for the native sachemship that was abandoned. Each Indian who adopted Eliot's system of government in the praying towns meant a loss for the sachem who had previously held his allegiance. Each Indian who adopted the Christian faith meant a diminution of the influence of the native powwows, which played a large role in tribal religious culture. While Eliot and the colonial authorities saw the growth of the praying towns as evidence of the advance of civility and the laying out of a place for natives in the godly kingdom, Metacom and other native leaders viewed this as yet another threat to their traditional way of life.

Tensions between the Wampanoags and the English authorities grew during the early 1660s. The Plymouth authorities summoned Wamsutta to answer various charges laid against him and compelled him to come when he declined to do so voluntarily. Sassamon likely accompanied Wamsutta and was likely with him when the sachem died while returning to his people. Many Indians believed that Wamsutta had been poisoned. Metacom certainly harbored a grudge against the English for humiliating his brother and, at the least, contributing to his death. The English commissioners who had identified Narragansett lands as part of a "King's Province" in 1664 visited Metacom and may well have asserted that he was a subject of the king and not of the Plymouth colony.

In 1671, a dispute arose between the Wampanoags and the Plymouth authorities over a new English settlement at Swansea, which Metacom believed encroached on native land. Sympathetic to Metacom and fearing that the actions of Plymouth might push the native ruler toward war, John Eliot arranged for the Natick Indians to send Sassamon and two other missionaries to persuade the Wampanoag leader to avoid any rash action. Those native emissaries persuaded Metacom to seek the good offices of Massachusetts and Connecticut in his quarrel. But when the representatives of those two colonies sided with Plymouth, Metacom was forced to sign a treaty acknowledging himself as a subject to the Pilgrim colony, to surrender all his English arms to the colonial authorities, to desist from selling any further land without the approval of Plymouth, and to pay a hefty fine.

The arbitration Eliot had helped to arrange thus proved a further provocation. Like his brother before him, Metacom felt humiliated by the Plymouth authorities. The fact that John Sassamon would have accepted the views that the Wampanoags were subjects of the English would have frayed their relationship. Furthermore, Sassamon began to be concerned about meetings that Metacom held with various neighboring tribes, meetings that Sassamon interpreted as efforts to forge new alliances and strengthen existing ones. The relationship between the two Indians broke down. Some contemporaries charged that Metacom rejected Sassamon's efforts to convert him and came to view Sassamon as an English spy. Other accounts claimed that Sassamon had taken advantage of his literacy to draft a will for Metacom that the sachem discovered to be fraudulent.

The exact reason for their falling out will never be known, but after a quarrel between them, Sassamon journeyed to Plymouth, where he warned Governor Josiah Winslow that "Philip . . . was endeavoring to engage all the sachems around him in a war." Winslow disregarded the report, as he had ignored similar warnings from other praying Indians. He also was reported to have said of native reports that "one can hardly believe them even when they speak truth." Sassamon, fearful of the consequences of having betrayed Metacom, left for home. A few weeks later his bruised and bloated body was found under the ice of Assawompsett Pond.

In many ways the career of John Sassamon is the perfect illustration of the difficulties of bringing the Native Americans into the puritan kingdom of God. John Eliot remembered Sassamon as a "man of eminent parts & wit," and if we can be objective, we have to be impressed with him as an individual who made the adjustment to losing his parents and, being taken in by an English couple as a young teenager, mastering the English language, accepting the challenge of attending Harvard, making himself into a skilled interpreter, developing the religious as well as the linguistic skills to play a key role in translating the Bible into his native tongue, serving as a puritan preacher, and becoming a trusted intermediary between the two cultures. But Winslow's explanation for refusing to take his warnings seriously was testimony to the fact that, despite his commitment to the Christian faith, his native birth denied him full acceptance by all Englishmen.

Sassamon's relationship with the Indians was also difficult. While he played an important role in the convert communities of Natick and Namasket, those Indians who resisted conversion saw him as deceitful and a traitor, judgments that have been adopted by many later writers who are sympathetic to the fate of the native population. He would not have been the first native New Englander who alienated other Indians by seeking to parlay his skills and his unique contacts between the two peoples into a position of importance. The fact that he sought to live among the Wampanoags as a Christian and to bring the gospel to them has been dismissed by some as ambivalence, while it may very well have been a sign of his commitment to blending the two cultures. Ironically, his death brought about a fierce conflict between those peoples that he had devoted much of his life to bringing together.

The discovery of Sassamon's body in a frozen pond gave credence to the warnings that the colonists had thus far ignored, for it was generally believed by the English that he had been murdered for revealing Metacom's plans. Increase Mather traveled to Plymouth to attend the inquest held to determine the cause of death of his one-time classmate. The coroner's jury concluded that Sassamon had not accidently fallen into the pond but had been murdered. Based on the testimony of a single Indian witness who then came forth, three of Metacom's men were indicted for

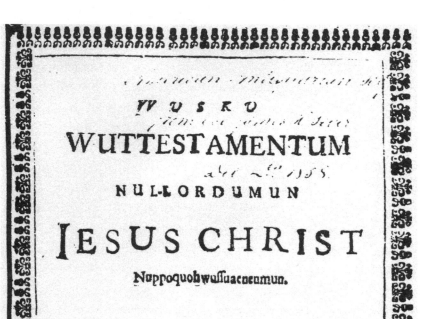

WUSKU
WUTTESTAMENTUM
NULLORDUMUN
JESUS CHRIST
Nuppoquohwuſſuacoeumun.

2d edition

CAMBRIDGE,
Printed for the Right Honourable
CORPORATION in London, for the
propogation of the Goſpel among the Indians in New-England 1680.

Title page of the Indian Bible

murder. It was William Nahauton, a Christian Indian who ministered to the praying town of Punkapoag, who had first heard the eyewitness account and brought the man to the Plymouth authorities. A jury that consisted of twelve Englishmen and six native Christians found the three accused Indians guilty, and the court sentenced them to death in June 1675. Metacom voluntarily came to Plymouth to deny any involvement in the death. The English had taken jurisdiction over a crime—if it was such—that the Wampanoags believed they had the right to deal with, had stretched the bounds of their own legal procedures, and had passed a judgment that did not accord with Wampanoag concepts of justice.

Attempts to reconcile the different interests of the two peoples collapsed. Among many tribes in the region the younger generation of Indians was increasingly insistent on striking out at the English, and on June 19 young Wampanoag warriors attacked Swansea, looting and plundering homes that the English settlers had quickly abandoned. Five days later the first English blood was drawn, and on June 29 Swansea was virtually destroyed. While it is not clear that Metacom actually ordered these attacks—in fact he seems to have been considering a Rhode Island proposal for arbitration—these incidents marked the start of a war, and the Wampanoag leader quickly moved to gain the support of other tribes.

King Philip's War, as it came to be known, began in 1675 and essentially came to an end in southern New England when Metacom was killed and beheaded in August 1676, though fighting continued sporadically after that date on the northern New England frontier. It was devastating for both the English and the natives. English battle losses may have amounted to over 10 percent of the forces engaged. Overall, colonial casualties represented a higher percentage of the population than that experienced by Americans in any subsequent war down to the present day. Over a dozen towns were abandoned or destroyed. Many more suffered the losses of homes and livestock. The material cost to the colonists was immense and effectively crippled any thoughts of forcibly resisting the revocation of the Massachusetts charter in 1684. The cost to the native population was even greater. One estimate placed Indian casualties at over 6,000, counting those who perished from disease and from starvation that resulted from the colonial strategy of destroying native fields and killing their livestock in addition to those who died in battle. Many more natives were captured or surrendered and forced to live as servants or slaves.

The war, which can be said to have been triggered by John Sassamon's murder, revealed the extent to which the overwhelming majority of New Englanders rejected the idea of a godly community with native citizens—even Christian native citizens. On the eve of the war it was evident that the Plymouth authorities did not trust John Sassamon because he was an Indian. The war only increased such attitudes. A sense of how the colonists were divided over whether to trust the natives can be illustrated by examining the activities of two of the most popular English leaders in the fighting. Samuel Moseley commanded a company of troops identified by some as recruited from servants and former pirates. Moseley consistently demonstrated hostility toward all Indians and was responsible for atrocities committed against praying Indians on more than one occasion. He pushed the Penacocks into war by an unprovoked attack on one of their settlements. He turned over an Indian captive to be torn apart by dogs after extracting information. His reputation was such that when the residents of Concord were nervous about Christian Indians being sheltered near their town, they called on Moseley for assistance. Citing his commission to "kill and destroy the enemy" he broke into the Indian homes, stole their possessions, and marched them off to Boston.

Benjamin Church had grown up on the Plymouth frontier in an area heavily populated by natives. He formed a number of friendships with his Indian neighbors, particularly with Awashonks, the female sachem of the Sakonnets. Church sought to learn from the Indians how to fight the type of frontier warfare the colonists found themselves engaged in. He "enquired of some of the Indians that were become his soldiers, how [the natives] got such an advantage often of the English," and learned from them that the colonial forces were vulnerable because they "always kept in a heap together, [so] that it was as easy to hit them as to hit a house." As a result, Church's forces "always marched at a wide distance,

one from another." He sought the assistance of natives as scouts and soldiers, and consistently advised offering favorable terms to those natives
who would desert Metacom.

The divisions over how to deal with ostensibly friendly natives were
highlighted in an incident in August 1676, when four English soldiers
murdered three native women and three children near Concord—"some
shot through, others their brains beat out with hatchets." All were praying Indians. The Englishmen were arrested and brought up on charges
before the Massachusetts Court of Assistants. The four acknowledged
their act and were unrepentant. Increase Mather confided to his diary
that "if justice be not done upon the murderers, God will take ven-
geance." The magistrates must have agreed, for they found the accused
guilty and sentenced them to death—the only time during the war that
Englishmen were punished for actions against Indians. But the brazen-
ness of the murderers and the popular outcry at the court's decision was
evidence of the deep hostility that could be found toward all Indians in
New England.

Less than a year later an even more horrific incident further reflected
colonists' fears of and animosities toward Indians. Some of the Waba-
naki people along the northeastern coast of New England had attacked
and captured fishing and trading vessels based in the region's ports. In
July 1677 the crew of one such ship turned the tables on their Indian cap-
tors, regained control of the vessel, and returned to port in Marblehead.
That town was crowded with refugees from frontier towns that had been
destroyed by native attacks, and by families of sailors lost in previous attacks. According to an eyewitness, when the native captives were taken
off the ship a mob of angry women "laid violent hands upon the captives.
. . . Then with stones, billets of wood, and what else they might, they
made an end of these Indians." Increase Mather also recorded how "the
women in a boisterous rage set upon and killed them," adding, "This
done upon the Sabbath day coming out of the meeting house." In this
case, likely because the natives murdered had clearly been active in the
war, no one was prosecuted.

Despite this, early in the conflict Daniel Gookin had successfully recruited Christian natives to fight with the colonial forces. Gookin was one of the Massachusetts magistrates and superintendant for Indian affairs. In that capacity he supervised efforts to maintain law and order in the praying towns, largely by overseeing native constables. He also traveled to the towns to support the catechizing efforts going on. Five natives accompanied the first Massachusetts expedition to Plymouth and by all accounts acquitted themselves well. Fifty more were fighting with the Bay soldiers early in July 1675. But in that same month use of praying Indians came to a halt. Many of the English troops were uncomfortable fighting alongside natives, fearful that their erstwhile allies might betray them. Some charged that praying Indians gave warning to the enemy, others claimed that the native allies held back from the fighting.

In August 1675 the Massachusetts General Court ordered that all praying Indians "against their own reason and inclination" be confined to five praying towns and prohibited from journeying more than a mile from those towns without explicit permission. The policy also made it easier to keep tabs on the Indians. Then, after a native attack near Natick, the Court ordered that the inhabitants of that settlement be interned on Deer Island in Boston harbor. Just as Japanese American citizens guilty of nothing more than their ancestry would be interned in the United States during World War II, Deer Island and other islands in Boston harbor became the places where the New England authorities confined Native Americans whose loyalty was suspect. The Court further declared that no Indian "shall presume to go off the islands voluntarily, upon pain of death," and that "it shall be lawful for the English to destroy those that they shall find straggling from the said places of their confinement."

Defending the praying Indians was not without risk. Eliot may have experienced an attack on his life. Gookin had his life threatened and was called an "Irish dog." Both he and Thomas Danforth, another magistrate who spoke out against the mistreatment of the praying Indians, were subject to a libel circulated in Boston in February 1676. The attack read "Reader, thou are desired not to suppress this paper but to promote its design, which is to certify those traitors to their King and country,

Gookin and Danforth, that some generous spirits have vowed their destruction. As Christians we warn them to prepare for death, for though they will deservedly die, yet we wish the health of their souls." It was probably English soldiers who destroyed Indian Bibles, leading to the surprising failure of all but a few of these texts to survive.

The appalling losses the English suffered in the winter of 1675–1676 forced a reconsideration of native auxiliaries. In April 1676 the Massachusetts General Court agreed to release Indians from Deer Island to serve as soldiers and scouts, though their families remained confined in miserable conditions for an additional time. As the war progressed, the English, aided by such native scouts, began to focus on striking at their enemy's food supplies, raiding fishing villages and destroying recently planted crops. A major June offensive by the forces of the United Colonies succeeded in forcing the natives from many of their bases. English victories mounted, and skilled native leaders were killed or captured. The Narragansett sachem Canonchet was captured and executed in April 1676. Over a hundred natives were killed or captured at Wausaccum Pond in June. The Connecticut militia achieved success in July. By now the value of employing the praying Indians was obvious. Referring to one of the battles in the summer of 1676, Increase Mather reported, "The praying Indians did approve themselves faithful to the English & did very good service at this as well as at other times, inasmuch many who had [had] hard thoughts of them begin to blame themselves & to have a good opinion of the praying Indians, who have been so generally & so sinfully decried." On August 11, 1676, Church and his native soldiers surprised Metacom on Aquidneck Island. One of the Indian auxiliaries shot and killed the Wampanoag sachem, whose body was decapitated and quartered. The head was paraded through the streets of Plymouth town on August 17.

IN THE AFTERMATH of the war Daniel Gookin declared that "John Sassamon was the first Christian martyr of the Indians, for it is evident that he suffered death upon the account of his Christian profession, and fidelity to the English." Like other puritans, Sassamon was not perfect in his efforts to lead a godly life. We could wish to know how he viewed his spiritual pilgrimage and what he preached to his native congregation at Namasket. But his tragedy is that if becoming a true Christian required, as Gookin implied, that one give fidelity to the English and not just to their God, that loyalty was not appreciated by the colonial authorities to whom he gave it.

✴

JOHN LEVERETT

Defending the Ways of the Fathers

John Leverett was the governor of Massachusetts at the time of King Philip's War. He is one of the least known of the colony's political leaders, a neglect attributable to the fact that he clashed frequently with the clergyman Increase Mather, whose son Cotton Mather did so much to define the history of New England in his monumental *Magnalia Christi Americana (1702)*. But Cotton Mather notwithstanding, Leverett was one of the more important governors of the seventeenth century. His career illustrates the Atlantic dimension of New England puritanism. But it also illuminates how the debates over congregational autonomy and the definition of the religious perimeter fence continued into the last decades of Massachusetts under its original charter.

JOHN LEVERETT was part of the New England establishment. He was born in Boston, Lincolnshire, England, in 1616 and baptized there in St. Botolph's Church. His father, Thomas Leverett, was a Boston alderman and a prominent member of St. Botolph's. Thomas was a strong supporter of John Cotton and an opponent of what were deemed unjust royal policies. He helped to protect Cotton against interference with his ministry. He was one of those who resisted the royal effort to raise funds that became known as the "forced loan." John likely began his education at the Boston grammar school. The Leverett family accompanied John Cotton when the clergyman immigrated to New England. The Boston, Massachusetts, church quickly admitted Thomas and selected him as a ruling elder of the congregation. In March 1634 he was granted the status of freeman, and in September of that year he was chosen for the first of a number of terms as a town selectman. In 1636 Thomas was chosen to be the recorder of the Boston church.

John Leverett was admitted to the Boston church in 1637, at the age of twenty-one. In 1639 he married. The same year saw his admission to the Boston Artillery Company, the militia organization, membership in which signified social distinction as well as military interest. In 1640 he was admitted to freemanship. John began his career as a merchant and appears to have engaged in intercolonial trade, on one occasion losing a valuable cargo off the coast of Virginia. But his true future was to be in public service. In 1642 he was chosen along with Edward Hutchinson to be one of the colony's emissaries to the Narragansett sachem Miantonomo. The two envoys temporarily defused a growing tension between the sachem, the Mohegans, and the English authorities, but hostilities flared in 1643 when Miantonomo invaded Mohegan territory.

Shortly after the outbreak of the English Civil Wars Leverett joined other colonists who were returning to England to join in the struggle against Charles I. By August 1644 he had a commission as captain in the foot regiment of Thomas Rainsborow. The Rainsborow family had lived briefly in Massachusetts and were close to the Winthrops—Thomas's sister Judith married Stephen Winthrop around this time, and the elder John Winthrop would marry another Rainsborow sister following Margaret's death. That connection goes far to explain the large presence of New Englanders in Thomas Rainsborow's regiment. In addition to Leverett, Israel Stoughton was lieutenant-colonel and Nehemiah Bourne held the rank of major. It has been estimated that somewhere between eighty and one hundred fifty New Englanders served in the ranks of the regiment. In 1645 Stephen Winthrop accepted a commission in Thomas Rainsborow's brother William's regiment.

Leverett may have been with Rainsborow's regiment when it captured Crowland, in Lincolnshire (not too far from his native Boston) in 1644. In June of 1645, serving as part of the New Model Army under Sir Thomas Fairfax, the regiment captured Gaunt House, near the king's Oxford base. Two weeks later, it participated in the battle of Naseby. Though the New Model Army's victory there turned the tide of the First Civil War, the fighting continued. Rainsborow's regiment took part in the siege of Sherborne, and then took the lead in the assault on Prior's Hill Fort, which defended Bristol. Oliver Cromwell considered that the regiment had "the hardest task of all" in that attack. "There was great despair of carrying the place," but Rainsborow's "resolution was such, that notwithstanding the inaccessibleness and difficulty, he would not give it over." Some of the troops "were two hours at push of pike, standing upon the palisados." In September 1645 the regiment captured Berkeley Castle, and in December joined the renewed siege of Oxford. Charles I surrendered in May 1646, but some royalist strongholds continued to resist. Following the capitulation of Oxford in June 1646, the regiment was dispatched to serve under then colonel Edward Whalley in the siege of Worcester.

The year 1647 saw a growing rift between the army and the leaders of Parliament regarding the terms to be offered the king and the ideal form of government settlement. In May 1647 Thomas Rainsborow accepted a parliamentary commission to occupy the island of Jersey. While he was still in London his regiment mutinied. Prompted by the radical element in the army, it marched to seize the artillery lest it be secured under the control of the parliamentary leadership. Forced to choose sides, the more conservative army leaders such as Fairfax and Cromwell sided with the troops. While the army was temporarily unified, the debates at Putney and Whitehall demonstrated that deep divisions remained. Thomas Rainsborow was one of the more radical leaders, pushing for much of the Leveller agenda of a broader franchise and religious toleration. At the Putney Debates late in 1647 Rainsborow argued, "Really I think that the poorest he that is in England hath a life to live as the greatest he; and therefore truly, Sir, I think it's clear, that every man that is to live under a Government ought first by his own consent to put himself under that Government." Rainsborow was one of the first to advocate the trial of the king. His radicalism led to a temporary breach with Cromwell and the more conservative leaders of the army. In October 1648, while engaged in the siege of a royalist garrison holding out at Pontefract, Rainsborow was killed in his lodgings by royalists who were attempting to abduct him.

John Leverett was back in Massachusetts by the time Rainsborow was

murdered. He was chosen in 1648 to be one of Boston's two delegates to
the colony's General Court. It is possible that he had made brief trips
back to Massachusetts prior to this, always returning to his command. A
lengthier return may have been precipitated by the news of the death of
his wife, who, he indicated, died in July 1647. Whether or not he was at
Putney to hear his commander's stirring remarks cannot be established.
As with Stephen Winthrop, his military service remained a part of his
reputation, and his political views were clearly shaped by his engagement
with the debates in and around the army during the time of the Civil
Wars.

Thomas Leverett died in March 1650, and John moved to his father's
house just to the east of the meetinghouse. John soon took his father's
place as a Boston selectman. In 1652 he was chosen to be one of the
Bay colony's commissioners appointed to bring the settlements of what
is today Maine under the jurisdiction of Massachusetts. At this time
England and the Netherlands were at war (the First Anglo-Dutch War,
1652–1654) and the southern boundaries of New England were being
threatened by the Dutch in New Netherlands. Leverett was one of the
New England commissioners who met with the Dutch governor in New
Amsterdam in May 1653 to discuss disputes. But even while negotiations were going on, the Commissioners of the United Colonies had instructed Leverett to evaluate what size force would be needed if fighting
broke out, and the New Haven and Connecticut authorities sought assistance from England. Oliver Cromwell, who became Lord Protector
in 1653, appointed Robert Sedgwick, the commander of the Boston Artillery Company and of the Massachusetts forces, to lead an expedition
against the Dutch colony, dispatching three English naval vessels and a
small body of troops to supplement forces that were expected to be raised
in New England. Leverett, who was known to Cromwell, was named
second-in-command of the expedition. He and Sedgwick, of course,
knew each other as fellow members of the Artillery Company.

Though recruiting was slow in Massachusetts, New Haven and Connecticut proved eager to support the expedition and a force of about
seven hundred troops were raised. Before an attack on the Dutch could
be launched, however, word was received of the treaty that ended the

war. The commanders decided to turn their attention to Acadia, held by the French but claimed by England. A brief campaign led to the capture of the French garrison at St. John, after which the English moved on to defeat the garrison at Port Royal. Cromwell endorsed their action and soon appointed Sir Thomas Temple to govern what the English called Nova Scotia.

Sedgwick's enterprise impressed Cromwell, who elevated him to major-general and gave him command of English reinforcements for the Protector's "Western Design." Sedgwick helped to establish the colony of Jamaica and died there in 1656. Meanwhile, in 1655 the Massachusetts authorities appointed Leverett to represent the colony's interest at Cromwell's Court. This stay in England would last until 1662. Leverett, who had known Cromwell from the days of the New Model Army, was an effective advocate for the colony. He gained for New Englanders exemption from the Navigation Acts. He explained to the Protector why New Englanders were reluctant to embrace Cromwell's invitation that they resettle in Jamaica. Though Leverett himself was inclined to tolerate some nonorthodox religious views, he was able to defend the Bay's more restrictive policies, so that when one of the colony's enemies complained of Massachusetts in Leverett's presence, Cromwell responded that he was "very much in favor of them [the New Englanders], that they had acted like wise men, and God had broken the designs of evil instruments, bearing witness with them against evil seducers which had risen up against them."

When Oliver Cromwell died, Leverett presented the Bay's respects to Richard Cromwell, the new Lord Protector, who remarked that "he had a deep sense how dear the people of New England were to his dear father, and that he should be ready in all things to lay forth himself for the good of that people." Unfortunately for New England, Richard soon resigned his post. Leverett kept the colony's officials informed of the changes in English affairs, culminating in the Restoration of the Stuart monarchy. The new king's Privy Council summoned Leverett before them and demanded if it was true that Massachusetts planned to cast off its allegiance and subjection to the king, a charge the agent denied. Leverett reported to the Massachusetts authorities the flood of complaints about the colonies that were submitted to the new king. He bemoaned the changes that had come to England itself—"Episcopacy, common prayer, bowing at the name of Jesus, sign of the cross in baptism, the altar, and organs are in use, and like to be more." He expressed his hope that "the Lord keep and preserve his churches [in New England], that they might not be faint in the day of trial."

IN THE REMAINING years of his life, Leverett would distinguish himself both for his defense of Massachusetts charter rights and his defense of lay congregational authority. Both positions were controversial. In the aftermath of the Restoration, the leaders of Massachusetts were divided over what attitude the colony should take toward the new royal regime. Some individuals favored a firm defense of the colony's traditions, while others urged the adoption of a conciliatory stance. According to John Hull, in a fast day sermon likely preached in the Boston church in February 1661, John Wilson emphasized allegiance, saying, "Our religion doth not teach us to be disloyal to our native land, the parliament, or our sovereign." Yet Wilson also asserted that it was equally important to ensure that religion continue to prosper.

While Wilson may have been unsure as to what position the colony should take, John Norton, his colleague in the First Church Boston, was a prominent spokesman for conciliation. In a 1661 election sermon Norton urged reconciliation with the crown. He advocated "an address to the supreme authority [the king] and a just apology" for the colony's past offenses. He also asserted that it was "neither Gospel nor English spirit for any of us to be against the government by Kings, Lords, and Commons." Humphrey Davie, an observer who was opposed to Norton's stance wrote to John Davenport that "truly the eyes of most begin to be opened and to see plainly the design to extirpate the profession and professors of the pure and right ways of the Lord out of this colony, if not out of the country, and to make all to receive the mark of the beast and his image." Davie feared that "a timorous and fearful spirit hath surprised men (and it is without cause) though some are desperately designed to overturn civil and spiritual liberties, which if they do effect, multitude of people and families will certainly remove to some other places of freedom, and the presence of the Lord with them." Yet Davie was thankful that there was still "a remnant that have not (would not) defile their garments, nor bow down to the image of Baal, and it may be the Lord may hear prayer and stand by them for preventing the evil." Leverett would be one of those who refused to bow to Baal.

In 1662 the Massachusetts General Court selected John Norton and Simon Bradstreet as agents to the crown. Their arrival in England released Leverett to return to Massachusetts. Faced with royal demands that included changes to the franchise and strict adherence to the Navigation Acts, the agents conceded more than many colonists believed they had to or should have. Having made these concessions, Norton lost the esteem of many colonists, including Leverett and other lay leaders of the Boston First Church.

On his return to Massachusetts in 1663 Leverett was again chosen to represent Boston as one of the deputies in the General Court and was also appointed major-general commanding Massachusetts forces. In 1665 he was voted by his peers to be speaker of the house of Deputies in the General Court. Meanwhile, in 1664 Charles II had sent a four-person commission to New England, ostensibly to settle boundary disputes. None of the colonists would have been reassured if they had seen the secret instructions to the commissioners. The king ordered the commissioners to examine the existing Massachusetts charter and "inquire into all laws passed during the late usurping government" and "to press the Governor to call a General Assembly, and to do their utmost to have members chosen who are most inclined to promote the king's service." They were to seek agreement that the king would have approval of governors and militia commanders. The secret instructions did acknowledge that it would "not be rational to appear solicitous to make any changes in matters of religion," but that was certainly a long-term objective.

Further insight into the royal strategy is to be found in a memorandum concerning the commission that is believed to have been drafted by the king's principal advisor, the Earl of Clarendon. In it he expressed his concern that the colonies would "harden in their constitution, and grow on nearer to a commonwealth, towards which they are already well-nigh ripened" if nothing was done to reduce them. England's circumstances required it at this time to use "means of insinuation [rather] than of force." Clarendon's suspicion that force might be met with force was not unfounded. Anticipating royal intervention in their affairs, in October 1663 the Massachusetts General Court had ordered the Boston militia committee to see to the condition of the fort in the harbor, and in March of the following year Captain Richard Davenport was officially ordered to make sure that Castle Island and the battery placed there, as well as the ammunition, officers, and soldiers was made ready for "the defense of this jurisdiction and the authority thereof." Steps were also taken to conceal the charter lest an attempt be made to forcibly seize it. Leverett was one of three men assigned the task of securing the precious document.

Governor Endecott and his fellow magistrates managed to thwart the more serious efforts of the commissioners, but in an attempt to reconcile protection of colonial privileges with recognition of the authority of the crown, the General Court appointed Leverett, Francis Willoughby, and the Rev. Jonathan Mitchell to prepare a new appeal to the king. The petition, adopted in October and entrusted to Leverett and Daniel Gookin to transmit to London, accepted the just authority of the king. However, having reviewed the struggle of the early colonists to establish this portion of the king's dominion, and the steps Massachusetts had recently taken to accommodate the king through the enlargement of the franchise, the petition went on to claim that the royal commission threatened their "power and privilege of government within themselves, as their undoubted right in the sight of God and man." It ended with a plea to the king: "Let our government live, our patent live, our magistrates live, our laws and liberties live, our religious enjoyments live." The language was typical of the position that Leverett would consistently take in asserting the virtual independence of Massachusetts.

The petition was not well received. The king, the colonists were informed, was "not pleased with this petition and looks upon it as the contrivance of a few persons who have had too long authority there." He believed that the majority of the colonists were "well affected to his service and obedient to his government," and reassured the colonists that the commissioners were not in New England to threaten the charter but "to see that the charter be fully and punctually observed." He wished to thwart "the power of any malicious person to make you miserable by entertaining any unnecessary and unreasonable jealousies," and therefore, having "much reason to suspect that Mr. Endecott, who hath during all the late revolutions continued the government there, is not a person well affected to his majesty's person or his government, his majesty will take it very well if at the next election any other person of good reputation be chosen in the place, and that he [Endecott] may no longer exercise that charge." The willingness of the colonists to follow this pointed request was not tested, for Endecott died in Boston on March 15, 1665, after months of declining health.

While the king would have liked to curtail the liberties of the colonists, and some colonial "royalists" sought to convince the English authorities that as many as two-thirds of the colonists would welcome such action, even longstanding opponents of the Day government such as Samuel Maverick counseled that forcibly reducing the colonists to obedience would be extremely difficult. A report recorded by the Council for Foreign Plantations in 1665 noted that Massachusetts had 27,000 fighting men; Plymouth 2,500; Connecticut 4,800; and New Haven and Providence Plantations 5,400. Among those fighting men were an undetermined number of veterans of the English Civil Wars, such as Leverett, Nathaniel Bourne, and, of course, the exiled regicides Whalley and Goffe. Given the challenges of reasserting royal rule in England itself, it was impossible to even consider the forcible reduction of the colonies. While King Philip's War would change things, in the 1660s a policy that mixed offering reassurance while trying to chip away at New England's independence seemed more likely to succeed.

Leverett was an Assistant, a member of the upper house (the Council) of the colony's General Court from 1665 to 1670, then deputy governor from 1671 to 1673. He was then elected governor every year from 1674 until his death. His rapid rise to the colony's top office was seen as "a little remarkable" by Cotton Mather. Throughout these years he continued to stand up for the colony's rights vis-à-vis England. Leverett corresponded with Connecticut's governor John Winthrop Jr. and New Haven's patriarch John Davenport. He discussed with Winthrop conflicts in Europe and their implications for the colonies, the transit of comets and other scientific matters, outbreaks of smallpox, and the religious situation in England. His exchanges with Davenport focused more on the religious situation throughout the world. The two men shared a belief that it was important for New Englanders to resist challenges to their political rights and religious heritage. Leverett admired Davenport's efforts to shelter the regicides (whom Leverett knew from his service in the New Model Army and had visited and communicated with in Hadley), his defense of congregational principles, and his relative moderation toward Baptists and Quakers. These were among the reasons Leverett strongly supported Davenport's call to the ministry of Boston First Church.

AS GOVERNOR during King Philip's War, Leverett mobilized the Bay resources as soon as he heard from Plymouth's Governor Winslow of the attack on Swansea. While he did not take the field himself, he did play a key role in appointing those who led the colony's forces and helped to shape the overall strategy. Confined to supervising the war, he would have taken great pleasure at the news that during a native attack on the town of Hadley, "a grave, elderly person" emerged from his seclusion to rally the colonists against the Indians as once he had rallied the forces of Cromwell against the royalist foe. According to an eighteenth-century account by Thomas Hutchinson, who claimed as his authority an account handed down in the family of Governor Leverett, at the height of the attack, with the colonists in confusion, this mysterious figure, dressed in the fashion of the mid-century, "not only encouraged them to defend themselves, but put himself at their head, rallied, instructed, and led them on to encounter the enemy, who by this means were repulsed." The mysterious stranger, the "grey champion" as Nathanial Hawthorne termed him, was presumably Leverett's old colleague in the English Civil Wars, Major General William Goffe. While the story may be mere legend, the fact that it entered into the folklore of New England reminds us that for the American puritans, the war against the Indians was part of a larger, cosmic struggle for the kingdom of God that they, like their fathers before them, were engaged in.

When the initial flood of volunteers to fight the war dried up, Lev-

erett had to deal with the difficult politics involved in requiring towns
to impress and send townsmen to join colony forces at the cost of weak-
ening their own local defenses. He recognized the futility of trying to
defeat the natives with the tactics that had worked at Naseby, and urged
that the soldiers "be commanded to attend the enemy's method, which
though it may seem a rout to ours, is the best way of fighting the enemy
in this brushy wilderness." Leverett authorized the use of native forces,
but did nothing to curb the harsh tactics of Captain Samuel Moseley,
his kinsman. At the conclusion of the war he approved the sale of native captives into slavery in the West Indies. He also used contacts with
English friends such as the Earl of Anglesey to solicit aid to assist those
colonists devastated by the war.

ONE OF THE consequences of the war was that New England was weakened both by loss of life and by the enormous financial burden of fighting
the conflict. The enemies of the puritan colonies, discouraged by the
failure of the 1664 commission to topple the Bay colony, renewed their
efforts to undermine the Bible Commonwealths. In 1675 the Council
for Foreign Plantations was replaced by a Privy Council Committee
for Trade and Plantations, generally referred to as the Lords of Trade.
Edward Randolph put together a case against the Bay—the colonists
denied Anglicans freedom of worship, harbored the fugitive regicides
Whalley and Goffe, ignored England's trade and navigation acts, illegally coined their own money, and in general conducted the affairs of
Massachusetts as if it were an independent commonwealth. The Lords
of Trade dispatched Randolph as an emissary of the king to investigate
the reported offenses of Massachusetts and to strengthen the resolve
of those colonists who were sympathetic to the crown's objectives. The
number of such men had grown since the Restoration, as many of those
who had come to the colony had done so for the chance of profit and
had no sympathy with puritan values. But some of the sons and grand-
children of the founders—men such as Joseph Dudley and Fitz John
Winthrop—had also begun to recognize that their futures would be
brighter if they cooperated with the crown.

Randolph arrived in Boston in June 1676, presented himself to Gov-

John Leverett
Courtesy of the Byrd family; photo by Mark Andrew Higgins

ernor Leverett, and announced that he had a letter from the king to read
to the assembled magistrates. Leverett invited him to address the magistrates, who were meeting that afternoon on other business. During the
reading of the king's letter, Randolph complained, only three of the colony's leaders "put off their hats and sat uncovered" as a sign of respect to
the king, while "the Governor and the rest continued to keep their hats
on." In the letter the king had set forth numerous charges against the
colony and demanded that the Bay send new agents to England. Having

heard it, Leverett told his fellow magistrates that "the matters therein contained were very inconsiderable things." The magistrates agreed to respond to the king with a letter, but not necessarily to send agents.

In the days that followed Randolph witnessed the arrival of ships from various parts of the Atlantic that clearly were in violation of the Navigation Acts. He complained of this to Leverett, who, according to Randolph's report to the king, "freely declared to me that the laws made by your majesty and your Parliament obligeth them in nothing but what consists with the interest of that colony." Leverett further asserted that the ability to make laws for Massachusetts rested solely with the colony's General Court and that decisions made by the colony's courts could not be appealed to England. The governor claimed that these rights had been granted by Charles I in the charter he granted to the Massachusetts Bay Company. Charles II could not retrench their liberties, but may enlarge them if your Majesty please!" While this is a position that the Bay's leaders had consistently taken from the time of John Winthrop, it was a striking assertion to make in the post-Restoration, post-King Philip's War era. Having proclaimed the colony's autonomy, Leverett proceeded to chastise Randolph for his efforts to stir up the disaffected elements in the colony.

Leverett understood the working of English government perhaps better than any of his fellow colonists. Having boldly asserted an extreme position, he turned to the task of delaying any actions that the king might take in response to it. A committee of the General Court drew up an address to the king which demonstrated a willingness to respond to some of the charges that their enemies had laid against them. The Court designated William Stoughton and Peter Bulkeley to present the address to the king, but denied them authority to negotiate on behalf of the colony. The hope was that actions against the colony could be delayed until, as had happened with past threats to the charter, other events seized the attention of the crown. Randolph, having returned to England, proved a formidable foe, building a case against the colony and particularly against Leverett, whom he referred to as an "old soldier" who "served in the late rebellion, under the usurper Oliver Cromwell." In addition to criticizing the Bay for asserting control over northern parts (what became New Hampshire and Maine) contrary to the claims of the Mason and Gorges families, he highlighted violations of the Navigation Acts, and indicted the colony for enacting laws that violated the laws of England, such as forbidding the observation of Christmas Day and the solemnization of marriage by anyone other than a civil magistrate.

In the end the Massachusetts General Court agreed to observe the Navigation Acts (which would be enforced by the Court's decision to do so, not on Parliament's authority), and the English Lords of Trade recommended not a revocation of the Bay charter, but the issuance of a supplementary charter to clarify disputed issues (which did not happen). But the failure of the colony's leaders to make additional concessions, such as agreeing to make all colonists take an oath of allegiance to the king, allowed Randolph to push matters further. Charles ordered that the oath of allegiance be administered in Massachusetts, and the colony bowed to the need in October 1678. This was not enough, and the Lords of Trade recommended that proceedings be undertaken to revoke the Bay charter. And Edward Randolph was appointed Collector of Customs for Boston to ensure observation of the Navigation Acts. But just when it appeared that the independence of Massachusetts might come to an end, the revelation of a (supposed) Popish Plot that sought the murder of Charles II and the resultant ascent of his Catholic brother James Stuart to the throne cast the English political scene into turmoil. As fears escalated and Parliament debated legislation to exclude all Catholics from the succession, the issue of Massachusetts ceased to be pursued.

It is difficult to know how the colony would have responded to a recall of the charter at this time, particularly since Leverett died in March 1679. History would show that he was the last governor to have asserted, as had Winthrop and Endecott before him, the virtual autonomy of Massachusetts and to take a hard line against making any concessions to England. Others, such as Thomas Danforth, would take on the mantle of defending the godly kingdom against external threats, but none who did so would be elected governor. Simon Bradstreet, who succeeded Leverett, was a godly man, but one who was easily influenced by strong men and personally inclined to be conciliatory. The next time that an attack was mounted on the charter, the outcome would be different.

JOHN LEVERETT was known as a staunch defender of the charter rights of Massachusetts, but he was also noted as a defender of the autonomy of individual congregations and the role of the laity in the governance of individual congregations. Over the course of the seventeenth century, in their efforts to preserve a united New England Way the colonists had continued to debate the fine balance between promoting consultation between autonomous congregations, and allowing assemblies of churches to have power over individual congregations. Over time they also debated the role of the clergy in the affairs of a particular church—Samuel Stone's assertion that church governance involved "a speaking [clerical] aristocracy in the face of a silent democracy" was an extreme expression of one side of the argument.

The Boston First Church had been a defender of congregational autonomy and lay authority from its first days. It had only reluctantly agreed to participate in the Cambridge synod of 1637 that had condemned the errors of the time. In the 1640s the church had been slow to embrace the call for an assembly to define the region's religious practices, and John Leverett himself had been one of the fourteen deputies in the General Court that voted against promulgating the resultant *Cambridge Platform*. The call of John Norton to join John Wilson to the ministry of that church in 1656 proved to be divisive. To the evident surprise of many who had supported his call, Norton proved to be a strong proponent of clerical and synodical authority. In a 1661 election sermon to the Massachusetts General Court he asserted the necessity of synods and complained of what he saw as a ministry that was overly compliant to the people. Some of his dissatisfaction stemmed from the fact that his own congregation failed to follow his lead. Along with Wilson, Norton unsuccessfully tried to bring the Boston church to adopt the proposal known as the Half-Way Covenant, which would have expanded church membership. Leverett, along with Edward Hutchinson and other lay members of the congregation, stood opposed to Norton and to these new directions. Leverett's belief in the importance of lay authority was rooted in his own piety. He was a zealous member of the Boston church who carefully recorded sermons for later review even till shortly before his death.

In the 1650s and 1660s the First Church Boston also divided over issues of toleration. Norton and his followers became noted as harsh opponents of the Baptist movement that had emerged in the colonies. Leverett and others in the congregation sought more moderate treatment of the Baptists. It was because John Davenport represented the positions they espoused that Leverett and the majority of the church called Davenport to the ministry of the church in 1667 following the death of both Norton and Wilson.

Leverett had developed broader views on toleration during his army service in England, and after his return to Massachusetts had remained in touch with lay and clerical friends across the Atlantic who encouraged him to treat Baptists mildly. In 1674 the members of the local Baptist congregation began to meet without disturbance in private houses in Boston itself. As governor, Leverett accepted this and subsequently did nothing to prevent the Baptists from building their own meetinghouse in Boston. His position was not universally popular, however, and in 1679, shortly after his death, "the Council ordered the doors of the meetinghouse which the Anabaptists have built in Boston to be shut up."

At the time of King Philip's War Leverett's views brought him into conflict with the most prominent religious leader in the colonies, Increase Mather. Mather, the son of the first-generation clergyman Richard Mather and father himself of Cotton Mather, had, like Leverett, spent time in England during the period of the Puritan Revolution. Also like Leverett, he had strong friendships with English political and religious leaders. In the 1660s and beyond Mather consistently fought for clerical authority and in many ways believed that the magistrates should be the instruments of the clergy in defending the principles of the founders. He demanded that the civil rulers step up their prosecution of evildoers. Leverett feared that this agenda would involve the civil authorities in interfering with religious affairs. He believed that the responsibility for moral improvement should continue to be placed on individuals and that infringements needed to be policed by their congregations. The confrontation between the two men became clear as the colony was facing the challenge of King Philip's War.

Mather believed that the war was a punishment from God for the failure of New England to uphold its standards. In October 1675 it was his turn to deliver the Boston lecture. The General Court was in session and so he could expect that the deputies and magistrates would be in attendance. He called on them to correct those things which God found "displeasing to him in the country," and the General Court appointed a committee of both houses along with some of the clergy "to consider about Reformation of those evils which provoke the Lord against New England." The result was a measure attacking the "provoking evils" that had called down God's wrath, a list including long hair, fashions that displayed "naked breasts and arms," and similar transgressions. However, this did not go as far as Mather had wished, largely because of the more moderate stand insisted on by Leverett and the assistants.

Reveling in his success, but frustrated at the limited nature, Mather preached again to a lecture day audience that included the colony's political leadership on January 27, 1676. This time Mather singled out drunkenness as a sign of the backsliding of the region: "Our fathers were patterns of sobriety, they would not drink a cup of wine nor strong drink more than should suffice nature and conduce to their health," whereas men in his own time "could transact no business, nor hardly engage in any discourses, but it must be over a pint of wine or a pot of beer." As was customary, the lecturer was invited to dine with the magistrates. There, Governor Leverett took Mather to task, saying, "There was more drunkenness in New England many year ago than there is now," particularly "at the first beginnings of the colony." Returning home Mather wrote in his diary, "As for the governor, he hath been the principal author of the multitude of ordinaries which be in Boston, giving licenses when the townsmen would not do it. No wonder," he concluded, "that New England is visited, when the head is so spirited." The next day he expanded on what was at the heart of his difference with Leverett, confiding in his diary that "magistrates have no heart to do what they might in order to [further] reformation, especially the governor. Nor will they call upon the churches to renew their covenant with God."

Leverett acknowledged that New England had changed since he had arrived with his family in 1633, but he did not accept the fact that change necessarily meant moral declension. As a member of First Church he had been raised under the ministry of Wilson and Cotton, had known John Winthrop well, and had been a supporter of the call to John Davenport. He had been one of the magistrates who had attempted to stop the formation of the Third Church. If anything, he saw declension in the effort to diminish the authority of individual congregations. Leverett suggested that if the churches did need to renew their covenants and the people did need to be reformed, it was the task of the ministers to persuade their congregations of the need.

Mather wanted the magistrates to push for the expansion of church membership, to further suppress heretical groups, to pass new laws, and—underlying all of this—to recognize the authority of the clergy as the arbiters of the New England Way. For Mather, opposition to the clergy was opposition to God. In many respects, Mather was using the crisis of the times to establish himself as the foremost American puritan. Originally opposed to the Half-Way Covenant, he had reversed himself on that issue and became a major promoter of the reform he had initially opposed. He had also crafted for himself a role as the broker for a network of correspondents in England, Europe, and New England.

The clash between Leverett and Mather flared again when the deputies invited Mather to preach the election day sermon in May 1677. Mather accused the magistrates and some ministers of turning a blind eye to New England's decline into sinfulness. "Certainly," he claimed, "if your blessed fathers and predecessors were alive, and in place, it would not be so. If Winthrop, Dudley, Endecott were upon the bench, such profanness as this would soon be suppressed." Mather was frustrated about the reluctance of the civil magistrates to institute further reforms. He warned them that if they had "become cold and indifferent in things of God . . . you may believe it, that God will change either you or your government ere long." Having failed to get the passage of all of the laws he sought, Mather had changed his tune—the primary fault was not in the laws, but in the failure of the magistrates to execute them. Not surprisingly, Leverett and the magistrates refused to have the sermon printed.

At about this time, Mather hit upon the notion of "covenant renewal" as a means of renewing New England. He wanted the magistrates to call upon each congregation to observe a day of fast and humiliation, acknowledge its apostasy from the path laid down by the founders, and renew its contract with God. He was successful in promoting the idea among some of his clerical friends in Connecticut, and he influenced the Plymouth General Court to recommend that the churches in their colony renew the covenant. Leverett was not against the idea of covenant renewal, but did oppose the idea that churches should be ordered to carry this out. He and his allies refused to order such a day of humiliation. Instead, the General Court called for a day of thanksgiving for the victory over the natives. In February of 1678 Thomas Jollie wrote to Mather from England and suggested that the colonists call a synod to organize a campaign for reform. Mather seized upon this idea, but again found himself frustrated, as Leverett and the magistrates declined to issue such a call. But in March 1679 the political situation changed in a way that opened the door for Mather to succeed. Leverett died.

Leverett had been ill and had anticipated his death, writing, "I have fought a good fight, I have finished my course, I have kept the faith; henceforth there is laid up for me a crown of righteousness, which the Lord, the righteous judge, shall give me in that day." He was remembered by his fellow colonists for his courage in arms during the wars in England, and praised for pursuing "God's cause [and] his country's welfare, not his own." Samuel Willard preached a sermon to remember the governor, in which he extolled Leverett as a "pious and zealous ruler," a "public spirited man . . . of skillful, discerning spirit," "a man of courage and undaunted resolution," who was yet "a man of tender heart," and "a man of fervent spirit of prayer." His loss created a "gap in the hedge" that guarded the godly kingdom. This could be a sign of the "plucking up of pillars" for the "pulling down of the house." The large procession of friends and citizens that accompanied him to his grave attested to his popularity.

With Leverett's death, the way was open for Mather to advance his plans. The General Court issued a call for a synod. In September the gathering of clergy and lay members met in the Boston townhouse. This "Reforming Synod" reaffirmed New England's commitment to the Cambridge Platform, because, as Mather expressed it, "Coming from a synod in their joint concurring testimony will carry more authority with it than if one man only, or many in the single capacities, should speak the same things." The Cambridge Platform had, of course, recognized congregational autonomy and the authority of the laity, but while endorsing this, the effect of the Reforming Synod was to strengthen the hierarchical elements in New England congregationalism. So too, in its own way, was the synod's call for covenant renewals, uniting the laity in a commitment ceremony to the goals of their founding fathers—but goals being explicated by Increase Mather and his fellow clergy. The synod also, as would have been expected, pointed to the sinful fashions and practices of the day that needed reform.

✳

ANNE BRADSTREET

Puritan Wife and Mother

There is no question that Anne Bradstreet's most important legacy was as a poet—the first published American poet, the first English woman to publish a book of poems, and the first English poet to publish explicitly marital love lyrics. But the purpose of this chapter is to look at her life for insights into the varieties of puritanism. While puritan governors such as John Endecott and John Leverett and puritan clergymen such as John Davenport and Increase Mather struggled to define the public character of New England's kingdom of God, the heart of the effort to transform society remained the little commonwealth that was the family. Ultimately, puritanism was a personal quest. Anne Bradstreet's life and writings offer one of the best windows through which we can peer into and understand that quest in the setting of the puritan household.

A NNE WAS the daughter of Governor Thomas Dudley and the wife of Simon Bradstreet, who succeeded John Leverett as governor of Massachusetts. She was born in England in 1612. Her mother, born Dorothy Yorke, was a gentlewoman who undertook the early education of Anne and her siblings. She was also a woman of strong religious sensibilities whom Anne remembered for being "religious in all her words and ways," for spending many hours in private meditation, and frequenting lay religious meetings. It is likely that she often led the household in its daily religious exercises. Dorothy set her children an example of "a loving mother and obedient wife," who was friendly to her peers and charitable to the poor.

When Anne was about six years old the family moved to the Sempringham estate of the Earl of Lincoln, who had just employed Thomas

Dudley as his steward. The Countess of Lincoln allowed Anne to study with her own daughters under their tutor, the physician and poet Thomas Lodge. Equally important, Anne was given the opportunity to use the library at the Sempringham estate. While still young she was drawn to the study of history and to poetry.

Anne's domestic religious training was supplemented by sermons preached by the Earl's chaplains and by preachers who visited, such as John Preston. And she joined her parents and siblings when they journeyed the fifteen miles to Boston to worship at St. Botolph's and listen to John Cotton. Typically, they travelled on Saturday, spent the evening at one of the Earl's town properties, and attended services on Sunday. In around 1626 the family moved to Boston, though Thomas continued to serve as the Earl's steward. Anne later remembered that as a young girl she began to be conscious of her behavior and to recognize certain things "as sinful, as lying, disobedience to my parents, etc." When she succumbed to evil impulses it troubled her, and she "could not be at rest till by prayer I had confessed it to God." She found herself too often neglectful of her household duties, but "found much comfort in reading the scriptures, especially those places I thought most concerned my condition; and as I grew to have more understanding, so the more solace I took in them."

Like John Winthrop and many other puritans, Anne's teenage years found her tempted by new thoughts and desires. She later told her children, "About 14 or 15 I found my heart more carnal, and sitting loose from God. . . . Vanity and the follies of youth took hold of me." At around the same time she became seriously ill. She feared death and was fearful that her sinfulness would damn her. She "besought the Lord" and confessed her "pride and vanity" and though God restored her to health, she believed that she was remiss in thanking him.

In 1627 Anne married Simon Bradstreet. He was the son of the Rev. Simon Bradstreet, a moderate puritan clergyman who had managed to conform sufficiently to retain his living in the diocese of Lincoln until his death in 1621. The young Simon had received his BA and MA degrees from Emmanuel College, Cambridge. He then was employed by the Earl of Lincoln as an assistant to Thomas Dudley, and at Sem-

pringham he met Anne. In 1627 the dowager countess of Warwick hired
Simon to serve as her steward. This provided him with a situation that
made it possible for him to ask for Anne's hand. The couple lived on
the countess's estate at Leighs Priory in the county of Essex. Perhaps
influenced by his father-in-law, Simon Bradstreet became involved in
the Massachusetts Bay Company and in February 1630 was appointed
secretary of the company. When he decided to immigrate he was chosen
to be one of the Assistants. He also would serve as the colony's secretary.

As examined in earlier chapters, the first colonists experienced numerous obstacles as they struggled to establish themselves in the New
World. The challenges were particularly great for women. It is not surprising that in later years Anne remembered that in confronting "a new
world and new manners" her "heart rose." This was a woman who had
been raised on the Sempringham estate of the Earl of Lincoln, where
she was surrounded by all the comforts of civilization available to the
English aristocracy. Having married, she spent the following years in
equal comfort at Leighs Priory. During her first years in Massachusetts
she was forced to adjust to living in a crude dwelling, with few servants
and shortages of food and other necessities. The surrounding wilderness with its pine trees two hundred feet tall seemed forbidding, and
the climate posed unexpected challenges. She was bitten by mosquitoes,
which did not exist in England, and she saw many other creatures that
were new to her. In time, "convinced it was the way of God," she "submitted" to it.

Simon and Anne settled first in Boston, where they were admitted
into the church soon after its formation. In 1634 they moved to Newtown, which Thomas Dudley had hoped would become the capital of
the colony, and then to Ipswich in 1636. The move to Ipswich must have
been difficult for Anne, taking her away from the very modest comforts
that by then had been established in Boston and Newtown to a frontier
village almost thirty miles north of Boston and thirteen miles north of
Salem. She may have taken some comfort from the friendship she was
able to form with Nathaniel Ward, who served as the town's clergyman. Ward, who had also been a lawyer, resigned as minister in 1636
but continued to live in the town. He was a scholar and an author with a

considerable library that Anne was able to use. John Winthrop Jr., who was one of the town founders, had left Ipswich to travel to England following the death of his wife and newborn daughter in 1634. When he came back to New England he did so as the governor of the Saybrook Colony. It is believed that the Bradstreets lived in his Ipswich house on their first arrival.

The Bradstreets were in Ipswich when the Free Grace controversy disrupted the peace of the Bay colony. The Dudleys and Bradstreets had likely encountered William and Anne Hutchinson in the old Boston, at St. Botolph's, and they certainly would have interacted with them in the new Boston. Anne's father, Thomas Dudley, played a key role in seeking to root out the errors that he believed threatened the colony. In memorializing her father in later years, Anne wrote that Dudley was "to truth a shield, to right a wall, to sectaries a whip and maul." But she remembered her mother's active participation in religious meetings, and in a letter of advice written to her children toward the end of her own life she expressed the sorts of questions it is hard to imagine her father having asked, though she did worry that in her lifetime the world had "been filled with blasphemy and sectaries." Simon, as one of the Assistants, was involved in the civil trial of Anne Hutchinson. His contributions were minimal, though he did make a point that while there might be doubts about the meetings Hutchinson conducted, he was not in principle against religious meetings held by women. Until the controversy erupted Anne Bradstreet would have likely seen Anne Hutchinson in a positive light, and perhaps was thinking of her when she noted, "Some who have been accounted sincere Christians have been carried away" with errors. She wrote, "[I have asked myself], 'Is there faith upon the earth?' and have not known what to think; but then I have remembered the words of Christ that so it must be, and if it were possible, the very elect should be deceived."

Anne acknowledged an uncertainty over her own spiritual state that was alien to her father. Perhaps his ability to achieve certitude was what led her to admire him and write that his "love to true religion ever shall shine." For her part, she confessed that she had "often been perplexed that I have not found that constant joy in my pilgrimage and refreshing which I supposed most of the servants of God have." Indeed, her own spiritual musings remind one of John Winthrop's struggle to know that he was loved by God. Anne wrote that God had given her "the witness of the Holy Spirit, who hath oft given me His word and set to His seal that it shall be well with me," and that she "sometimes tasted of that hidden manna that the world knows not," yet admitted that she had experienced "many times sinkings and droopings, and not enjoyed that felicity that sometimes I have done." There were times when she was "in darkness and seen no light."

In times of darkness, she wrote, "Satan troubled me concerning the verity of the Scriptures." Many times she was tempted "by atheism, how I could know whether there was a God." At such times her observation of the wondrous things of creation would "resolve me that there is an Eternal Being," but she still asked "how should I know He is such a God as I worship in Trinity, and such a Savior as I rely upon?" She even wondered on occasion "why may not the Popish religion be right?" After all, she reflected, "they have the same God, the same Christ, the same word. They only interpret it one way, we another." She was saved from such dangerous musings by remembering "the vain fooleries that are in their religion, together with the lying miracles and cruel persecutions of the saints." In the end she found comfort by building her faith in Christ, and saw God's will in the blessings he bestowed on her and the trials he placed on her.

Anne believed that God shaped her life and she saw illness and setbacks as corrections to bring her back to righteousness. "God doth not afflict willingly, nor take delight in grieving the children of men," she wrote. "He hath no benefit from my adversity, nor is he the better for my prosperity, but he doth it for my advantage, and that I may be a gainer by it." This does not mean that the pains were not deeply felt. On July 10, 1666, the Bradstreet home caught fire when one of the household maids put hot ashes in a barrel on the porch. Anne wrote that she was "wakened . . . with thundering noise, and piteous shrieks of dreadful voice, that fearful sound of 'Fire!' and 'Fire!'" Though the family escaped unharmed, when the fire was quenched she saw her "goods now in the dust." She saw places in the ruins "where oft I sat and long did lie."

There was nothing left of her possessions — "my pleasant things in ashes lie, and them behold no more shall I." No longer would guests gather under her roof, no longer would the family sit around the table recounting the tales of everyday life. Yet in the closing lines of the poem she focused on the heavenly home prepared for the saints in heaven. "The world no longer let me love," she asked God, "my hope and treasure lie above." Likewise, she viewed illnesses as corrections, telling her children that she hoped that they would remember "the many sicknesses and weaknesses that I have passed through, to the end that if you meet with the like you may have recourse to the same God that heard and delivered me, and will do the like for you if you trust in Him."

WHILE HER DEEPEST musings on the nature of religious faith are to be found in a letter to her children, she also learned at an early age to express her thoughts in poetry. Some poems may have been written while she was still in England, most were clearly composed during her life in America. The early poems reflected Renaissance traditions as found in the works of men such as Guillaume Du Bartas, Edmund Spenser, and Philip Sidney — all of whose works she was familiar with — though with little of the rhetorical elaborations found in their works. In 1647 her brother-in-law, the Reverend John Woodbridge, returned to England, where he initially became a chaplain to parliamentary negotiators. He evidently carried manuscript copies of Anne's poems with him and arranged for their publication, noting that he feared the "displeasure of no person in the publishing of these Poems but the Author's, without whose knowledge, and contrary to her expectation, I have presumed to bring to public view what she resolved should never in such as manner see the Sun." The volume appeared in 1650 as *The Tenth Muse Lately Sprung Up in America, or, Several Poems . . . by a Gentlewoman in Those Parts*. *The Tenth Muse* featured a number of four-part poems on the four elements, the four humors, the four ages of man, and the four seasons of the year.

The volume also included "A Dialogue between Old England and New" in which Anne expressed her support of the Parliament in England's evolving conflict. In it she blamed the king and his supporters for the fact that the "Gospel [was] trodden down." She noted that some of the godly "lost their livings, some in prison spent, some fined," and others "to exile went," and that sermons had "cried destruction" on England if her path did not change. In the poem New England blessed "the nobles of thy noble land," and the "commons, who for common good . . . have boldly stood," and "blessed be thy preachers who do cheer thee on." "Let's bring Baal's vestments forth," she wrote, "to make a fire, their copes, rochets, crosiers, and such empty trash."

While Anne might not have anticipated publication, she had put the collection together as a gift to her father, so that Woodbridge had little to do other than solicit some prefatory poems by Nathaniel Ward and other friends. Her reluctance to see the verse published was undoubtedly due to a realization that most of her contemporaries did not see such endeavors as suitable for a woman. In her poetic prologue to the collection she acknowledged that she was "obnoxious to each carping tongue, who says my hand a needle better fits" and her fears that because of the "despite they cast on female wits, if what I do prove well . . . they'll say it's stolen, or else it was by chance." The dedicatory poem to Thomas Dudley was dated in 1642, so it can be assumed that most of the poems were finished by that time. She continued to write poetry, however. Her later work was predominantly short lyric poems focusing on members of her family and domestic affairs. It is these that give us our insights into her life as wife and mother.

AS A WOMAN striving to live a godly life and feel God's caress, Anne found a partner in Simon Bradstreet, who would reinforce her search for grace and support her in her times of doubt. This was, for puritans, a central purpose of marriage—bringing a man and a woman together to form a little commonwealth that strengthened them and provided inspiration for others. Anne's prose and poetry offers an unparalleled insight into what such a bond meant, and should dispel the myths that puritans were cold, unemotional, and suspicious of sexuality.

Even more than the story of John and Margaret Winthrop, the sources illuminating the marriage of Simon and Anne Bradstreet reveal the importance of physical and emotional love that was the foundation of the puritan family. In a poem addressed "To My Dear and Loving Husband," Anne wrote:

> If ever two were one, then surely we.
> If ever man were loved by wife, then thee;
> If ever wife was happy in a man,
> Compare with me, ye woman, if you can.
> I prize thy love more than whole mines of gold
> Or all the riches that the East doth hold.
> My love is such that rivers cannot quench,
> Nor ought but love from thee, give recompense.
> Thy love is such I can no way repay,
> The heavens reward thee manifold, I pray.
> Then while we live, in love let's so persevere
> That when we live no more, we may live ever.

Elsewhere she referred to Simon as "my head, my heart, mine eyes, my life, nay, more, my joy, my magazine of earthly store." He was "more loved than life." His warmth "frigid colds did cause to melt," and in a clearly sexual reference said that their children "through thy heat I bore."

Simon's role in the political life of the colony led to his frequent absences from his family. Once they had moved to Ipswich his attendance at the meetings of the Court of Assistants and the General Court required him to spend much time in Boston. For thirty-three years he served as one of the Massachusetts commissioners of the New England Confederation, travelling to meetings in Hartford, New Haven, and Plymouth as well as Boston. In 1662 he was sent as one of the colony's agents to the court of Charles II. During his time away from the family Anne supervised the household affairs and the raising of their children.

Anne felt deeply Simon's absence on these occasions and wrote a number of poems expressing her loss. In "A Letter to Her Husband, Absent upon Public Employment," she urged him to "return, return," and told him that with him gone "I weary grow the tedious day so long." In another poem she referred to her "dumpish thoughts, my groans, my brackish tears, my sobs, my longing hopes, my doubting fears." Yet again she wrote of "the absence of her love and loving mate, whose loss hath made her so unfortunate." She composed a poem to Simon, her "dear and loving husband" on his departure on the colony embassy to England. In it she begged the Lord to "keep and preserve my husband, my dear friend" and asked God's help to accept what she anticipated to be his long absence. It is important to remember that in an age with no electronic communication and with very uncertain mail, it was impossible to know if loved ones had safely reached their destination and how they were managing. During this time, Anne relied more on God providing her strength, writing, "Though husband dear be from me gone, whom I do love so well, I have a more beloved one whose comforts far excel," and yet pleading with God, "Bring back my husband, I beseech." She composed a poem "In Thankful Acknowledgment for the Letters I Received from My Husband out of England," and another "In Thankful Remembrance for My Dear Husband's Safe Arrival" back in New England at the conclusion of his mission.

COMPLETING THE little commonwealth that was the family were children. In looking back at her life Anne remembered, "It pleased God to keep me a long time without a child, which was a great grief to me and cost me many prayers and tears before I obtained one." That was Samuel, born in 1632. In all, she would write, she "had eight birds hatched in one nest; four cocks there were, and hens the rest"—Samuel, followed by Dorothy (1634), Sarah (1636), Hannah (1638), Simon (1640), Mercy (1647), Dudley (1649), and John (1652). Over the years she "nursed them up with pain and care" sparing neither cost nor labor till they grew up. All children at this time were subject to disease and accident, and the New World carried its own dangers. Like other mothers Anne feared "lest this my brood some harm should catch." As great as was her "pain when I you bred," so "great was my care when I you fed. Long did I keep you soft and warm, and with my wings kept off all harm." She taught them "what was good, and what was ill; what would save life, and what would kill." As they grew she suffered pains equivalent to childbirth as she waited to see if they would be reborn in Christ.

Toward the end of her life, in meditating on raising children, she remarked that "children have their different natures: some are like flesh which nothing but salt will keep from putrefaction, some again like tender fruits that are best preserved with sugar. Those parents are wise that can fit their nurture according to their nature." At the heart of her efforts to raise her own children was a determination to provide them with the ability to shape their behavior by conscience rather than by fear of external consequences. She referred to the heart of each man as "the little commonwealth," and wrote that in that commonwealth was "a great court of justice erected, which is always kept by conscience, who is both accuser, excuser, witness, and judge, whom no bribes can pervert nor flattery cause to favor." If one's "conscience condemn us, He also who is greater than our conscience will do it much more."

In 1664 she told her son Simon that "parents perpetuate their lives in their posterity and their manners," and she prepared for him a set of seventy-seven "Meditations Divine and Moral" which he could refer to when she had passed away. It offers insights into the lessons she tried to teach all of her children when they were young. She believed that "a negligent youth is usually attended by an ignorant middle age, and both by an empty old age," and was determined to raise her children to avoid such a fate. Drawing on her own spiritual experience, she wrote, "There is no object that we see, no action that we do, no good that we enjoy, no evil that we feel or fear, but we may make some spiritual advantage of all; and he that makes such improvement is wise as well as pious." She was undoubtedly troubled by her sister Sarah's departures from godliness, making her more concerned that her own children would learn to avoid such transgressions. She offered numerous warnings against self-regard and self-seeking—"A ship that bears much sail and little or no ballast is easily overset, and that man whose head hath great abilities and his heart little or no grace is in danger of foundering"; "The finest bread hath the least bran, the purest honey the least wax, and the sincerest Christian the least self-love" were among her cautionary messages. A relationship to God was more important than anything else—"It is the absence and presence of God that makes heaven or hell."

Anne emphasized to her children the importance of the Christian duty of caring for others. Using an analogy similar to what John Winthrop employed in his "Christian Charity" sermon, she wrote that "God hath by his providence so ordered that no one country hath all commodities within itself, but what it wants another shall supply that so there may be a mutual commerce throughout the world. As it is with countries," she continued, "so it is with men; there was never yet any one man that had all excellencies. Let his parts natural and acquired, spiritual and moral, be never so large, yet he stands in need of something which another man hath." The lesson, she concluded, was that "God will have us beholden one to another."

Like any mother, Anne feared for her children. She was very fortunate in that all eight of her children survived her. How unusual this was made clearer in the 1660s by the deaths of grandchildren. In August 1665 she mourned her grandchild Elizabeth Bradstreet, a "fair flower that for a space was lent, then taken away unto eternity" at the age of one and a half. In June 1669 she commemorated her grandchild Anne Bradstreet—"a withering flower that's here today, perhaps gone in an hour"—who died at the age of three years and seven months. In November 1669 her "dear grandchild Simon Bradstreet" died a month and a day after birth, making "three flowers, two scarcely blown, the last in the bud cropped by the Almighty's hand." She was consoled by the thought that they were in heaven, but still viewed these as "bitter crosses."

Equally bitter must have been the signs that despite her efforts, her children were capable of straying from their upbringing. In May of 1672, four months before she died, two of her sons were brought before the county court. John, who was nineteen at the time, was cited for creating a disturbance by smoking and carousing at night with some of his friends. Dudley, who was twenty-three, was charged with being drunk and disorderly, shooting off pistols along with friends. Anne was likely already suffering from a debilitating disease which caused her to lose weight so that it was said that she was "wasted to skin and bone." Simon continued to play an important role in the colony's history.

AFTER ANNE'S DEATH, marriage being such an important ingredient of puritan life, it was not unusual that Simon, who deeply missed Anne, would marry again. He wedded a daughter of Emmanuel and

141

423

THE
TENTH MUSE
Lately ſprung up in AMERICA.
OR
Severall Poems, compiled
with great variety of VVit
and Learning, full of delight.
Wherein eſpecially is contained a com-
pleat diſcourſe and deſcription of

The Four $\begin{cases} \textit{Elements,} \\ \textit{Conſtitutions,} \\ \textit{Ages of Man,} \\ \textit{Seaſons of the Year.} \end{cases}$

Together with an Exact Epitomie of
the Four Monarchies, *viz.*

The $\begin{cases} \textit{Aſſyrian,} \\ \textit{Perſian,} \\ \textit{Grecian,} \\ \textit{Roman.} \end{cases}$

Alſo a Dialogue between Old *England* and
New, concerning the late troubles.
With divers other pleaſant and ſerious Poems.

By a Gentlewoman in thoſe parts.

Printed at London for *Stephen Bowtell* at the ſigne of the
Bible in Popes Head-Alley. 1650.

Title page of Anne Bradstreet's *The Tenth Muse*

Lucy Winthrop Downing in June 1676. Simon succeeded John Leverett as governor of Massachusetts in 1679. As noted previously he was more amenable than his predecessor to Increase Mather's insistence that the colony magistrates call for a Reforming Synod. Though he was less determined to resist English encroachments on the colony than Leverett had been, he was reelected governor each year until 1684. In that year the English authorities finally secured a writ calling in the Massachusetts charter. Edward Randolph carried the writ to the Bay along with letters appointing Joseph Dudley (the son of Thomas) as acting governor. Joseph had thrown his lot in with those embracing greater royal authority. On May 17 the General Court met in the crowded Boston Town House. Dudley "made a speech [to the Court] that [he] was sorry [he] could treat them no longer as governor and Company," and produced and showed to the gathering the judgment and his commission. After Dudley and his new Council members left, the representatives of the old charter regime continued a desultory discussion. Some urged a protest, but with little support. Others called upon the clergy to offer prayers.

Dudley's appointment as the man to take over from the old puritan regime was a masterstroke. Had a known enemy of the puritans been sent as the new governor of Massachusetts, resistance may have been possible. But Dudley, despite his unpopularity in many quarters, was one of New England's own—the son of one of the colony's early leaders, a member of the Roxbury church, and a graduate of Harvard. And the fourteen men named as members of his Council included not only newcomers unsympathetic to puritanism such as Richard Wharton, but New Englanders of distinguished pedigree—Simon Bradstreet, William Stoughton, Peter Bulkeley, Nathaniel Saltonstall, John Pynchon, Wait Winthrop, Fitz John Winthrop, and Dudley Bradstreet (though Saltonstall and both Bradstreets declined the honor). It was hard for many to imagine that such men would agree to undermine the liberties of the colony. But any who had hoped that conditions would remain the same in the former godly kingdom were quickly disillusioned.

On September 25, 1684, the queen's birthday was celebrated by the firing of ships' guns and cheering. The following month, on October

14, "many guns [were] fired, and at night a bonfire [lit] on Noddles Island in memory of the King's birthday. . . . Some marched through the
streets with viols and drums, playing and beating by turns." All of these
developments rankled the godly, but the worst was yet to come. Charles
II died in 1685 and was succeeded by his Roman Catholic brother James
Stuart. James II had already established a reputation for autocratic instincts and proceeded to alienate many of his subjects on both sides of
the Atlantic. On December 20 Sir Edmund Andros arrived in Boston
as the new king's governor with about sixty redcoat soldiers. Dudley's
administration was being replaced and Massachusetts merged with the
other New England colonies into the Dominion of New England. Massachusetts was already under royal authority. The rest of the region soon
accepted their fate. Joseph Dudley was named the head of the Dominion
Council and chief justice.

Under the Dominion, New Englanders lost all semblance of control-
ling their affairs. Not only was there no assembly, but the Council was
appointed and purely advisory. The press was licensed, with Edward
Randolph the official in charge. Fees for probating wills and other official actions were raised to exorbitant levels. Individuals anywhere in
New England seeking to settle estates had to travel to Boston to do so.
The incorporation of towns and Harvard College by the old charter
government was deemed an infringement on the king's prerogative and
thus invalid. Land grants derived from the illegally incorporated towns
(virtually all colonial landholdings) were declared invalid. Settlers had to
pay fees and petition the Dominion for affirmation of title to the lands
that their families may have farmed for half a century. Those who alienated Andros or other officials of the new regime might find their petitions denied and their land given to others. Portions of town commons
were also distributed to friends and allies of the governor-general. Town
meetings, which were the bedrock of local government, were allowed
only once a year and were prohibited from doing anything but electing
local officials. Taxes were imposed by the governor and collected in each
town by a taxing commissioner chosen by the citizens. The collection
of town rates for the support of congregational clergy was prohibited.

The walls of the kingdom had been breached. Within the short space of two years the puritans had discovered that without control of the political process it would no longer be possible to keep out fashions and practices that threatened to undermine the moral standards to which the founders had committed themselves and their posterity. Reflecting on the situation New Englanders found themselves in under the Dominion of New England, Thomas Danforth wrote, "Our rulers are those that hate us and the churches of Christ, and his servants in the ministry." Andros and his minions "daily scorn, taunt, and reproach" the godly, he continued. "We, our lives, and liberties, civil and ecclesiastical, [are] in their hands, to do with us as they please. . . . Some of the chief of them have said . . . [we are] no better than slaves, only they had not power to sell us for slaves. We are deprived of the privileges of Englishmen, of the benefit of the great Charter [Magna Carta] of our nation. Our lands and possessions [are] seized and limited to strangers." The Danforth, as other puritans, never gave up hope that God would redeem them.

The prayers of New England seemed to be answered when news was received of the Glorious Revolution of 1688 in England. William of Orange had landed a Dutch army in England to assert his and his wife Mary Stuart's rights to the English throne, and most Englishmen embraced their cause. James II, his wife, and newborn son fled the country, and William and Mary were soon enthroned. Increase Mather, who was in England trying to negotiate an easing of the burdens of the Dominion, sent word of the events to Massachusetts, and the result was a colonial uprising. April 18, 1689, was the day for the Thursday lecture at Boston's first church, an event that gave settlers from the outlying districts a reason to enter the town. What was different is that on this occasion many who came to Boston came armed. Samuel Prince, in the North End, "saw boys run along the street with clubs in their hands, encouraging one another to fight." Soon "the drums began to beat, and the people hastening and running, some with and some for arms." A band of colonists raised a flag on Beacon Hill. Another group seized the captain of the royal frigate, the *Rose*, who was found on shore. Others captured and jailed Randolph and other officials of the Dominion. A militia band escorted leaders of the old charter government, including Simon Bradstreet and Thomas Danforth, to the Town House. When

Bradstreet, the living symbol of the colony's first leaders, was spotted, the crowd broke out in cheers. By the end of the second day Andros and all of the Dominion officials who had been in Boston were incarcerated, some in the fort and some in the castle.

The leaders who had gathered in the Town House declared themselves a Council of Safety with Bradstreet at their head, and temporarily assumed governing powers. On May 2 the Council of Safety called a convention where representatives of the Massachusetts towns voted to resume the old charter government. On May 22 elections were held for new deputies, and Bradstreet resumed his governing authority. Everyone was concerned about whether these actions would be approved by William and Mary or if the crown might see the overthrow of the Dominion as an act of rebellion against duly appointed authorities that would merit the leaders being punished as traitors. Increase Mather, with the help of English friends of New England, was able to prevent any such outcome. He failed to gain the restoration of the old Bay charter, but through his efforts the Dominion was broken up and Massachusetts granted a new royal charter in 1691. Bradstreet was over eighty years old when he was restored as governor, and he was more than willing to hand over authority to the first royal governor appointed under the new charter, William Phipps, when Phipps arrived in 1692. Bradstreet settled in Salem, where he died in March 1697.

＊

Samuel Sewall

The Conscience of a Puritan

In its origins puritanism had focused on reforming men and society by example and persuasion. The establishment of the Bible Commonwealths of New England—and the puritan Commonwealth and Protectorate in England—presented puritans with the challenge of how to use governing authority to shape God's kingdom. Samuel Sewall was raised and reached maturity in a society where puritan magistrates wielded their power to nurture the church, define the boundaries of acceptable behavior, and advance a culture of discipline. The loss of the Massachusetts charter brought such practices to an end. Once again puritans could draw only upon their example and words to shape their world. His story is one in which we can trace the end of one era and the beginning of another.

S AMUEL SEWALL was born in England in 1652. His father, Henry, had actually immigrated to Newbury, Massachusetts, in 1634, and there married Jane Dummer. But the couple had returned to England in 1647 because the harsh New England climate did not agree with Jane's parents, and it was in England that Samuel was born. In 1659 Henry returned to the colony to settle estate matters. Shortly thereafter the Restoration of the monarchy and the adoption of policies meant to suppress puritanism in England convinced him to stay in Massachusetts. In 1661 Jane joined him, along with Samuel and his siblings, and the family settled in Newbury. Samuel was nine years old at the time and had begun his education at Romsey grammar school in England. In Newbury he prepared for college with the town's pastor, Thomas Parker. Parker and his ministerial colleague James Noyse had been the region's principal advocates of presbyterian church practices. Isolated in a sea of congregationalists, they were still able to administer their own church in keeping with their views and over time influenced the move in New England toward greater clerical authority and a greater role for synods and assemblies.

Samuel entered Harvard College in 1667. On graduating four years later he remained at the college as a fellow and tutor, and supervised the library. He strongly considered a career in the ministry and received an invitation to be pastor of the church being formed in the newly settled town of Woodbridge, New Jersey. The town had been established by former residents of Newbury and named after John Woodbridge, a nephew of Thomas Parker. Reluctant to leave Massachusetts, Samuel declined the invitation. He did, however, substitute for the ailing Parker in preaching to the Newbury church in the spring of 1675. Thoughts of a clerical career were abandoned following his marriage in February 1676 to Hannah Hull, the only surviving child of John Hull, a wealthy merchant, silversmith, and the colony mint-master. The newlyweds moved into Hull's home, and Samuel began to learn the "manner of merchants" as he expressed it in his diary. Hull had been one of the leading figures in the secession from First Church Boston and one of the leaders of the new Third Church. Samuel was admitted to that congregation in 1677.

Samuel and Hannah would have fourteen children, only six of whom lived to adulthood. He was to prove a loving husband and a caring father. His detailed diary reveals his emotional responses to the birth of his various children, his watchful care at their sickbeds, and his grief when one of them died. He remained deeply invested in the lives of his adult children, counseling them and aiding them as they struggled to establish their own places.

Sewall became enamored of the natural landscape of eastern Massachusetts, and particularly Plum Island, the coastal barrier island near Newbury which he had explored as a youth. He took his children there, and also to Hogg Island (which he owned) and other sites for outings. On a summer Saturday afternoon in 1685 he and his wife traveled to Dorchester to gather and eat cherries and raspberries. On another occasion they travelled to the family property at Sherborn, where they walked through the meadow, ate apples, and drank cider. A few years later he took five of his own children and some of their friends on a picnic to Hogg Island, where they feasted on "turkey and other fowls." Occasionally he took his sons fishing. The children, particularly his sons, were allowed to go swimming, sleigh-riding, and skating, and to play games such as wickets. His diary discredits the stereotype of puritans as harsh parents seeking to break the wills of their children by physical punishment. Cotton Mather, whom Sewall knew well, argued against the use of physical punishment for children, writing that "the slavish way of education, carried on with raving and kicking and scourging (in schools as well as families) is abominable." Sewall was diligent in correcting his children's faults, but only recorded one instance in which he actually raised a hand to one of his children. On one occasion he chastised an acquaintance for using physical force against one of her family members.

None of this means that Sewall did not share the concerns of the Winthrops and the Bradstreets that their children be raised in godliness. He and Hannah gathered their household daily for religious instruction. Children were to be made aware of their sinfulness and to contemplate the horrors awaiting the reprobate. They were encouraged to consider how their sins separated them from the love of God. Seeing how their transgressions hurt their parents led children to speculation on how they also hurt God, and helped them to develop a sense of conscience that focused on how their behavior affected others. But at the same time, Sewall sought to model God's love through the affection and care he bestowed on his children.

SEWALL'S LIFE STORY reinforces the puritan concern for making the family a godly commonwealth that has been seen in the lives of the Winthrops and the Bradstreets. But this chapter is focused on what his life tells us about how puritans coped with the challenges facing New England in the last decades of the seventeenth century and the first decade of the eighteenth. Three episodes in particular are important to examine: Sewall's response to the changes wrought in the government of Massachusetts following the revocation of the original charter, the challenge of witchcraft in Salem and the surrounding towns in 1692, and the moral issues raised by the growing slave trade of the period.

Sewall became a freeman of the colony in 1678, and joined the Ancient and Honorable Artillery Company the following year. He did not emerge as a major figure in the colony's public life, however, until he took over John Hull's business affairs following the death of his father-in-law in 1683. As a merchant he was very successful. He never experienced the criticism that plagued Robert Keayne, though in part this was due to the fact that the puritan attitude toward commerce had shifted in the intervening years. Samuel Willard, Sewall's pastor at Third Church, like many of his contemporaries, had come to view economic expertise positively. Merchants were regarded as agents of public prosperity. The British Empire was seen as a bulwark of Protestantism. Ambitious overseas trade was a national, religious, and even moral good. A new emphasis was placed on the rights of Englishmen as defining characteristics of a godly society. The demands of the marketplace were no longer a subject of clerical oversight. Merchants should make money, provide for their families, and contribute liberally to civic and religious causes. Certainly Sewall was comfortable with this role. He ordered his ship captains to see that God was properly worshipped on their vessels and particularly that the Sabbath was observed. While he used his wealth to surround himself with luxuries that his father would have been amazed by, he also used his wealth to provide free catechisms and religious tracts to ordinary colonists.

IN THE YEAR that John Hull died, Samuel was elected to be a deputy to the General Court, and the following year he was chosen as one of the Assistants and a justice of the peace. Hardly had he achieved this prominence than the whole political structure of the colony would collapse with the revocation of the Massachusetts charter. There was considerable debate during the summer of 1685 as to how the colony should respond when a royal governor would actually appear and demand the charter. Sewall heard Increase Mather preach, "The church of God shall stand and abide forever, and [it is] probable that the New England Church shall do so." A few months later Sewall crossed the river to Cambridge where Michael "Wigglesworth preach[ed] excellently from those words, Fight the good fight of faith; Lay hold on eternal life." But the clergy were no more united than the colony's political leaders. And at the General Court there were "very sharp debates about submission." Reflecting on the discord on one occasion, Sewall wrote, "This Monday we begin palpably to die." Tensions continued high. On October 5, 1685, a "cloudy, lowering day," the Artillery Company, with Sewall commanding the company from South Boston, crossed the river to Charlestown and trained at storming and defending one of the hills behind the town (likely what became known as either Bunker Hill or Breed's Hill). Two weeks later the local militia companies drilled on Boston Common and also practiced "taking of the fort."

After Joseph Dudley arrived as the new, acting governor of the colony, Sewall wondered, "If the foundations [are] being destroyed, what can the righteous do?" When Sewall met with his fellow magistrates to discuss how to respond to Dudley's instructions, it was clear that most had no heart for resistance. Samuel Nowell bitterly "prayed that God would pardon each magistrate and deputy's sin." Those gathered "thanked God for our hitherto of mercy 56 years." Sewall was "moved to sing, so sang the 17 and 18 verses of Habbakkuk"—"Although the fig tree shall not blossom, neither shall fruit be in the vines; the labor of the olive shall fail, and the flesh shall yield no meat; the flock shall be cut off from the fold, and there shall be no herd in the stalls: yet I will rejoice in the Lord, I will joy in the God of my salvation."

An old dispute that was revived during Dudley's brief supervision of the colony concerned the flag used by the colony's trainbands. The new Council determined to restore the use of the royal ensign with the red cross in it, which had been discontinued after Endecott's cutting the cross from the flag in the 1630s. Samuel Sewall, who was no longer an Assistant but continued to serve as a captain in the militia, was "in great exercise about it" and "afraid if I have a hand in it whether it might not hinder my entrance into the Holy Land." Sewall had spoken against the use of the cross in the flag when one of the military commanders had suggested its restoration in 1681. Now he reviewed his copy of John Cotton's arguments against that use which the Boston clergyman had prepared when Endecott had cut the cross from the ensign used at Salem. He consulted with Increase Mather, who judged it a sin by those who gave the order, but not necessarily by a militia captain who was ordered to use it. Sewall, however, "could hardly understand how the command of others could wholly excuse" the captains, "and especially me who had spoken so much against it in April 1681," and so resigned his commission.

Andros continued the efforts begun by Randolph to establish the presence of the Church of England in the region. In a confrontation that would directly involve Sewall, shortly after arriving in Boston Andros called the ministers of the three churches into his presence and proposed that two of the congregations join together so that the Church of England could use the third meetinghouse. After meeting together, the clergy and lay elders determined that they "could not with a good conscience consent that our meetinghouses should be made use of for the Common Prayer worship." In the spring Andros sent Randolph to the Third Church to demand the keys to the meetinghouse. Sewall and other members of the congregation went to see the governor-general and explained that the land and meetinghouse were the private property of the congregation, but despite this the sexton was "prevailed upon to ring the bell and open the door to the Governor's command." Thus began the practice of the Church of England using the Third Church on Sabbath mornings, with the puritan congregation waiting outside to be allowed into their meetinghouse for afternoon services. Sewall recorded that "it was a sad sight to see how full the street was with people gazing and moving to and fro because [they] had not entrance into the house." The contention continued for the remainder of the Dominion era, with Andros at one time ordering an investigation into the legality of the congregation's title to the land. A threat to deprive Sewall of some of the lands he had sought a new deed to likely derived from the layman's ardent defense of his church.

In addition to their sense of political oppression, the colonists' concerns about the sins of the land continued into the period of the Dominion. Some, but not all of this was attributable to the change in political regime. Puritans were distressed by new fashions brought from England that they no longer had the power to stop. Sewall was highly offended to learn that one official, a public notary, had cut off his hair and was wearing a periwig of a different color. The troops that accompanied Andros to "keep the country in awe" were, according to a contemporary account, "a crew that began to teach New England to drab, drink, blaspheme, curse, and damn; a crew that were every foot moving tumults, and committing insufferable riots amongst a quiet and peaceable people." Sewall recorded in his diary an occasion when some of the new royal officers came "in a coach from Roxbury about 9 o'clock one night, singing as they come, being inflamed with drink." The party stopped at the home of one of the new judges and "drank healths, curse, swear, talk profanely and baudily, to the great disturbance of the town and grief of good people." Sewall judged that "such high handed wickedness was hardly ever heard of before in Boston."

Holidays and holy days began to be observed. An almanac published in Boston in 1687 listed the holy days of the Church of England and next to January 30 noted "King Charles murdered." It became common for many to celebrate Christmas, prompting Increase Mather to observe that "such vanities . . . are good nowhere, but in New England they are a thousand times worse." At First Church James Allen referred to the practice as Antichristian. The English authorities celebrated the anniversary of the king's coronation with bonfires and fireworks in April 1687. What made it worse was that the date fell that year on the Sabbath "The rattling of the guns during almost all the time [of the church services] gave them great disturbance," Sewall pointed out, writing, "It was never so in Boston before." A maypole was raised in Charlestown on May 1, 1687. Bad as it was that Church of English worship had been introduced in the colonies, Thomas Shepard Jr. noted that there were "pictures and images of Christ, of the Virgin Mary, and other canonized popish saints . . . sold in some shops." On January 2, 1686, Samuel Sewall recorded in his diary that the previous night he "had a very unusual dream." He dreamed "that our Savior, in the days of his flesh when upon earth, came to Boston and abode here sometime." Sewall "admired the goodness and wisdom of Christ in coming hither and spending some part of his short life here." But most recognized that any idea of a visible godly kingdom in New England could only have been a dream. While they did not give up the hope that God would deliver them from the Dominion and all that went with it, it became evident to New Englanders that informal methods would once again become the primary means whereby puritans sought to advance God's kingdom.

In the fall of 1688 Samuel Sewall returned to England seeking to deal with lands that he had inherited there and to reinforce some of his business connections. He welcomed the chance to see some of the interesting sites of the country he had left as a youth. He visited Stonehenge, Salisbury Cathedral, St. Paul's in London, the University of Oxford, the city of Coventry, where his great-grandfather had held municipal office, and other places of interest. But he was also determined to lend his assistance to Increase Mather, who had sneaked out of Boston a few months earlier to petition King James against the harsh policies of the Andros regime. While Mather was in England, the political situation changed with the Glorious Revolution that put William and Mary on the throne. Increase Mather vigorously called upon all his English friends to assist in lobbying the new regime for a restoration of the old Massachusetts charter. Sewall sought to assist, but was shunted aside by Mather, and so Samuel returned to Boston, arriving early in December 1689 after his fellow colonists had toppled the Dominion and called back the last elected government. He resumed his seat on the Council along with his colleagues, who were exercising the authority they had been elected to in 1685.

One of the consequences of King William's accession to the throne of England was the outbreak of war between England and France. For the first time the French in Canada were a threat to New England. In 1690 rumors of French collaboration with northern Indians became a reality. While Governor Bradstreet was dining at Samuel Sewall's home on February 24, news was brought to the governor of a French and Indian attack on "Schenectady, a village 20 miles above Albany, . . . [where] 60 men, women, and children [were] murdered. Women with child ripped up, children had their brains dashed out." Less than a month later, a force of French and Indians attacked the village of Salmon Falls on the Maine frontier within the jurisdiction of Massachusetts. Over twenty houses were burned and close to a hundred settlers were killed or captured.

Sewall and his fellow magistrates determined that the best strategy to relieve these attacks was to strike at the French. Consequently William Phipps, a Massachusetts sea captain who had become famous and wealthy for recovering part of the treasure from the sunken Spanish galleon the *Concepcion*, was put in command of an expedition to seize the French outpost of Port Royal on the coast of Acadia. At the same time, Sewall and William Stoughton were sent to New York to discuss with Jacob Leisler and the other leaders of New York a joint attack on Montreal. Phipps won an easy victory at Port Royal. Heartened by this victory, the leaders of New York, Massachusetts, and Connecticut advanced their plans for a two-pronged attack on the heart of New France. Phipps would lead a sea and land assault on Quebec, while a New York and Connecticut force under the command of Fitz John Winthrop would move north from Lake Champlain to capture Montreal.

The dual assault on Canada failed, but the willingness of the colonists to attack the French helped Increase Mather persuade King William to accept the overthrow of the Dominion of New England and grant Massachusetts a new charter. The Charter of 1691 incorporated the former Plymouth colony into Massachusetts, but it did not restore all the autonomy the colonists had claimed under its original charter. Massachusetts was now a royal colony with a governor appointed by the king. The Council was no longer elected by the people but appointed by the governor on the nomination of the deputies. After consulting Mather, the king appointed Sir William Phipps as the first royal governor. The king also deferred to Mather in naming the first Council (pending elections), and Sewall was one of those named.

WHEN INCREASE MATHER and William Phipps arrived in New England bearing the new charter, they were confronted with news of disturbances in Essex County. The jails were filled with men and women who had been bound over for trial as witches. Most men and women of this time, in America as in England, believed that the devil was a malevolent force who could possess and afflict men and women. The unexplained death of livestock, inexplicable diseases of men and women, hideous fits suffered by young and old—all of these suggested the agency of the devil or someone in league with the devil, a witch. The same system of belief included folk techniques to tell fortunes, discover lost property, heal the sick, and ward off witches. The puritans who first settled New England brought with them belief in possession, affliction, and exorcisms. They heard news of further outbreaks of witchcraft in England after they left. Those who had friends and relatives in East Anglia were undoubtedly concerned by the reports of the more than two hundred witches ferreted out by Matthew Hopkins, the "Witchfinder General" in that region of the country in the 1640s.

Given this background, it is perhaps surprising that so few individuals were accused of witchcraft in New England in the seventeenth century. In each of the New England colonies the law defined the crime of witchcraft as making a compact with the devil. Because it was a capital crime, punishable by death, two witnesses were required, which made convictions difficult. Magistrates were cautious in allowing cases to proceed. The first trial for witchcraft in New England did not occur until 1647. In all there were only sixty-one known prosecutions for the crime in the region prior to the Salem episode. At most sixteen of those cases led to convictions, four of those following confessions—fewer than one in five who proclaimed their innocence were found guilty.

All of this makes the Salem episode exceptional. What explains it? Historians have pointed to various factors that combined in some brew to lead to the widespread hysteria. The crisis originated in Salem Village (now Danvers), a farming community that was a part of the larger seaport town of Salem. This was a community struggling economically and bitterly divided between those who wished to remain a part of Salem and those who wished to form a separate town and thus control their own destiny. The village had been given permission to have its own meetinghouse. The preacher at the time—the best they could find for a poor living—was Samuel Parris, who had failed to complete his Harvard education, failed as a planter and sugar broker in Barbados, failed as a Boston merchant, and finally accepted the call to Salem Village. His appointment was opposed by many and his harsh denunciations of his opponents from the pulpit fueled the divisions in the community. The village had become the poster child for everything that could go wrong with John Winthrop's vision of men and women knit together in brotherly love.

In the last years of the 1680s and the first years of the new decade, the tensions peculiar to Salem Village had to have been aggravated by the general concerns felt by New Englanders about the Dominion, its overthrow, and the uncertainly as to how the English authorities would deal with the colonies. The flare-up of war generated fear of Indian attacks throughout Essex County. This was an area exposed to possible attacks; an area filled with refugees from the frontier and their horrific stories of family members killed or captured, and homes burned. Indeed, one of the key accusers in the Salem trials was Mercy Lewis, who had been three years old when the town of Falmouth was attacked by Indians in 1676. In all, thirty-four men, women, and children were killed or captured in that incident. This was but one of many connections between the Indian wars and those who were to play critical roles in the unfolding of the 1692 trials.

In mid January 1692, Betty Parris, the young daughter of the Salem Village minister, and her young cousin Abigail Williams began to experience fits, choking sensations, pain in their limbs, and other symptoms that would disturb any parent. The local medical practitioner, elderly and self-taught, could find no natural cause for their suffering. One explanation of such behavior was possession, the devil actually taking up residence in the person (as modern moviegoers are familiar with from *The Exorcist*). The other explanation was that the person was being tortured (afflicted) by a witch who had received the power to do so through a compact with the devil. Since possession could imply that the person involved was in some way guilty of having welcomed the devil into his or her soul, this was an explanation that few parents or friends wished to entertain. In Salem Village the conclusion was quickly reached that young Betty and Abigail were indeed afflicted by a witch or witches. A critical point came when Tituba, the Carib Indian female slave in the Parris household, on being accused of witchcraft, confessed and claimed that other witches were at work in the region as well. Over the following months others claimed to be afflicted, and the web of accusations spread, with the contagion spreading well outside the confines of Salem Village.

The circumstances the colony found itself in made prosecution and possible containment of the crisis difficult. Because the courts at that time were still operating under provisional authority granted them by King William, pending the resolution of the request for a charter, there was no interest in prosecuting capital cases until a new court structure was properly constituted. Magistrates heard official complaints starting in February, and bound over for trial those against whom there appeared to be a case to be answered. When Governor Phipps arrived in May the jails were filled with women and men awaiting trial, but the courts called for in the new charter would not be constituted until after elections and the meeting of the new legislature. Unable to wait that long, Phipps appointed a special Court of Oyer and Terminer—"Oyer," to hear; "Terminer," to decide.

Phipps named William Stoughton to head the court, which included nine councilors, among whom were Samuel Sewall, John Hathorne (ancestor of Nathaniel Hawthorne), Nathaniel Saltonstall, Wait Still Winthrop, and Jonathan Corwin. In all, 144 people (106 women and 38 men) had legal action taken against them, 54 confessed to witchcraft, 14 women and 5 men were hanged. No one was more responsible for the outcome than William Stoughton. Opinionated and assertive, Stoughton flouted all previous English and New England precedent, and the views of numerous clerical writers in allowing the use of spectral evidence. This meant that if an accuser claimed to see the spectral image of a living person afflicting them, the testimony was accepted as proof that the person whose specter was seen was a witch. Accepting this meant not only accepting that the witness indeed did see what only he or she could see, but also asserting that it was impossible for the devil to assume the shape of an innocent person.

Increase Mather and the Bay clergy were slow to publicly reject this position, probably because they needed the magistrates' support to advance their own reform agendas and were reluctant to alienate Stoughton, who was also lieutenant-governor. Others did speak out. Thomas Danforth criticized the Court of Oyer and Terminer. Nathaniel Saltonstall stepped down from the court. Simon Bradstreet was also critical, and his son Dudley Bradstreet, a magistrate in Andover, stopped issuing warrants for the apprehension of accused witches in September 1692.

Among the clergy, Sewall's pastor, Samuel Willard, was one of the first to raise doubts. Finally, in early October, when the majority of the clergy had publicly come forth to criticize the court's use of evidence, Governor Phipps suspended the Court. By the end of the month, over the bitter objections of Stoughton, Phipps brought its existence to an end. In December, the Massachusetts Council appointed the judges to the new Superior Court of Judicature, recently established by the legislature, which would hear the cases of those still in jail.

There are a few popular misconceptions about the episode that should be cleared up. The accused Giles Corey was not tortured to extract a confession, nor was any other person accused tortured to confess. In English and colonial law a trial could not proceed without the accused entering a plea, and, unlike our court system, the court could not enter a "not guilty" plea on behalf of the accused. Pressing the gradual application of weights to the recumbent body of the accused—was allowed as a means of extracting not a confession, but a plea. Giles Corey refused to enter a plea, perhaps to protect his estate from being denied to his heirs, which would have been a consequence of being guilty. His body broke before his will did.

A second misconception is the notion that false confession was a way to avoid execution. Of course, lying under oath was a sin no true puritan would have considered. But there is no evidence that confessing would lead to anything more than a delay in execution. Those who confessed were to be given time to make their peace with God and kept available as witnesses against others accused. They would have expected to eventually be hanged. They would have had no reason to think that the trials would be ended and the jails opened before they met their fate.

Lastly, many authors have claimed that two of the key principles—the judge Samuel Sewall and the accuser Anne Putnam—confessed that they had knowingly victimized those accused. It is true that years later both asked God's forgiveness for what they had come to recognize as a miscarriage of justice. But a careful reading of their statements indicates that they both continued to believe that the devil had been at work in Salem Village—just not as they had originally believed. Anne Putnam

Samuel Sewall
Courtesy of the Massachusetts Historical Society

eventually acknowledged that she must have been possessed by the devil (as opposed to being afflicted) and under his power accused innocent people.

Before Putnam's recantation, Sewall had come to believe that he and his fellow judges were deluded and had condemned innocent people to die. In January 1697 Samuel Willard, the pastor of Third Church, read a statement from Sewall while Sewall stood in his place in the front of the congregation: "As to the guilt contracted upon the opening of the late Commission of Oyer & Terminer at Salem . . . he . . . , upon many accounts, more concerned than any he knows of, desires to take the blame & shame of it, asking pardon of men, and especially desiring prayers that

God, who has an unlimited authority, would pardon that sin." Sewell, like others who similarly looked back on the events, appears to have concluded that the young women at the center of the dispute were likely not afflicted, but possessed, and that it was the devil who had spoken to them. The court, in accepting their testimony, had done the devil's will and not God's.

ALTHOUGH THE key figures that conducted the Salem witch trials were puritans, the events occurred after the puritans had lost political control of their society. Samuel Sewall believed that Christ's Second Coming would usher in the millennium in New England, but most of the godly were not willing to wait for divine intervention and turned to traditional tactics to shape their world. With the transformation of Massachusetts from a godly kingdom controlled by puritan magistrates to a royal colony with a large puritan population, reform, as it had been in the England of the 1620s, had to be achieved by persuasion rather than power. In the new Massachusetts, the nurturing of faith among the godly again depended on private voluntary associations. It is likely that the tradition of private religious meetings of godly friends, such as encouraged by Richard Rogers and practiced by John Winthrop and Brigit Cooke, had never died in New England. Early in the region's history, John Eliot had described the practice of the faithful: "We have our private meetings, wherein we pray and sing, and repeat sermons, and confer together about the things of God." The meetings made it seem that they were "in heaven almost every day." But the practice became even more important as puritan control over the institutions of the society weakened. Samuel Sewall recorded his regular attendance at such sessions, which rotated among the homes of the members. Typically, a scripture verse would be chosen for discussion. One of the gathered laymen would speak to the text, and then everyone was encouraged to enter into a discussion of its meaning. Prayer was another key element of the sessions. On one occasion Sewall recorded, "The exercise was such, preaching and praying, as if God did intend it for me." He added, "I prayed earnestly before I went, that God would show me favor at the meeting," and afterwards hoped "he will set home those things that were by him carved for me." In exercises such as these, lay people were able to wrestle with the meaning of faith, employing the spiritual gifts that in public settings were reserved for the clergy. Sewall was still attending such meetings in 1708, when he attended such a gathering at the home of Josiah Franklin (Benjamin's father), who had recently joined the church.

Another practice that had a long history among puritans trying to advance god's kingdom was sermon gadding and taking sermon notes. These were lifelong habits that died hard, and John Leverett was still taking notes on sermons he heard in the last years of his life. Here too, Sewall's diary provides us evidence of the vitality of this tradition in the last part of the seventeenth century and the beginning of the next. Not only did Sewall listen to sermons at his own Boston church and at the Boston lecture, but he travelled to neighboring towns such as Dorchester, Cambridge, and Charlestown to feed his appetite for sermons.

Yet another tradition that was used to sustain the faith of the godly was family exercises. Many families gathered in both the morning and evening, "wherein having read the scriptures to our families, we call upon the name of God, and every now and then carefully catechize those that are under our charge." Roger Clap, one of the early settlers of Dorchester who died in 1691, advised his children, "Worship God in your families. Do not neglect family prayer, morning and evening. And be sure to read some part of the word of God every day in your families. . . . And be sure to instruct your families in the grounds of religion. And be yourselves patterns, by your holy lives and conversation unto your children." Family prayer was to be conducted soon after the evening meal, so that there would be time before retiring for individual devotions. Catechizing was another practice of piety often conducted in a family setting.

Individuals also spent time alone reading scripture or works of devotion or theology, praying, and meditating. According to Cotton Mather, "A Christian that would thrive in Christianity must be no stranger to a course of meditation." Many spoke of going into their "closet" to do so. This was often simply a private space they set apart, but occasionally was a specially built room. Anne Bradstreet regularly meditated on her life and her hopes for eternal life, and often used these meditations as springboards for her poems. On one occasion she depicted herself as a "weary pilgrim" anticipating a final rest. On another she asked the Lord to prepare her for her death, urging Christ to "Come dear bridegroom. Come away." Meditation was often prompted by scripture readings and was a means by which the godly tried to apply the lesson of the text to their own life.

Samuel Sewall, who frequently meditated on divine things, also took it upon himself to distribute religious publications. He frequently "carried a half dozen catechisms" in his pocket and "gave them to such as could read." He also lent and gave away books by English and New England divines to friends he felt could benefit from them. It was Sewall who arranged for the Boston publication of John Bunyan's *Pilgrim's Progress.* Sewall also wrote works in which he advanced his own views. In his *Phaenomena quaedam Apocalyptica, . . . or, some few lines towards a description of the New Heaven* (1697) he asked why New England might not become the New Jerusalem. Whereas John Davenport believed that the colonies had a role to play in the Middle Advent, Sewall believed that their role was more central, writing that "the New English churches are a preface to the New Heavens," and that America (not just New England) would be where Christ came to establish his millennial kingdom. He explored both history and scripture to support his cause. He offered further such analysis in his 1713 *Proposals Touching the Accomplishment of Prophesies.*

SEWALL'S MILLENARIAN beliefs have not commanded much attention from later generations. This is not true, however, of his attack on the growing slave trade. Black slaves had been brought to New England by 1638, and a reliable account exists of the rape of a black woman by Samuel Maverick, who had settled in the Boston area before the puritans and was an opponent of their rule. Emmanuel Downing, John Winthrop's brother-in-law, had argued for the extensive use of slave labor in New England. Though Downing failed to win this argument, a small number of slaves continued to be brought to the colony. Nothing about his upbringing made Samuel Winthrop disinclined to use slaves on his Antigua plantation. Most slaves in New England were incorporated into households and were included in family prayers. John Winthrop noted in his journal the admission of a black woman to the church in Dorchester in 1641. At that time there were likely fewer than 150 slaves in New England. A recent study documents the use of slaves in what had been John Winthrop's Ten Hills farm by the Royal family in the late seventeenth and eighteenth centuries. The growth of slavery in the region accelerated during Sewall's lifetime, the number of slaves growing from about 200 in 1676 to 550 in 1708. Close to three-quarters of them lived in Boston. Many Boston merchants (though not Sewall) entered the slave trade when the English government suspended the Royal Africa Company's monopoly on the trade in 1696.

One response to the growing Black population was Cotton Mather *Rules for the Society of Negroes* (1693). Puritans had always insisted that slaves, like all other servants, be taught to read and be provided with religious instruction. John Eliot, the Apostle to the Indians who died in 1690, bequeathed a portion of his estate for the support of a school to teach Indian and African, as well as English, students. More than thirty black slaves were members of the Mathers's Second Church, and they were the core group involved in the Society of Negroes. The members of that society announced that in order that they "may be assisted in the service of our heavenly master, we now join together in a society." They pledged to meet in the evening of every Sabbath to "pray together by turns, one to begin, and another to conclude the meeting." Between the two prayers a psalm would be sung and the members would discuss that day's sermon. Their status as slaves was recognized by their noting that they would only gather with the consent of their masters and end their session by nine in the evening so "that we may not be unseasonably absent from the families whereto we pertain." Only those who had "sensibly reformed their lives from all manner of wickedness" would be admitted to the society. Any members guilty of drunkenness, swearing, lying, stealing, disobedience, fornication or other sins would be admonished by the society and excluded from the sessions until he displayed true repentance. These slaves, like all servants, were supposed to have been taught to read, and they pledged to learn the catechism, stating, "It shall be one of our exercises, for one of us to ask the questions, and for all the rest in their order to say the answers."

The Society for Negroes allowed slaves to help shape their religious lives. But Cotton Mather did not question the fact that they were slaves. In 1700 Samuel Sewall went further when he published *The Selling of Joseph*. This was the first published tract against slavery in American history—the Germantown Pennsylvania protest of 1688 was a petition presented to the local Quaker meetings in the region. Sewall's brief work was directed at the slave trade. He wrote that it was "most lamentable to think how in taking Negroes out of Africa and selling of them here, that which God hath joined together men do boldly rend asunder; men from their country, husband from their wives, parents from their children. He rejected the notion that slaves were the spoils of just wars—"Every war is upon one side unjust. An unlawful war can't make lawful captives." He likewise rejected the argument that slavery brought heathens to a Christian society where they would learn of God—"Evil must not be done," he wrote," that good may come of it." This did not mean that Sewall regarded blacks as equal. Like most Englishmen of his time, he believed that Africans were inferior and could never take their place in New England society. But, in a world in which liberty was connected to Protestantism and New England puritans had begun to conflate godly values and the rights of Englishmen, Sewall proclaimed, "Liberty is in real value next unto life: none ought to part with it themselves, or deprive others of it, but upon the most mature consideration."

Sewall's case did not gain widespread support. His fellow merchant, John Saffin, was perceived to have the better argument in his *Brief and Candid Answer* to *The Selling of Joseph*, also published in 1700. Yet Sewall was articulating a view of human rights that would continue to be a part of the New England heritage that led to the Revolution of 1775. And his moral critique of slavery represented a puritan contribution to that heritage that would also inspire the New England antislavery movement of the nineteenth century.

SAMUEL SEWALL died in 1730, recording his views and tokens of his faith in his diary until 1729. Raised in a world controlled by puritan magistrates and ministers, he came to epitomize the use of moral example and persuasion that were the only weapons available to the godly in the decades after Massachusetts lost its initial charter.

Conclusion

Civil Society and the Godly Kingdom

What unites virtually all of the stories of the men and women (I'm not sure about Sarah Keayne here) is their commitment to fashion themselves into godly individuals and to reform those around them. They did not all agree on what doctrinal beliefs constituted a true faith. Indeed, some of them viewed their lives as a pilgrimage not only in search of grace, but of understanding. And they trusted their fellow believers to find their own way. Certainly some were found to have abused their freedom to seek God, to have crossed the boundaries of acceptable beliefs, and such individuals were banished or worse if they would not conform to the community consensus. But what is truly remarkable is how little hierarchical control existed in this society. Magistrates were elected annually, and not even a John Winthrop could be assured of being returned as governor. Every colony had a legislature which was assured of meeting regularly—unlike the world they had left where until the Puritan Revolution the king and the king alone determined if a Parliament should be called. Laws had to be approved by the people's representatives meeting in those legislatures. At the local level it was town meetings of the residents that decided who was to hold local offices, how land was to be divided, and issues such as where a bridge over a local stream would be built.

Suspicion of established hierarchical authority shaped the formation of church life. Congregationalism meant that the lay believers chose their ministers and could dismiss them. Admissions to the church had to be approved by the believers, not simply the elders. Changes in church policies required congregational approval, and the debates over the Half-Way Covenant provided many examples of lay believers rejecting the advice of long-established clergy. As the previous pages have shown, over the course of the seventeenth century there was a movement to vest greater authority in the hands of the clergy, and eventually this would succeed. But the movement was contested as clergy such as John Davenport and laymen such as John Leverett fought to preserve the participatory elements of church polity.

Part of the religious legacy of these men and women was the belief that at the essence of Christianity was the commandment to love one's neighbor. A godly kingdom was one in which, as John Winthrop expressed it, each was expected to "delight in each other, make others' conditions our own; rejoice together, mourn together, labor and suffer together—always having before our eyes our commission and community in the work, our community as members of the same body." Or, in Anne Bradstreet's words, "God will have us beholden one to another." To advance the common good meant that each person and each family must proclaim godly values and live according to those values. True liberty was constrained by an obligation to care for others. One consequence of this was a determination to subject public affairs to moral scrutiny. Another was the insistence on insuring that all individuals—rich and poor, free and unfree, women as well as men—were taught to read and given access to the scriptures and to copies of the laws. Because, as the Massachusetts School Law of 1642 expressed it, "the good education of children is of singular behoof and benefit to any Common-wealth," each colony required parents to see that all in their households learn to read, and mandated the employment of schoolmasters to facilitate that policy.

Every step taken in establishing this legacy was contested, and that is one of the lessons of approaching the larger story through the individual stories of men and women who made their own unique contributions to the society's evolution. An analysis of other lives, beyond those treated in this book, would reveal additional nuances in the shaping of New England. But such stories would also contribute to an understanding of what makes colonial New England important in the shaping of American values. The seventeenth-century puritans were truly founders in that they imparted to future Americans an insistence on the importance of self-examination and self-improvement, on the importance of participatory government in state and church, and on the need for individuals to sacrifice for the advancement of the common good. They subjected public behavior to the demands of a higher morality, and insisted that children be educated to assume the responsibilities of citizenship. We see their legacy throughout the centuries that followed, not least in John Adams's invocation of John Winthrop in defense of American liberties, in Samuel Adams's call that the newly independent America be as a Christian Sparta, in Horace Mann's crusade for universal public education, in the zeal of a John Brown in attacking slavery, and in John F. Kennedy's call that we ask what we can do for our country. The puritans would be the last to demand that we slavishly follow their example or accept their views, but understanding who we are does require that we come to grips with who they were.

A good starting place to understand puritanism and its impact on England and America is Francis J. Bremer, *Puritanism: A Very Short Introduction* (New York: Oxford University Press, 2010). Francis J. Bremer, *The Puritan Experiment: New England Society from Bradford to Edwards* (Hanover, NH: University Press of New England, 1995) in many ways complements *First Founders*. That earlier work is a narrative overview of New England history that brings the story down to the Great Awakening of the eighteenth century. There is still value in Samuel Eliot Morison's *Builders of the Bay Colony* (Boston, Houghton Mifflin, 1930), a collection of biographical sketches of various puritans, which was the inspiration for this work. David D. Hall has written with great insight into the seventeenth-century New England world. Highly recommended are *Worlds of Wonder, Days of Judgment: Popular Religious Belief in Early New England* (Cambridge, MA: Harvard University Press, 1990) and *A Reforming People: Puritanism and the Transformation of Public Life in New England* (New York: Knopf, 2011). Stephen Foster's *The Long Argument: English Puritanism and the Shaping of New England Culture, 1570–1700* (Chapel Hill: University of North Carolina Press, 1996) offers an important discussion of its subject.

There is still much value to be derived from Cotton Mather's 1702 work, *Magnalia Christi Americana*. Mather, the son of Increase Mather, had available to him numerous sources that have since disappeared. His closeness to the subject makes his judgments suspect, but he recorded details of the lives of the early puritans which can be found nowhere else. In writing this book I have turned frequently to John G. Palfrey's five-volume *History of New England to the Revolutionary War* (1859–1890). Like Mather, the judgments have been surpassed by subsequent scholarship, but the level of detail and the inclusion of documents in the notes make it a valuable source.

John Winthrop and the Struggle to Lead a Godly Life

Quotes in this chapter are taken from *The Winthrop Papers*, five volumes to date (Boston, 1929–). The Massachusetts Historical Society plans to put these volumes as well as a new volume of *Religious Writings* and future volumes online on their website (masshist.org). Richard S. Dunn, James Savage, and Laetitia

Yaendle, eds., *The Journal of John Winthrop, 1630–1649* (Cambridge, MA: Belknap Press of Harvard University Press, 1996) is the definitive edition of Winthrop's account of the public events of his time in the colony. Francis J. Bremer, *John Winthrop: America's Forgotten Founding Father* (New York, Oxford University Press, 2003) is the most recent full-length biography of John Winthrop. Still valuable are the insights in Edmund S. Morgan, *The Puritan Dilemma: The Story of John Winthrop* (Boston: Little, Brown, 1958).

John Endecott: Godly Magistrate

The only biography of Endecott is Lawrence Shaw Mayo, *John Endecott* (Cambridge, MA: Harvard University Press, 1936). The Pequot War and Endecott's role in it are explored in Alfred Cave, *The Pequot War* (Amherst: University of Massachusetts Press, 1996). His role in cutting the cross of St. George from the English ensign is the focus of Nathaniel Hawthorne's short story "Endicott and the Red Cross." Accounts of the early trials of the settlers can be found in Everett Emerson, ed., *Letters from New England: The Massachusetts Bay Colony, 1629–1638* (Amherst: University of Massachusetts Press, 1976). The quote from Stephen Foster is from his *The Long Argument.* The court cases are to be found in George Francis Dow, ed., *Records and Files of the Quarterly Courts of Essex County, Massachusetts: 1662–1667,* which is available in modern reprints.

John Wilson: Puritan Pastor

Despite his importance as minister of the Boston church from its founding until his death in 1667, there has been no scholarly study of Wilson. Alexander W. M'Clure's *The Lives of John Wilson, John Norton, and John Davenport* (1846) draws much of its information from Mather's *Magnalia.* A valuable source is Richard D. Pierce, ed., *The Records of the First Church in Boston, 1630–1868* (Boston, The Colonial Society of Boston, 1961). The account of Wilson's speech to the troops is in Edward Johnson, *Wonder Working Providence* (1653), which is available in reprints.

Thomas Dudley and Thomas Shepard: Hammers of Heretics

There has been no scholarly study of Thomas Dudley. He is an important figure, however, in Bremer, *John Winthrop,* in Michael Winship's studies of the Free Grace Controversy noted in the suggestions for the following chapter, and in treatments of his famous daughter, Anne Bradstreet. The best starting place to understand Shepard is Michael G. McGiffert, ed., *God's Plot: Puritan Spirituality in Thomas Shepard's Cambridge* (Amherst: University of Massachusetts Press, 1994), which includes the clergyman's diary and autobiography.

Four Strong Women: Anne Hutchinson, Mary Dyer, Lady Deborah Moody, and Anne Eaton

There have been numerous works dealing with Anne Hutchinson. The most recent biography is Eve LaPlante, *American Jezebel: The Uncommon Life of Anne Hutchinson, The Woman Who Defied the Puritans* (New York: HarperCollins, 2004), though in my opinion it downplays religious issues and makes the protagonist seem more modern than she was. Less detailed but more grounded in the context of the period is Timothy D. Hall, *Anne Hutchinson: Puritan Prophet* (Upper Saddle River, NJ: Prentice Hall, 2009). The documents of the controversy are published with excellent commentary in David D. Hall, *The Antinomian Controversy, 1636–1638*, 2nd ed. (Durham, NC: Duke University Press, 1990). The best treatment of the controversy is Michael P. Winship, *Making Heretics: Militant Protestants and Free Grace in Massachusetts, 1636–1641* (Princeton, NJ: Princeton University Press, 2002). There are no comparable works covering the lives of Mary Dyer, Lady Deborah Moody, or Anne Eaton. John Hull's diary provides insight into the events of his time, and particularly the Quaker presence.

The Troubled Keaynes

The best starting point for Robert Keayne is Bernard Bailyn, ed., *The Apologia of Robert Keayne: The Self-Portrait of a Puritan Merchant* (New York: Harper & Row, 1964). Mark Valeri's *Heavenly Merchandize: How Religion Shaped Commerce in Puritan America* (Princeton, NJ: Princeton University Press, 2010) has a valuable chapter on Keayne. Also useful is Stephen Innes, *Creating the Commonwealth: The Economic Culture of Puritan New England* (New York: Norton, 1995). Sarah Keayne's story is told in D. Brenton Simons, *Witches, Rakes, and Rogues* (Boston: Commonwealth Editions, 2006).

Stephen Winthrop: Soldier of the Lord

There is a chapter on Stephen Winthrop in Lawrence Shaw Mayo, *The Winthrop Family in America* (Boston: Massachusetts Historical Society, 1948). Correspondence to and from Stephen is to be found in the published and unpublished Winthrop Papers of the Massachusetts Historical Society. Good introductions to the English Civil Wars include Michael Braddick, *God's Fury, England's Fire: A New History of the English Civil Wars* (London: Penguin, 2008); Ian Gentles, *The English Revolution and the Wars in the Three Kingdoms, 1638–1652* (London: Pearson Education, 2007); and Blair Worden, *The English Civil Wars, 1640–1660* (London: Weidenfeld and Nicolson, 2009). For the Protectorate see David L. Smith and Patrick Little, *Parliaments and Politics during the Cromwellian Protectorate* (Cambridge: Cambridge University Press: 2007).

Hugh Peter: Regicide

The standard biography of Hugh Peter is Raymond Phineas Stearns, *The Strenuous Puritan: Hugh Peter, 1598–1660* (Urbana, University of Illinois Press: 1954). The general works on England's Puritan Revolution in the previous section help to understand the context of his English career.

John Davenport and the Middle Advent

My study of *Building a New Jerusalem: John Davenport, a Puritan in Three Worlds* (forthcoming from Yale University Press) is the first full biography of the New Haven clergyman. His life and career is a major part of Isabel M. Calder, *The New Haven Colony* (New Haven, CT: Yale University Press, 1938). Calder also edited *The Letters of John Davenport, Puritan Divine* (New Haven, CT: Yale University Press, 1937).

Samuel Winthrop: From Puritan to Quaker

There is no full-length study of Samuel Winthrop. Larry D. Gragg, "A Puritan in the West Indies: The Career of Samuel Winthrop," *William and Mary Quarterly* (1993) is a valuable study. The context is set in Gragg's *The Quaker Community on Barbados* (Columbia: University of Missouri Press, 2009) and *Englishmen Transplanted: The English Colonization of Barbados 1627–1660* (New York: Oxford University Press, 2003), and Natalie Zacek, *Settler Society in the English Leeward Islands, 1670–1776* (Cambridge: Cambridge University Press, 2010). C. S. Manegold, *Ten Hills Farm: The Forgotten History of Slavery in the North* (Princeton, NJ: Princeton University Press, 2009) offers a fascinating look at connections between New England and Antigua.

John Sassamon: A Puritan between Two Cultures

A good starting point for understanding the general story of the colonists' relations with the native population remains Alden T. Vaughan, *Puritan Frontier: Puritans and Indians, 1620–1675*, 3rd ed. (Norman: University of Oklahoma Press, 1995). The effort to convert the natives is examined in Richard W. Cogley, *John Eliot's Mission to the Indians before King Philip's War* (Cambridge, MA: Harvard University Press, 1999). King Philip's War is best approached through Daniel R. Mandell, *King Philip's War: Colonial Expansion, Native Resistance, and the End of Indian Sovereignty* (Baltimore: Johns Hopkins University Press, 2010); Yasuhide Kawashima, *Igniting King Philip's War: The John Sassamon Murder Trial* (Lawrence: University Press of Kansas, 2001); and Jill Lepore, *The Name of War: King Philip's War and the Origins of American Identity* (New York: Knopf, 1998). Daniel Richter's *Facing East from Indian Country: A Native His-*

tory of Early America (Cambridge, MA: Harvard University Press, 2001) offers important insights into how natives viewed the events of the time.

John Leverett: Defending the Ways of the Fathers

There are no modern studies of Leverett. I have relied on early studies such as Mather and Palfrey, and examined the official *Records of the Governor and Company of the Massachusetts Bay* in five volumes, edited by Nathaniel B. Shurtleff in the nineteenth century and available in modern reprints. Further material is to be found in the manuscript records in the Massachusetts Historical Society and the Commonwealth Archives.

Anne Bradstreet: Puritan Wife and Mother

The quotes of Anne Bradstreet are taken from Jeannine Hensley, ed., *The Works of Anne Bradstreet* (Cambridge, MA: Belknap Press of Harvard University Press, 1967). Among the various studies of her life and poetry are Charlotte Gordon, *Mistress Bradstreet: The Untold Life of America's First Poet* (New York. Little, Brown, 2005) and Rosamund Rosenmeier, *Anne Bradstreet Revisited* (Boston: Twayne, 1991).

Samuel Sewall: the Conscience of a Puritan

The diary of Samuel Sewall is available in various editions. Recent biographies include Richard Francis, *Judge Sewall's Apology: The Salem Witch Trials and the Forming of an American Conscience* (New York: HarperCollins, 2005); and Eve LaPlante, *Salem Witch Judge: The Life and Repentance of Samuel Sewall* (New York: HarperCollins, 2007). Judith Graham's *Puritan Family Life: The Diary of Samuel Sewall* (Boston: Northeastern University Press, 2000) offers valuable insights. The most insightful study of the witch trials is Mary Beth Norton, *In the Devil's Snare: The Salem Witchcraft Crisis of 1692* (New York: Knopf, 2002).

INDEX